T0347080

WIDOWS OF VIDARBHA

WIDOWS
OF
VIDARBHA
Making of Shadows

KOTA NEELIMA

OXFORD
UNIVERSITY PRESS

OXFORD
UNIVERSITY PRESS

Oxford University Press is a department of the University of Oxford.
It furthers the University's objective of excellence in research, scholarship,
and education by publishing worldwide. Oxford is a registered trademark of
Oxford University Press in the UK and in certain other countries.

Published in India by
Oxford University Press
2/11 Ground Floor, Ansari Road, Daryaganj, New Delhi 110 002, India

ISBN-13 (print edition): 978-0-19-948467-6
ISBN-10 (print edition): 0-19-948467-8

ISBN-13 (eBook): 978-0-19-909363-2
ISBN-10 (eBook): 0-19-909363-6

Typeset in Bembo Std 11/15
by The Graphics Solution, New Delhi 110 092
Printed in India by Replika Press Pvt. Ltd

To
Pawan

Contents

Illustrations

illustrations

Abbreviations

APL	Above Poverty Line
BPL	Below Poverty Line
Bt	*Bacillus thuringiensis*
CAG	Comptroller and Auditor General of India
gm	Gram
ICDS	Integrated Child Development Services
ITI	Industrial Training Institute
MPSC	Maharashtra Public Service Commission
NABARD	National Bank for Agricultural and Rural Development
NCRB	National Crime Records Bureau
NOTA	None of the Above
PAC	Public Accounts Committee
PTA	Part-Time Attendant
RBI	Reserve Bank of India
SBI	State Bank of India
SDO	Sub-Divisional Officer
VJAS	Vidarbha Jan Andolan Samiti
VNSSM	Vasantrao Naik Sheti Swavlamban Mission

Preface

*O*ne early winter morning I found myself in a small room of
a half-built house in a village in Yavatmal district where a
farmer had committed suicide the year before. The morning light
came in from the open front door and there was a faint fragrance
of hay from the cattle shed. A just-lit wood stove gave off smoke
that smelled of a familiar tree. The room held the father, mother,
and brother of the deceased farmer. I said I wanted to speak to
the wife, which turned out to be an unexpected request. She was
busy, with two children to send off to school, food to cook for
the family, and errands to run before she went to work as farm
labour at Rs 100 per day. When I finally got a chance to talk to
her, she answered my questions in a guarded, measured manner; but whenever her responses were simple and direct, she was
impatiently interrupted by her family members. When I asked
about her life after her husband's death, the sunlight from the
open door reflected in the unshed tears of her brown eyes. The
men answered on her behalf, and I told them that I wanted her
version. Abruptly, she stood up and left the room, and I wondered if I had probed too far. The men explained that she did not
know anything about what killed her husband and that there was
no point in asking her questions.

Giving up, I decided to leave, when she returned carrying two
cups of tea. She handed one teacup to her surprised father-in-law
and the other to me. A confused silence reigned in the room as if

she did not have the authority to decide whether or not to serve tea to guests. Then, she settled in her corner and began speaking about her life in her own way—simply and directly. No one interrupted her again.

It was the best tea I ever had.

★★★

There can be no generalization, even for the sake of a preface, about the women of Vidarbha. Each of them had a story of grief and torment of living in poverty in India. Each time they spoke, it was in a voice unused to expression. Their grief and tears swept away every claim of the greatness of this nation. Each time they asked a question, they silenced every compelling speech by our political leaders. And these were simple questions: What will happen to my children? Why does no one care for us? Why am I so unfortunate?

The women I followed since 2014 led me on a journey into a land of shadows. They lived in the undefined space left by the men of the society. They were considered physically weak, socially redundant, and electorally insignificant. They were colonized peripheries, whose lives were at the disposal of men to do as they pleased. This was how this nation was built: by relegating the woman behind the man, glorifying her sacrifice in that overused saying that behind every man, there must be a woman.

I learnt they did not compare themselves to men, they did not consider themselves equals. So they did not deal with men, and their reluctance was considered feminine and made men feel protective towards them. When the men died, the women lost their only access to the world; they needed a male escort to go to panchayat offices, tehsil offices, banks, krishi kendras, even their children's schools. They told me they would not be 'allowed'. I later understood what that meant. One of the widows faced intense social backlash—mainly from her own family—when she single-handedly managed to get approval for a house loan, under a 2016 government scheme. Another woman, who found financial independence because of employment through the government in 2007, was advised to remarry as she had only daughters, but no sons.

These women's spirits were tamed every day in a continuous exercise of control over their choices and freedom. Forced to walk a few paces behind the man, like his shadow, the woman did not exist without him. But when he died, he left his shadow behind.

The woman, however, may be the best part of the man. One rainy day in 2015, a mother of several children living in a mud-and-thatch house said that her husband had loved her. She knew that it did not explain his suicide, which left her alone to handle the consequences and the distress, but she said it for the children. She wanted him to be honoured and remembered by them, and praised his efforts to help the family.

The children also knew what killed their fathers and shackled their mothers to their circumstances. I would often ask them about their dreams for future, and only one said agriculture. The children imagined being professionals, artists—one, even a busi-nessman—but their aim was respect, not wealth; no one said they wanted to be rich. Many wanted to be part of the state system, so that they could bring justice for others like them and make it more humane and responsive. These children were witnesses to the state's neglect of their fathers when they were alive, and, the harsh investigation after their deaths. Their anger cannot be reconciled; they know the state could have saved their fathers, just as it could now support their mothers.

One evening in August 2016, a frail widow heard my con-versation with her young son while we all sat in her front yard. The son spoke enthusiastically about what he dreamt of doing when he grew up, and how he would like to be an engineer. His mother interrupted him curtly, asking him what was the point of such plans if they were never realized. When her son grew upset, she explained that she was saving him from disappointment. He nodded, and did not speak again. His silence that evening echoed with a desperation unarticulated by the powerful orators of our nation. No one represents the helplessness of the farmer driven to suicide, and the family he leaves behind.

Through the years of research that went into the *Widows of Vidarbha: Making of Shadows,* I learnt the meaning of strength. Women who escaped from the constraints they had inherited from their mothers, and cultivated the desire for freedom among their daughters. Women whose will was so strong that they waited, sometimes for years, for the state to acknowledge them. Women who were so resolute that they worked double shifts as farm labour under the scorching sun and did not have the energy to even stand on their feet when they returned home. These women were the role models of a new generation in Vidarbha.

The widows are not remembered in policy and politics, and neither are they remembered by the media when their husbands commit suicide. It is a half-democracy that does not recognize half of its population. India is a long way from being a great nation if it cannot take care of a grieving widow who struggles to keep her children alive. I have often wondered how the elected representatives have the heart to return to Vidarbha and campaign for the votes of these invisible people. Who did the members of Parliament and Legislative Assembly represent? And if the sweeping electoral results were despite the tears of the poor, then is India really a democracy? Is the state that treats a farmer suicide with suspicion and distrust really constitutional? The answers, however, were not in the purview of this research; these are merely the questions that come to my mind every time I travel on the patchy roads of Vidarbha.

I would like to thank the kind and patient people of Vidarbha, and the time they spent sharing their stories for this research. Even when they were still grieving for the loss of a husband, the women were collected, polite, and kind. In the course of my visits, I had seen too many eyes fill up and always hoped I would never see another teardrop fall again. On some visits, my hopes came true and I was greeted with smiles instead. I thank the sunlight and rain that makes the people of Vidarbha smile.

A great deal of knowledge about farmer suicides and farming can be found among the bureaucracy of Yavatmal and Amravati at the level of the tehsils and district collectorates. Through the experiences of the officers who handled the crisis for the state, I learnt about the region and its peculiarities in agriculture over the years. Many officers shared information about farmer suicides beyond their call of duty and with heartfelt empathy with the farmers' families. I would like to thank these officers for the time they spent in guiding this research. In Yavatmal, I am forever grateful to the officers of the District Collectorate in-charge of farmer suicides, the district information officers, the Department of Women and Child Development, the Baliraja Chetna Abhiyan, and the officers at the tehsil headquarters at Ner, Arni, and Ghatanji. In Amravati, I am grateful to the office of the divisional commissioner, the district information officers, the Vasantrao Naik Sheti Swavalamban Mission, and the officers at the tehsil headquarters at Morshi, Chandur Bazar, and Bhatkuli.

The Vidarbha Jan Andolan Samiti has been instrumental in keeping a tab on farmer suicides and compiling data independent of the state's categorizations of eligibility. I would like to thank its members, especially Kishore Tewari, for his insight into the farm crisis. The research was assisted by Marathi translators and I thank Rahul Subhashrao Raut in Yavatmal, and Subodh Krishnarao Deshmukh and Gaurav Khond in Amravati. I owe a special thanks to Shashi Kant Sharma, Ajay Gawande, Richa Choudhary, and Vinod Nangia for their support. I am grateful to Dr K.R. Kranthi, formerly of the Central Institute for Cotton Research, now the head of the Technical Information Section of the International

Cotton Advisory Committee, for sharing his vast experience with cotton crops in India and the world. I am grateful to my friend Premanka Goswami for helping me conceptualize the research about farm widows.

For making this book possible, I would like to thank the entire team at Oxford University Press, India. I have been fortunate to work with research assistants hailing from different parts of the country who were keenly interested in Vidarbha and diligent while researching about it. For the period 2014–17, I am grateful to Sudhir Choudhary for his enthusiasm and dedication throughout the project. For 2016, I thank Prince Bhandari for statistical support and Ritika Popli for contribution during one of the field visits. For 2017, I thank Ragini Pant and Venkata Narayana for their assistance with finalizing the text.

In the end, I remember my father, K.V.S. Rama Sarma, whose life will always be an inspiration to me. I am also grateful to my husband, Pawan Khera, for his conviction and optimism, which helped me see this book through.

Kota Neelima

December 2017
New Delhi

Introduction

'It is easy to die.'
A widow from Vidarbha

hy do farmers commit suicide? Farmer suicides have been taking place across India for years now, and the studies of rural distress reveal the deeply rooted, tenacious causes, such as lack of irrigation, fragmentation of land, unsuitability of seeds, and inadequate sources of credit. Despite the democratically elected governments that claim to represent a country where over half the population is dependent on farming,[1] agriculture has been consistently ignored at a steep cost to farmers' lives. Remedies have been tried—the state waived loans to small and marginal farmers ahead of elections, and after elections, such sops were criticized for disrupting credit discipline among the borrowers.[2] The crisis provided an opportunity to try more adventurous 'remedies'; farmers were cornered into using expensive, genetically engineered seeds, even when these added heavily to the cost of cultivation of crops like cotton, further indebting the farmer. Although this generated hope, which helped the governments get re-elected, none of the remedies worked. The question remained: why did farmers commit suicide, bringing a bad name to 'popular' governments?

So it became prudent and necessary for the state that other causes of the suicides were discovered, such as alcoholism, depression, vices, etc. Farmers were blamed for being ambitious, extravagant, adventurous, lazy, cowardly, and too emotional. Camps were set up to help them cope with life's stresses, charities were organized and advice was dispensed. Additionally, the state found the usual way of containing the situation; not all farmer suicides would be recognized as such. There were rules to dying; only those deceased farmers who had unpaid bank loans in their name or in the name of their families, and had land in their name or in the name of their families, were considered to fall in the 'farmer suicide' category. These 'correct' suicides of the farmers, verified through this process, earned them compensation money, which was given to their widows. Once again the state expected that such monetary relief would make the farmers, and voters in general, appreciate the kindness of the politicians and re-elect them. And once again, it was not a remedy. The question still persisted: why did farmers commit suicide despite such 'generosity' of the state?

Again, it became imperative for the state to find other reasons to explain why it failed to contain farmer suicides. It was believed that the compensation itself encouraged the farmers to kill themselves; that the Rs 1 lakh might have increased the toll, and that farmers who died due to other reasons were shown as farmer suicides. It was insinuated that farmers could do anything for money, even die. But the state knew the truth, because the compensation procedure ensured that each farmer suicide was investigated in-depth. The state was aware that farmer suicides happened because of one essential reason—the farmer's sense of fairness and responsibility was hurt by his continued inability to repay debts. This explanation was in stark contrast to the ease with which the state and politicians tried arbitrary solutions to farm distress and blamed farmers for their own deaths. It was an inconvenient truth that would have shifted the guilt to the state and was, therefore, never told. Meanwhile, the question continued—why did farmers commit suicide, denting the image of every charismatic prime minister of the country and every dynamic chief minister of the state?

The farmers of India have no witnesses either in their life or in their death. The state, therefore, believed that the truth it sought to suppress was known only to the deceased farmer. But the state was wrong in making this assumption, because the truth was known to one other person—the farmer's widow. She was invisible to the state, as she was to society at large after the death of her husband. Her views were summarily represented in the opinions of the family, community, and the state; she could not speak in a voice separate from the male voice, and did not exist independent of the male identity. The state procedure gave the widow partial visibility during the investigation of farmer suicides by taking her statements or issuing the relief cheques in her name. This was mere procedure, and the state did not expect a woman to really know why her husband committed suicide.

But the wives *did* know. They knew how the state ignored their husbands while they were alive, how their desperate applications for welfare were dismissed, how many times their husbands visited the collectorates for relief, how much money was spent appeasing tehsildars,[*] gram sevaks, panchayat[†] members, talathis,[‡] etc. These wives had seen their husbands lose faith, and found the empty pesticides bottles that had ended their lives. These were the caring mothers who rescued the memories of their fathers for their children, shielding them from the painful facts. These were the grieving women who, within days of a suicide, convinced the state of the good mental condition of their husbands, signed documents attesting to the 'truth', and accepted the meagre cheques. But for the state, they did not exist. After all, what did the widows of farmers know about agriculture, crop management, bank

---

[*] A tehsildar is a deputy or assistant to an Indian district revenue officer.

[†] A panchayat is a village council.

[‡] A talathi is in charge of a village or group of villages, and represents the district administration.

loans, private debts, land documents, health bills, power connec-
tions, panchayat politics, children's education? The short answer
was—everything.

Losing the Invisible

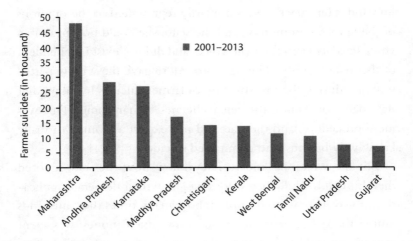

FIGURE 1   Top 10 states for farmer suicides in India from 2001 to
2013[3]
Source: National Crime Records Bureau

Farmer suicides, as given in Figure 1, reflect the crisis brew-
ing through the several phases of structural transformation of
the rural sector.[4] The first phase, from the early 1950s to the
mid-1960s, focused on land reforms, irrigation, and objectives
like supply of credit, which are yet to be uniformly achieved.
The second phase was the Green Revolution, during which the
implications for distribution of resources, and economic and
social development[5] were ignored, and agricultural development was measured through productivity, which turned into a
'trope for development itself'.[6] The last phase was the period of
economic reforms and globalization, which only widened and
deepened the inequalities.

During this time, and under the aegis of politically correct pro-farmer governments, agriculture had become particularly difficult in rain-fed areas due to a fall in public investment in irrigation and infrastructure, and in technological research and innovations.[7] Farmer suicides, as development economists D. Narasimha Reddy and Srijit Mishra argue, were the result of neglect of agriculture since the middle of the 1980s, followed by the economic reforms and the low institutional support to agriculture.[8] In this context, the state of Maharashtra presented the contradictory picture of extreme agricultural failure along with high non-agricultural growth.[9] This disparity was sharpest in western Vidarbha, where the farmer was entirely at the mercy of the weather, the market, and the state's indifference.[10] The wide regional as well as inter-district differences suggest the study of the region as a unit, like Vidarbha, which displayed the severe impact of farm neglect.[11] Further, owing to the intensity and length of the farm crisis, the study of Vidarbha could map the diversity of conditions and the common factors for farmers' distress, such as indebtedness, rising costs of cultivation, declining returns, and inadequate policy support. The region also indicated how small and marginal farming could not be sustained without substantial public infrastructure support, and that the solution had to include initiatives of both policy and civil society.[12] In what might be true for the entire nation, agricultural distress in Vidarbha was also worsened by the opportunism of the political class that used the crisis in blame games instead of meaningful and timely interventions. For example, the governments were challenged by the opposition on issues like tariff, where the suicides were only used as a 'weapon'[13] to attack politicians and their vested interests.

The causes of farmer suicide, as mentioned before, had also 'evolved' through research in the field. While analysing quantitative studies on the farm crisis in Vidarbha, Meeta and Rajivlochan found that there were a few 'attractive qualities'[14] to identify indebtedness as the cause: Debt, it was found, was not only tangible and quantifiable, but also the historically appropriate reason for farm crisis, where the 'rapacious moneylender, exploiting the farmer under the protection of a colonial or colonial-type bureaucracy and legal system, has been part of a nationalist common sense'.[15] It was found too simplistic to claim that the state schemes and loan waivers to those in distress were easy to announce, and it could not be known with certainty if they helped.[16] Such reasoning freed the state of its welfare responsibilities, first initiated under Article 371(2).[17] Other causes for farmer suicides—like depression—diverted the discourse towards the 'need to strengthen the National Mental Health Programme at primary health care level to offer support and counselling to vulnerable farmers in rural area'.[18]

The neglect of the farm crisis by the state administration might be partly due to the disinterest of the elected representatives towards the implementation of solutions, or for finding new ones. In the XVI Lok Sabha, in the first three years, there had been 17 questions on farmer suicides,[19] while during the entire tenure of the earlier Lok Sabha, there had been 20.[20] There were 29 questions raised in the XVI Lok Sabha over widows,[21] and addressed war widows, among others. Farm widows, however, were not included in the questions of the elected representatives, even though their numbers were increasing by the day. Perhaps, the state found this aspect covered in committee reports that examined the farm crisis from the view of the farmers and concluded, rather inevitably, that 'while economic indebtedness and its attendant economic distress is the main reason behind suicide by farmers, the root cause behind the suicides is the fact that farming in Vidarbha has no longer remained financially viable'.[22] In this July 2008 report on the progress of the government's Rs 1,075 crore package for the six districts of western Vidarbha as well as the prime minister's Rs 3,750 crore relief for Vidarbha, much time and space was spent to prove that Maharashtra was not 'the worst possible State'[23] in India with respect to farmer suicides.

Significantly, the farmer was analysed statistically and quanti-tatively so that distress could be tabulated and charted around his suicide. His living widow, however, was another matter. Even though her life was spent amid the same distress, it was invisible to the state. To be fair, the state also tried to make the farmer suicides invisible. Data on the suicides suffered from underestima-tion because it was linked only to cases where state compensation was paid. That was not considered a good measure, as Reddy and Mishra argued, because the 'official scrutiny often is known to treat even genuine instances of suicides as arising out of disease or old age or other reasons, with a view to restrict the payment of com-pensation'.[24] Death was separated into different categories in the data provided by the National Crime Records Bureau (NCRB)[25] in 2014, in which 'Farmers' sub-category recorded fewer suicides and 'Others' category showed a sudden increase.[26] This quantita-tively decreased farmer suicides, but increased the toll in another column. That, in a nutshell, was the trouble with numbers.

It might be difficult to research the invisible, especially when such invisibility is imposed and maintained by a consensus among the state, society, and family. Authors like B. Ratna Kumari[27] and Meena Karnik[28] have made incisive comments on the subject and provided access to the unexplored problems of farm widows. Ranjana Padhi[29] presented the sociological conditions prevail-ing around farmer suicides in Punjab, and the bitter struggle for survival by the women dependent on the hetero-patriarchal struc-tures of marriage and family, and how they supported themselves, their children, the elderly, as well as dealt with the wrath and harassment of lending agencies and commission agents. Factors for farmer suicides, as Padhi stated, could be hurt pride, humilia-tion at the hands of recovery agents, crop failure, and the 'torment of seeing one's children not having enough to eat, or facing one's inability to pay their school fees'.[30]

Agricultural crisis, manifested as farmer suicides, did not seem to include the crisis of women farmers. For instance, in Andhra

Pradesh, although women cultivated land in rural households and had even committed suicide due to farm distress,[31] they were not counted as farmers. This, however, did not stop the debt of the husbands to be transferred to the widows, as Ratna Kumari states.[32] The state and social custom seemed to deny legitimacy to even the distress of the farm widow.

The relationship of the state with gender was tumultuous, as development economist Bina Agarwal observed, because the state has the power to enhance cooperation or entrench discrimination.[33] Further, such cooperation and conflict[34] were evident within the state in its implementation of gender-based policy. This role of the state was also established in the research for this book, especially at the points of its interface with the farm widows. The state, in a way, endorsed the legitimacy of the custom and practice that was purposefully blind to gender interests. Widows had access, but not ownership of land, as Padhi states, which was either cultivated by the next senior male member of the family or her sons, or leased.[35] The invisibility of the widow was standardized without scope for response or contest. Further, daughters of farm widows do not seem to be headed to a different future. With tenuous rights over land, just like their mothers, the daughters too could not claim land meant for the sons. This may be the reflection of a larger reality existing in South Asia in relation to land rights and gender, as Agarwal states, where even families without male heirs waited for daughters to be married to pass on the land to the son-in-law.[36] The farm widow had no legitimate right over land belonging to her husband and even the time-bound ownership was subject to factors like, as Agarwal points out, 'whether or not she remains single and chaste; whether she has sons and her sons (if any) are minors or adults; whether the deceased husband has partitioned from the joint family estate before his death; and so on'.[37] When she had only daughters and no sons, she received maintenance in some cases, and when she had minor sons, she was trustee of the land until they were old enough to cultivate it.[38]

Interaction with the state as a male domain posed a deterrence against any assertion and contest by the farm widows. The mediation with the outside world through the male member of the family[39] deeply influenced the decisions of not just widows but women at different ages, and reflected in their condition socially and economically. Disputes against the late husband's family, therefore, had a low possibility of being initiated by the widow, as she would still need the cooperation and mediation of his family members. Some cases in this book bear out this reality.

There is an urgent need for an inclusive argument against the invisibility conferred by the state on the woman, whose conditional visibility as a wife is lost with the death of her husband. The research on farmer suicides might rightly stop with the farmers, but the research on farmer crises must necessarily include the widows. The impact of farm distress on the community and family has to be studied through complete visibility of the widow and her life. During the research of this book, I found the state unable to accommodate this difference in its evaluation of the farm crisis. This was borne out in the list of 43 questions asked during the enquiry into suicides by Vidarbha farmers, as given in Figure 2. It demonstrates what Judith Butler in her seminal book *Gender Trouble* states that 'the action of gender requires a performance that is repeated' in daily conduct through socially established meanings.[40] The questionnaire maintains gender in its given frame, as can be seen through the actions of the state before it decides to pay the compensation. A farmer's widow has to fix herself in a pre-decided role to be able to communicate with the state, as evident from the *bayaan* or the statement submitted by the widow to the tehsildar, which none of the women interviewed for this book had written themselves, but had to sign nevertheless. With each such signature under the words written by men, the state appropriated the right of the visibility of the widows of Vidarbha, without their knowledge or consent.

१) मृतकाचे नाव व वय   :-

२) राहण्याचे ठिकाण व तालुका   :-

३) मृत्युची तारीख व ठिकाण   :-

४) मृत्युची तारीख व ठिकाण   :-

५) मृत्यु कशाामुळे झाला   :-

६) शव विच्छेदन अहवाल प्राप्त झाला काय :-

७) त्यानुसार मृत्युचे कारण :-

८) मृतकाकडे शेतजमीन आहे काय   :-

९) बागायत किंवा कोरडवाहु क्षेत्र   :-

१०) मागील वर्षी काय पिक घेतले ?   :-

११) कुटुंबातील व्यक्तींची नांवे वय ,व्यवसाय :-

१२) कुटुंबातील व्यक्तीचे नावे जमीन आहे काय :
     किती , काठे , काय पिक घेतले   :-

१३) मृतक व्यक्तीने शेती ,मक्त्याने लागवडीने
     इतरास दिली आहे काय ? कुणाची कुठली
     कीती काय पिक होते उत्पन्न किती झाले ?   :-

१४) मृतकाच्या मालकीचे शेतात यंदा तथा मागील :-
     वर्षी पिकावर झालेले उत्पन्न

१५) मृतकाची सामाजीक व मानसिक स्थीती काय होती

FIGURE 2   A sample of the 43-question form of the Yavatmal
administration. The questions in Marathi are about the farmer's name,
age, address, date and place of death, post-mortem findings, cause of
death, farmer's land details and crop yield, family members' land details
and crop yield, the mental state and social status of the farmer, etc.
Source: Farmer Suicide Department, Yavatmal District, Maharashtra

Finding the Invisible

It was said that there was one suicide of a farmer every 30 minutes
in India,[41] and that, in turn, meant that a woman's life was suddenly
and irretrievably plunged into darkness and societal struggle. This
was true for every widow I interviewed in Vidarbha. There were
two main objectives of writing this book: to reveal the invisible
world of the widows from the inside, unmediated by the perception of the visible; and, to chart the various invisibilities that were
imposed on these widows at various stages of their life before and
after they lost their husbands. The method of the research was to
study individual cases during 2014–17, and follow their financial,

social, and agricultural plans, along with aspirations of education, employment, marriage, and business, among others.

Farmer suicides have taken place across the country, as mentioned before, but I chose to focus on Vidarbha, where the toll has been the highest since 2001. It provided a holistic and wide-ranging picture of the multiple hurdles in the path of a farm widow's survival after a farmer's demise. This book seeks to offer an interior view of the condition of farm widows with the optimism that it could be applicable to farm widows in other situations, despite the variations intrinsic to the diversity of the country.

The empirical study of suicides in 2014, when the research began, showed that of the 5,650 farmer suicides in India that year, the maximum—2,568, which was 45.5 per cent of the total—took place in Maharashtra.[42] The other four states with a high incidence were Telangana, Madhya Pradesh, Chhattisgarh, and Karnataka, which, together with Maharashtra, accounted for 5,056 of 5,650 farmer suicides in India that year.[43] Within Maharashtra, Vidarbha recorded the maximum farmer suicides, and of its 11 districts, Yavatmal, Amravati, Buldhana, Akola, Wardha, and Washim (in descending order) had the highest cumulative farmer suicides at 12,989 between 2001 and 2016.[44]

However, the government figures of farmer suicides for Maharashtra were exponentially reduced from those of earlier years, as given in Figure 3. According to the NCRB, there had been 47,915 farmer suicides in Maharashtra from 2001 to 2013.[45] Then, in 2014, the NCRB changed the data presentation, causing a drop in suicide numbers of farmers in India; as mentioned before, the decrease in the numbers in the 'Farmers' sub-category seemed to coincide with increase in the 'Others' category.[46] In 2014, suicides in India in the 'Farmers' sub-category fell to 5,650,[47] which was less than half the 2013 figure of 11,772.[48] The reorganization of statistics raised questions about suppression of the truth that only exposed the state's complicity, and encouraged similar trends in the future.[49] However, the increasing numbers of farmer suicides in the villages of Vidarbha and the resulting increase in the number of widows cannot be hidden by any methodological sleight of hand. Any attempt by the state to brush them aside statistically or reorganize them into categories of obscurity would not serve to diminish the problem, but only reveal the state's motives to cover up its guilt in the creation and neglect of the farm crisis. This was demonstrated by the fact that despite all attempts, Maharashtra still ranked the highest on the list of states where the tragic events took place from 2001 to 2013, as given earlier in Figure 1 and the number remained in thousands as seen in Figure 3.

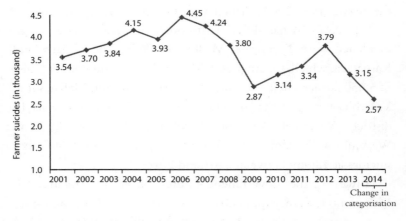

FIGURE 3 Farmer suicides in Maharashtra from 2001 to 2014
Source: Author compilation based on NCRB reports

Apart from state-owned statistical organizations, alternate sources of information were the media, civil society, and activists who worked in the districts of Vidarbha. The efforts of the non-state initiatives[50] had been in contrast to the efforts of the state (which had tried to underplay the suicides), and turned the nation's focus on the matter. Prominent among them was the Vidarbha Jan Andolan Samiti (VJAS) that had diligently collected and presented the data about farmer suicides in western Vidarbha, and shared it with this study for the years between 2009 and 2014, as given in Figure 4. The state administration in Maharashtra sought to provide compensation for farmer suicides based on an eligibility criteria of debt, land ownership, etc., and segregated the list of farmer suicides between those eligible and ineligible for such compensation. The non-state organizations compiled a single list of farmer suicides based on the person's occupation being agriculture, and whether the person worked on own or rented land, or as farm labour.

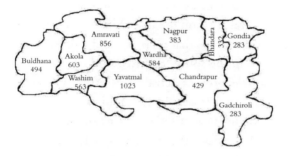

FIGURE 4 Map of district-wise farmer suicides in Vidarbha from 2009 to 2014
Source: Vidarbha Jan Andolan Samiti

The study of the data collected for both eligible and ineligible cases showed that the two districts, Yavatmal and Amravati, had the highest number of suicides. This fact was also supported by official figures about the suicide numbers in the two districts, in which 3,589 farmers had committed suicide in Yavatmal and 2,911 farmers in Amravati from 1 January 2001 till 22 August 2016.[51] Farmer suicides have been the result of historical and contemporary causes in the districts of Amravati and Yavatmal, as studies have shown.[52] Rain-dependent agriculture, decreasing profits, failure of procurement schemes, and stepping back of the state from agriculture, both in formal credit as well as investment, were some of the causes discovered.[53] While the study of

Yavatmal and Amravati served as a larger framework of districts for choosing the case studies, the specific framework was tehsils where the villages were situated. This selection of tehsils was based on two criteria: one, accessibility of the cases so that they could be revisited; and two, the distribution of the cases to represent all regional variations within the two districts. To address the first issue, tehsils were chosen based on their accessibility, that is, if they could be reached by the state or district roads and were within 100 km from the district headquarter towns or the district capitals of Yavatmal and Amravati. To address the second issue, the selected tehsils were located approximately in the north, south, and central areas on the map. Six tehsils were selected from the contiguous districts that were located, approximately, two in the north, two in the south, and two in the central area.

The final selection of tehsils was Arni, Ghatanji, and Ner from Yavatmal, and Bhatkuli, Chandur Bazar, and Morshi from Amravati. On the first criteria of accessibility, the tehsils were all within 100 km from the district capitals, and were approachable by road. The longest distance from the district capital was Morshi, at approximately 53 km from Amravati, and the shortest was Bhatkuli, approximately 21 km also from Amravati.[54] On the second criteria of distribution, Arni and Ghatanji represented the south, Ner and Bhatkuli represented the central region, and Morshi and Chandur Bazar represented the north.

Cases were chosen through four levels of selection based on the data of the district administration, the list of farmer suicides, the list of welfare schemes for children, and the farmer–suicide compensation process. First, the state lists[55] of the farmer suicides were referred to select the case studies. These had the name, age, date of suicide, and village address of the farmers who had committed suicide, and provided the first level of selection, based on which cases were shortlisted. The age of the widows in the case studies ranged between 26 and 63 years, as of 2017, while the time period was from 2002 until 2014. Second, a list of farmer-suicide cases with children who got support from the state was obtained from the administration.[56] This aspect was also studied to ascertain the impact of the state's intervention on the lives of widows and constituted the second level of selection, wherever applicable. Third, the shortlisted cases were visited in 2014 and deviations like unmarried cases were disregarded. As mentioned before, the accessibility and distribution criteria of the cases were crucial for the purposes of the book, and these were also addressed in this phase of selection. Finally, the shortlisted cases were studied through the state's investigation into the farmer suicide before award of compensation, and this formed the fourth level of selection.

To sum up, the criteria followed in the four levels were age of farmer, time of suicide, marital status, welfare schemes, accessibility by road, and availability of documentation for suicide compensation. The final list contained 18 cases that were recognized by the state or had been eligible for compensation. These constituted nine cases in each district, along with two ineligible cases that served as a reference to understand the state process. For an overview of the cases selected, please refer to Appendix 1 and 2. Of the 18 cases, two women had died of illness in 2006 and 2014. Among the remaining 16 cases, three widows had stopped working in the fields personally[57] while 10 widows now work only as daily wagers. Two widows worked as anganwadi workers and one worked as a part-time attendant in a medical dispensary. The loan at the time of their husbands' deaths was in the range of Rs 17,000 to Rs 2,50,000,[58] and the land was between 2 acres and 12 acres. Some widows had also leased out their land to other farmers. The main crop of cultivation was cotton, followed by soybean and pigeon pea (*tur*). Of the 18 farmer suicides, post-mortem reports revealed that 14 died of poisoning, 3 hung themselves, and one burnt himself to death.

The narratives of the widows were recorded several times during the research and the observations were mentioned in the case studies year-wise. This allowed tracking of the progress of work, agricultural productivity, construction projects, state of education and health, as well as state-related work like applications for irrigation schemes, Below Poverty Line (BPL) cards, anganwadi employment, deepening of wells, etc. The repeated visits, as envisaged, helped to achieve a deeper understanding that was, in most cases, at three levels. First, the lives of the widows remained unchanged not just from one season to the next, but from one generation to the next. Second, it was impossible for the widows to support their families without private loans and the generosity of others. Third, there was anger among the farmers' children who held the state and the political class responsible for their destiny. Fourth, there was evidence of the continuous neglect of the widows by the state, despite their need and their agency.

The first of the two objectives in writing this book, as noted before, was to speak in the voice of the widows of Vidarbha, unmediated by the perception of the visible. To ensure this, once the narratives were recorded through 2014–15, they were read out to the widows in August 2016. The text was reviewed by the women themselves so that it was their authentic view and the narratives were finalized; further updates until 2017 were added separately at the end of each narrative. The research provided a perception study of the invisible, and revealed the dynamic of the world of shadows in which the women survived. It also helped chart the different invisibilities of the widow, which was the second objective of this research. The question that was raised, and sought to be answered, was about how farm widows were restricted to their invisibility, conditionally released through social rituals like marriage, or partially released through state rituals like suicide compensation. The widows made an intervention into the working of the state, the community and the family that had never been heard before and, perhaps, never been sought.

Notes

1. 'State of Indian Agriculture, 2015–16', Ministry of Agriculture and Farmer Welfare, Government of India, 2016, p. 3, available at www.eands.dacnet.nic.in, accessed 28 June 2017. According to the report, 'around 50 per cent of the population' was dependent on agriculture.

2. In the words of Arundhati Bhattacharya, the then SBI chairperson in 2017, according to a newspaper report, 'Today the loans will come back as the government will pay for it but when we disburse loans again then the farmers will wait for the next election expecting another waiver.' *PTI*, 'SBI Farm Loan Waivers Upset Credit Discipline: SBI Chairman', *The Hindu*, 15 March 2017, available at www.thehindu.com/business/agri-business/sbi-farm-loan-waivers-upset-credit-discipline-sbi-chairman/article17466189.ece, accessed 28 June 2017.

3. The data is for undivided Andhra Pradesh until 2013. Telangana was formed on 2 June 2014 (see www.telangana.gov.in, accessed 3 July 2017).

4. C.H. Hanumantha Rao, *Agriculture, Food Security, Poverty, and Environment: Essays on Post-Reform India* (New Delhi: Oxford University Press, 2005), pp. 99–118.

5. A.R. Vasavi 'Contextualising the Agrarian Suicides', R.S. Deshpande and Saroj Arora (eds), *Agrarian Crisis and Farmer Suicides* (New Delhi: Sage Publications, 2010), p. 76.

6. Vasavi, 'Contextualizing the Agrarian Suicides', p. 76.

7. D. Narasimha Reddy and Srijit Mishra, 'Agriculture in the Reforms Regime', D. Narasimha Reddy and Srijit Mishra (eds), *Agrarian Crisis in India* (New Delhi: Oxford University Press, 2009), pp. 12–13.

8. Reddy and Mishra, 'Agriculture in the Reforms Regime', pp. 3–43.

9. Srijit Mishra, 'Agrarian Distress and Farmers' Suicides in Maharashtra', D. Narasimha Reddy and Srijit Mishra (eds), *Agrarian Crisis in India* (New Delhi: Oxford University Press, 2009), p. 126.

10. Mishra, 'Agrarian Distress and Farmers' Suicides in Maharashtra', p. 134.

11. Refer to Figure 4: Map of district-wise farmer suicides in Vidarbha from 2009 to 2014.

12. Srijit Mishra, 'Farmers' Suicides in Maharashtra', *Economic and Political Weekly* 41 (2006): 1538–45.

13. Neelima Deshmukh, 'Cotton Growers: Experience from Vidarbha', R.S. Deshpande and Saroj Arora (eds), *Agrarian Crisis and Farmer Suicides* (New Delhi: Sage Publications, 2010), p. 185.

14. Meeta and Rajivlochan, *Farmers Suicide: Facts and Possible Policy Interventions* (Pune: Yashwantrao Chavan Academy of Development Administration, 2006), p. 51.

15. Meeta and Rajivlochan, *Farmers Suicide: Facts & Possible Policy Interventions*, p. 51.

16. Meeta and Rajivlochan, *Farmers Suicide: Facts and Possible Policy Interventions*, p. 51.

17. To prevent a situation in which particular regions received inequitable distribution of state funds, resources, and opportunities, a 1956 amendment to the Constitution gave specific protections to Vidarbha, Marathwada, and other areas of Maharashtra and Gujarat under Article 371(2). Despite this, Vidarbha and Marathwada—a smaller region in south-central Maharashtra—have suffered exactly the kind of economic discrimination that they were to be safeguarded against. The Constitution (Seventh Amendment) Act, 1956, available at www.mha.nic.in, accessed 2 July 2017.

18. Amol R. Dongre and Pradeep R. Deshmukh, 'Farmers' Suicides in the Vidarbha region of Maharashtra, India: A Qualitative Exploration of their Causes', *Journal of Injury and Violence Research* 4, No. 1 (2012): 2.

19. Available at www.loksabha.nic.in, accessed 3 July 2017.

20. Available at www.loksabha.nic.in, accessed 3 July 2017.

21. Available at www.loksabha.nic.in, accessed 3 July 2017.

22. Narendra Jadhav, 'Farmers' Suicide and Debt Waiver: An Action Plan for Agricultural Development of Maharashtra', Farmers' Suicide Prevention Packages Evaluation Committee, Government of Maharashtra, 2008, pp. 6-16. The report was submitted by the Farmers' Suicide Prevention Packages Evaluation Committee, which was independently constituted by the Government of Maharashtra.

23. Jadhav, 'Farmers' Suicide and Debt Waiver: An Action Plan for Agricultural Development of Maharashtra', pp. 1-4.

24. Reddy and Mishra, 'Agriculture in the Reforms Regime', *Agrarian Crisis in India*, p. 33.

25. The National Crime Records Bureau was constituted in 1986, under the Ministry of Home Affairs, Government of India. The objective of the organization was to help the police with reliable

26. P. Sainath, 'The Slaughter of Suicide Data', *Frontline,* 21 August 2015, available at www.frontline.in/social-issues/the-slaughter-of-suicide-data/article7495402.ece, accessed 29 June 2017. Sainath revealed that the problematic categorization of farmer suicide by the government led to a decrease in the 'official' number of farmer suicides.

27. B. Ratna Kumari, *Farmers' Suicides in India: Impact on Women* (New Delhi: Serials Publications, 2009).

28. Meena Karnik, *Surviving Suicide: The Brave Women of Vidarbha* (Mumbai: Focus India Publications, 2011).

29. Ranjana Padhi, *Those Who Did Not Die: Impact of the Agrarian Crisis on Women in Punjab* (New Delhi: Sage Publications, 2012).

30. Padhi, *Those Who Did Not Die,* p. xvi.

31. P. Sainath quoted in Kumari, *Farmer's Suicides in India Impact on Women,* p. 82.

32. Sainath quoted in Kumari, *Farmer's Suicides in India Impact on Women,* p. 82.

33. Bina Agarwal, *A Field of One's Own: Gender and Land Rights in South Asia* (Cambridge University Press, 1994), p. 77.

34. Agarwal, *A Field of One's Own,* p. 78.

35. Padhi, *Those Who Did Not Die,* p. 40.

36. Agarwal, *A Field of One's Own,* pp. 249–50.

37. Agarwal, *A Field of One's Own,* pp. 254–5.

38. Agarwal, *A Field of One's Own,* p. 255.

39. Agarwal, *A Field of One's Own,* p. 268.

40. Judith Butler, 'Bodily Inscriptions, Performative Subversions', of Chapter-3 Subversive Bodily Acts in *Gender Trouble Feminism and the Subversion of Identity* (New York: Routledge, 2016), p. 191.

41. Between 1997 and 2005, one farmer in India committed suicide every 32 minutes, and since 2002, the figure has become 30 minutes. P. Sainath, 'One Farmer's Suicide Every 30 Minutes', *The Hindu,* 15 November 2007, available at www.thehindu.com/todays-paper/tp-opinion/One-farmerrsquos-suicide-every-30-minutes/article14875521.ece, accessed 25 June 2017.

42. 'Accidental Deaths and Suicides in India 2014', National Crime Records Bureau, Ministry of Home Affairs, Government of India, Chapter 2A, p. 266, available at www.ncrb.nic.in, accessed 29 June 2017.

43. 'Accidental Deaths and Suicides in India 2014', National Crime Records Bureau, Ministry of Home Affairs, Government of India, Chapter 2A, p. 266.

44. Data given by the Department of Land and Resettlement, Amravati District Administration, of the total number of farmer suicides from 1 January 2001 till 22 August 2016.

45. Compiled by author based on NCRB reports.

46. P. Sainath, 'The Slaughter of Suicide Data', *Frontline,* 21 August 2015, available at www.frontline.in/social-issues/the-slaughter-of-suicide-data/article7495402.ece, accessed 29 June 2017.

47. 'Accidental Deaths and Suicides in India 2014', National Crime Records Bureau, Ministry of Home Affairs, Government of India, Chapter 2A, p.266, available at www.ncrb.nic.in, accessed 3 July 2017.

48. 'Accidental Deaths and Suicides in India 2013', National Crime Records Bureau, Ministry of Home Affairs, Government of India, Part-II (Suicides in India), pp. 201–202, available at www.ncrb.nic.in, accessed 3 July 2017.

49. P. Sainath, 'The Slaughter of Suicide Data', *Frontline,* 21 August 2015, available at www.frontline.in/social-issues/the-slaughter-of-suicide-data/article7495402.ece, accessed 29 June 2017.

50. Kalpana Sharma, 'Media and the Agrarian Crisis', *Seminar,* 2009, available at www.india-seminar.com/2009/595/595_kalpana_sharma.htm, accessed 3 July 2017.

51. Data given by the Department of Land and Resettlement, Amravati District Administration.

52. Kumari, *Farmers' Suicides in India,* pp. 13–15.

53. Kumari, *Farmers' Suicides in India,* p. 70.

54. All distances were calculated on road and with the help of physical and online maps.

55. Accessed through the collectorate offices of Amravati and Yavatmal, respectively.

56. Accessed through the collectorate offices of Amravati and Yavatmal, respectively.

57. All the widows still depended on agriculture in one form or another.

58. Any bank or banks mentioned in the text refer to formal lending agencies like nationalized banks, cooperative societies, and finance companies, whereas informal loans are given by *shahukars* or private moneylenders.

SECTION I

Yavatmal

FIGURE 5   Map of Yavatmal district
Source: Yavatmal district website[1]

*T*he Yavatmal district of Maharashtra has an area of 13,582 sq km, with a total population of 27,72,348.[2] According to the District Census Handbook Yavatmal 2011, 21,74,195 of the total population lives in 2,137 villages.[3] At 82.8 per cent, Yavatmal's literacy rate[4] is higher than the 82.34 per cent[5] for Maharashtra and the 72.99 per cent[6] for India. The district has the highest sex ratio for the state at 952.[7] Agriculture is rain-fed and employs 79.2 per cent[8] of the total workforce, and cotton is the major crop. While there are three lakh farmers in the district, double the number are employed as farm labour. As found in this research, many farmers also worked as farm labour due to the unsustainability of agriculture on their own fields.

The district is divided into 16 administrative units called tehsils. Of these, the three tehsils of Ner, Arni, and Ghatanji were selected, as explained earlier in the Introduction. According to the District Census Handbook Yavatmal 2011, the largest total population among the tehsils is in Arni, followed by Ghatanji and Ner. Arni has a total area of 767 sq km[9] and has a total population of 1,61,833.[10] There are 111 villages[11] in Arni. The Ghatanji tehsil is spread over an area of 969 sq km[12] and has a total population of 1,17,294[13] across its 122 villages. Ner is spread over an area of 681sq km[14] and has a total population of 90,930;[15] there are 121 villages[16] in Ner.

Farmer suicide cases in the three tehsils for the years between 2001 and 2014 have been chosen for in-depth study. Among these, the earliest case of suicide was in 2002 in Ner; the latest, in Ghatanji in 2014. Most farmers I focused on were small and marginal, while most widows have not studied beyond Class 12. Many daughters of farmers excelled in schools despite the education system but were forced to think of marriage, and many sons did not want to be farmers, but were not qualified for other avenues of employment.

The narratives of the eight women in Yavatmal district in the following section reconstruct the invisibility of the widows of Vidarbha. No two stories are the same; every widow spoke of her life and battles—some that she won, and some that she lost.

≈

Notes

1. Available at: www.yavatmal.nic.in.
2. District Census Handbook Yavatmal, Maharashtra, Series-28, Part XII-B, Directorate of Census Operations, Maharashtra, 2011, p. 14, available at www.censusindia.gov.in, accessed 29 November 2017.
3. District Census Handbook Yavatmal, Maharashtra, Series-28, Part XII-B, Directorate of Census Operations, Maharashtra, 2011, p. 14, available at www.censusindia.gov.in, accessed 29 November 2017.
4. District Census Handbook Yavatmal, Maharashtra, Series-28, Part XII-B, Directorate of Census Operations, Maharashtra, 2011, Yavatmal, Maharashtra, www.censusindia.gov.in, accessed 29 November 2017.
5. Census of India, 2011, Office of the Registrar General & Census Commissioner, India, available at www.censusindia.gov.in, accessed 29 November 2017.
6. Census of India, 2011, Office of the Registrar General & Census Commissioner, India, available at www.censusindia.gov.in, accessed 29 November 2017.
7. This is the number of females per 1,000 males. District Census Handbook Yavatmal, Maharashtra, Series-28, Part XII-B, Directorate of Census Operations, Maharashtra, 2011, available at www.censusindia.gov.in, accessed 29 November 2017.
8. District Census Handbook Yavatmal, Maharashtra, Series-28, Part XII-B, Directorate of Census Operations, Maharashtra, 2011, p. 13, available at www.censusindia.gov.in, accesed 29 November 2017.
9. 'Geographical information of Arni Taluka', Yavatmal District, available at www.yavatmal.gov.in, accessed 30 November 2017.
10. District Census Handbook Yavatmal, Maharashtra, Series-28, Part XII-B, Directorate of Census Operations, Maharashtra, 2011, p. 24, www.censusindia.gov.in, accessed 29 November 2017.

11. 'Geographical information of Arni Taluka', Yavatmal District, available at www.yavatmal.gov.in, accessed 30 November 2017.
12. 'Geographical information of Ghatanji Taluka', Yavatmal District, available at www.yavatmal.gov.in, accessed 30 November 2017.
13. District Census Handbook Yavatmal, Maharashtra, Series-28, Part XII-B, Directorate of Census Operations, Maharashtra, 2011, p. 24, available at www.censusindia.gov.in, accessed 29 November 2017.
14. 'Geographical information of Ner Taluka', Yavatmal District, available at www.yavatmal.gov.in, accessed 29 November 2017.
15. District Census Handbook Yavatmal, Maharashtra, Series-28, Part XII-B, Directorate of Census Operations, Maharashtra, 2011, p. 24, available at www.censusindia.gov.in, accessed 29 November 2017.
16. 'Geographical information of Ner Taluka', Yavatmal District, available at www.yavatmal.gov.in, accessed 30 November 2017.

CHAPTER
ONE

Hope and Other
Temporary Things

Vandana Rathod, Ajanti Village, Ner Tehsil, Yavatmal District

A Widow Since 22 August 2013

There was no permanence about the house that farmer Ganesh Rathod had called home. The mud-and-thatch structure was built with the knowledge that it could dissolve in the next rain, and that the loosely repaired smooth walls could crack by the next summer. The thatched roof was too sparse, and the house too small to accommodate a family of five—Ganesh's widow Vandana and their four children. The repairs to the house seemed to be just another temporary way of holding back the inevitable. It was neither protest nor rebellion; the house did not stand with a determined will to survive or to battle against destiny. It was surrender, not immediate but the kind that slowly drained life from the living; almost like the mud that precariously held the structure together and waited to flow away with the monsoons. The roof of the house was low, as if the residents were not expected to stand tall inside its premises. The traditionally built floor was uneven but smooth, and felt cool under bare feet. The dilapidated door was barely shut and all the forces of nature were free to enter, just like every insidious twist of fate.

FIGURE 6   House of Vandana Rathod, January 2015
Source: Author

All things permanent had vanished with Ganesh, the post–mortem certified that. The report[1] stated that he was brought dead to the regional hospital of Ner at 1 o'clock in the morning on 23 August 2013 by the police. The post–mortem did not begin until noon the same day. The examination lasted for one hour and fifteen minutes, from 12.15 p.m. to 1.30 p.m. The clothes he wore for the last time were listed in detail, and he was described as moderately built, with no injuries, but with his fists clenched. Pieces of his intestine and stomach, along with their contents, were retained for further chemical examination. Also preserved were a piece of his liver, spleen, lung, and kidney. His body was returned to his family without his heart, which was retained in 'Bottle No.1'.[2] The examiners also found a tattoo on the right side of chest where his wife's name, Vandana, was written in Hindi. The examiners could not take that away from Ganesh, and those were the kind of permanent things that ended with him.

A picture of Ganesh now hung in the mud house with his name and date of death inscribed, as if made by a studio which had ample experience of framing such memories. He had dark, confident eyes, and sported a fashionable haircut and a red ceremonial *tilak* on his forehead. Adjoining his picture was a poster of bright roses and a phrase printed on the top right corner: 'Hope makes life meaningful …' Next to Ganesh's photograph, the slogan seemed ironic and impossible to bear. The photograph carried a garland of plastic flowers that would never wilt. Right beside that was a plastic container that held the tooth brushes of the family, which appeared, at first, to be a seemingly strange location for toiletries, on a wall that was almost a shrine for Ganesh. However, it was a way for Vandana to ensure that the children looked at their father's photograph first thing in the morning. The inscription on the poster now assumed great significance, as if it was a message that the mother wanted the children to believe in and live by. She did not just have to live without Ganesh, she had to deal with problems of survival and also ensure that the future was not lost to despair. She did not want the children to think of escape as an option.

There were two smaller photographs on the wall—one of Ganesh with Vandana and one with his younger daughter Tejal. In the first picture, Ganesh was sitting in a chair while Vandana was standing next to him with an arm around his shoulders, the way friends did. It was from another print of the same photograph that his final portrait had been cut out, separated from Vandana, framed, and garlanded. In the second photograph, Tejal was standing next to her father in her blue-and-white school uniform. He wore sunglasses, as if to humour his daughter's whim. There were no photographs of his other daughter Sonu, or of his sons Rohit and Vikram.

FIGURE 7   Vandana with her sons, January 2015
Source: Author

In 2014, when I first met them, Sonu was 16 years old, Rohit was 14, Tejal, 13, and the youngest, Vikram, was 10. Vandana was 32 years old, a frail woman with dark, introspective eyes that never smiled. In her statement to the police and the administration,[3] she described the day that Ganesh killed himself. On the morning of 22 August 2013, Ganesh had told her that he had to spray chemical pesticides in the field, and left home at 10 a.m. He returned around 7 p.m. and complained of extreme dizziness. As his condition worsened, Vandana asked a neighbour for help, and rushed him to the hospital in Ner where he was declared brought dead. She stated[4] that her husband had been anxious about the outstanding loan amount and had increasingly become despondent. She felt that this might have been a reason why he had committed suicide. Her mother-in-law, Yashodhabai, who was also at home at that time, said in her statement that Ganesh had been very quiet in the days preceding his death. His inability to repay the loan had made him pessimistic and taciturn. Ramesh

Rathod, the neighbour who helped take Ganesh to the hospital, revealed in his statement[5] the conversation they had regarding the loan. On 21 August 2013, Ganesh had complained to Ramesh about the low productivity of the field, and expressed the fear that he would not be able to repay the loan that year. He had also told Ramesh of his plans to spray pesticide in his field on the following day—the same pesticide he had consumed to kill himself. By all the official accounts, crops had been affected in the tehsil from 2010 to 2013 owing to bad weather. In his report, the deputy sarpanch of Ajanti had said that the repeated failure of the crops and the pressure to repay the loan might have left Ganesh hopeless and compelled him to commit suicide.

Since that day in 2013, Vandana has had to deal with all the problems that killed Ganesh, and deal with them alone. Records showed that they had a farmland of 13.59 acres, of which 2.98 acres was barren.[6] Ganesh had taken loans from a lending society in 2009 and 2010, which, together amounted to Rs 41,706 as of 31 March 2013.[7] Based on the statements of the family, the same report concluded that failed crops along with debt burden might have caused the suicide. At the top of this important document was the word 'patra', written in Hindi and underlined twice. That one word, which meant 'eligible', was written by a government employee to certify that Ganesh had indeed died due to debt burden and failure of crops. In other words, by dying for reasons that could be certified as 'appropriate', he became eligible for state compensation. The acceptance of his death by the system brought a semblance of permanence to his life. It stood like a tentative footprint amid the persistent erosion of everything else that belonged to the family.

After Ganesh's suicide, Vandana had rented out the land to another farmer at Rs 9,000 per year, which alleviated the financial burden per month only by Rs 750. Far from being a good bargain, it was a helpless compromise. As was the fact that a village road ran through their field and occupied almost two acres of the land, for which there had never been any compensation to a family that could not afford such a loss. Vandana was an intelligent woman who knew that these matters had to be resolved, but she neither had the time nor the assistance to pursue them.

Vandana was trained, like most girls in India are, to be a homemaker. That came with the handicap of not just financial dependence, but also a dependence on others for the general understanding of the outside world. Ganesh had managed all matters relating to loans, crops, and agricultural land. After his death, Vandana was plunged into these affairs about which she had no prior experience or information. Among the things she had to rapidly learn was how to fend for herself. 'There is no one left in the family to do farming,' Vandana said simply. 'My relatives helped us in the initial days after my husband's death. But they have their own families to look after, I understand that.' This understanding, however, could not have come without a hard and painful realization of her situation. She seemed indifferent to her fate; as if she knew all the choices were already made for her and the decisions already taken. 'I work as labour for daily wages, and earn about Rs 70 to Rs 100 per day. The work is sporadic and not available round the year. But I earn whatever I can during the sowing season, and later, during the harvest,' she said. All the money earned was already earmarked for various expenditures like education, health, and other costs of living. However, the money always fell short. Vandana explained the problem meticulously. 'My yearly expenditure is Rs 30,000 to Rs 40,000. I cannot get that money from either the rent on the field or from my work as labour. So I borrow money, sometimes from my parents and my brother.' She was unhappy about this, and seemed to share the same pride that had made Ganesh repay other pending loans with his hard work alone, without expectations of help from anyone. This was despite the fact that crops regularly failed, as if testing his confidence in his efforts and in his destiny.

The children continued going to school, and Ganesh's mother stayed at home due to ill health. Vandana toiled as farm labour to address the requirements of four growing children, bills for their education, health, transportation, and basic facilities. These were paid in slow, gruelling instalments, leaving no money for unforeseen expenditures that inevitably forced such families to borrow from private moneylenders. Besides the bank loan, Ganesh had also taken a private loan for agriculture of up to Rs 60,000, according to Vandana. But the cotton crop had stayed undependable, producing a yield of less than 10 quintals for the total land. Through 2012 and 2013, Ganesh had cultivated soybean, jowar, and tur, but without sources of irrigation, the yield was so low that it was almost a wasted effort. Despite the economic hardships he faced, a private loan taken four years ago had to be repaid by Ganesh at the rate of 2.5 per cent per month. The questions reminded her of the time when Ganesh had shielded her from such worrying details. Her smile lit up the little, dusty room, but it was short-lived.

'He used to worry too much. But there was never any money to save, any money to spare.' There was a brief silence, as she relived the hopelessness. 'He was that kind of man; he could not rest knowing that the failed crops meant the loan could not be repaid. I never knew about the state of the crops, he never burdened me with such things.' She had been stunned by his suicide—she still is. 'I never knew he contemplated killing himself. I would have never let him.' She had rushed him to the hospital on that night in August 2013. 'But I knew he had died on the way,' she said, her voice lost in the darkness of that journey that night. She knew he had come home to her to die; he had consumed the pesticide on their farm. Slow tears filled her eyes as she fell silent, engulfed by the memories. 'The family suffers more now than it had before, the troubles have only increased. I have to deal with everything—all my work, and all that used to be his. Now there is no one to share this burden. His death has solved nothing; it has only hurt all of us for the rest of our lives.' She did not speak in anger or complaint; it was not any other support she wanted, she wanted Ganesh's support. 'When he was around, I never faced

such anxieties because I was confident we both could find a solution to any problem. I feel very alone now, and I am the only one
who can take care of my children, their needs, and their future.'
She stopped speaking and withdrew into the silence of her own
world. She said briefly, 'I have no one.'

The compensation awarded to her by the government could
never include the cost of losing a proud, hardworking man, a
loving husband, an affectionate father. Of the Rs 1 lakh received,
Rs 70,000 was put in a fixed deposit bank account, while the rest
had been given in cash and spent on family expenses. The bank
loan had been rescheduled and she did not return to cultivating
cotton on the farm. It was an irreversible decision; she said, 'We
do not do agriculture anymore.'

Vandana's last stand against her present destiny was personified
in her four children, none of whom wasted a moment of their
life or a rupee of their mother's earning. Education was not a
matter of talent or opportunity for this family; it was a matter of
affordability. 'The school fees for Class 9 and higher classes are
expensive in the area, and I wanted my daughter Sonu to study
further,' Vandana said. Sonu had dropped out of school in Class
9 after the death of her father in 2013, and joined her mother as
a daily wager. It was not difficult to understand why, as Vandana
explained the odds. 'Although I want my children to study so that
they can have a better future, I do not have the money to support
them, and I do not get any work, other than as a daily wager.
The children study under the single light bulb, the bill for which
is Rs 300 for two months. The bus for the school costs Rs 200
per month.'

While we talked, the children stood leaning against the mud
walls, their eyes angry and sad as Vandana articulated her lack of
choices. Rohit had a sensitive face, much like his father. 'I will
never do agriculture,' he said calmly but firmly. Despite the lack
of facilities and basic requirements, he scored high marks in his
Class 9 examinations. He said, 'I want to be a policeman. I am

preparing by studying hard and I will sit for the examination.' There was a spirited defence of the profession of law enforcement, and also a certain belief in the stature it could provide. His younger brother Vikram was in Class 6 in 2015. 'I want to be the headmaster of my own school,' he said, after having clearly spent his day playing in the mud outside. While not providing any further explanation for his very specific desire, he keenly observed how the notes were being taken throughout the interview and cameras were being focused. The children knew their education was the key expenditure of the family and that Vandana struggled to help them. There was guilt on Rohit's sharp face as he said that there were medical bills to be paid, as he had complained of stomach pain. His playful smile was replaced by something serious, something like determination, and something permanent. These were not destiny's chosen children, but like their father, they wanted to be stronger than their present circumstances. Theirs were not indulgent dreams, but necessary ones.

The state played no role in the dreams of Vandana's children; if anything, it had rather curtailed them. According to the information provided by the sub-divisional officer (SDO) to the administration and other documents from the tehsildar, Ganesh was not given a loan waiver.[8] This was despite the fact that his crop had failed for three years and he had an unpaid bank loan on record. Though he had been ineligible for the debt waiver, he was eligible for compensation for his suicide. The administration always found a way to survive such oversights and move on to the next promotion, the next election, the next budget. It was as if the administration knew farmers like Ganesh were weaker than the state. Perhaps he had placed too much faith in the system, in agriculture, in god, in government, all of which proved to be more permanent than his own life.

It would be a mistake to think that Vandana and her children did not remember or were helpless about what killed Ganesh. It would be a mistake to consider his case compensated, stack the file away somewhere in the official corridors, and then move on to investigate the next suicide in Yavatmal.

★★★

My next meeting with Vandana and her children took place on an August evening in 2016. She and the children had returned from working on the fields in Ajanti village. Their home was dark, without electricity. She offered me some of the drinking water she brought in steel containers from the village tap; there was no direct water supply to their house, just as there was no drainage. The household seemed to be facing tougher times than it had seen in 2014 and 2015. They were tired from working in the sweltering heat of the day. Sonu had washed her hair for relief but it did not seem to help, as her young face was still fatigued. She was a trained beautician and now awaited an opportunity for employment or business in the same field.

FIGURE 8 Sonu, Vandana's daughter, August 2016
Source: Author

Sonu recalled how her father was harassed for repayment of loans by the banks and moneylenders. 'He was crushed by repeated home visits from people asking for the money,' she said. The pending loan had been restructured but remained unpaid and as the banks did not lend again to defaulters, Vandana had to borrow Rs 70,000 from a private moneylender. The only way she could repay the loan was by working as farm labour for daily wages along with her daughter. They got Rs 100 each day in the monsoons, and the rains had been kind in 2016. Besides this, Vandana received a monthly interest of Rs 500 from the compensation amount deposited in the bank. The difficult financial situation was clear to all the children and there was a collective effort to add to the income of the family.

The talk of the children's future brought tears to Vandana's eyes as she said, 'We have no plans, no dreams, and there is nothing to dream about.' Tejal, still in her pink-and-white school uniform, sat in silence at a distance. She did not comment until the end, when she said that it was pointless waiting for assistance from either the community or the government. There was conviction too mature for her years as she remarked, 'No one will help us. We are on our own.'

Notes

1. Memorandum of the post-mortem examination of Ganesh Rathod held at the Dispensary Hospital, Yavatmal on 23 August 2013.
2. Memorandum of the post-mortem examination of Ganesh Rathod.
3. Statement of Vandana Rathod in August 2013, recorded and presented to the district administration of Yavatmal by the tehsildar of Ner, in which the village of Ajanti is situated.
4. Statement of Vandana Rathod in August 2013, recorded and presented to the district administration of Yavatmal by the tehsildar of Ner.

5. Statement of Ramesh Rathod in August 2013, recorded and presented to the district administration of Yavatmal by the tehsildar of Ner, in which the village of Ajanti is situated.

6. According to the letters issued to the administration by the Sub-Divisional Officer (SDO) based on the reports gathered from Ner to the district collector of Yavatmal, on 13 and 22 November 2013.

7. According to the letters issued to the administration by the SDO based on the reports gathered from Ner to the district collector of Yavatmal, on 13 and 22 November 2013.

8. RBI notification issued on May 2008, available at www.rbi.org. in, accessed 2 July 2017. The 2008 Loan Waiver was called the 'Agricultural Debt Waiver and Debt Relief Scheme, 2008'. This was applicable to small and marginal farmers with less than 5 acres of land. However, under the same scheme, those farmers in the 'Others' category with more than 5 acres of land were eligible for debt relief under the One Time Settlement scheme of 25 per cent or Rs 20,000, whichever was higher.

CHAPTER
TWO

The Absence of Everything

Manjubai Rathod, Son Wadhona Village, Ner Tehsil, Yavatmal District

A Widow Since 28 September 2013

There was an unfinished look about this home, as if it was woken up in the middle of a dream. A young calf was tethered to a pole, pacing around it restlessly. The yard was clean but somehow also seemed empty, as if it awaited something more or someone else. The residence of the Rathod family was made of asbestos, concrete, brick, thatch, mud and anything else that could give them shelter. The roof that let in the sunlight from the gaps in between must have also let in the rain. The single source of electricity fed multiple points, so that the power consumed by one lamp could be stretched to two, perhaps even three. This was not a home; it was the place where a farmer's family precariously pieced together the semblance of a life. And yet, there were always some pieces missing.

Manjubai Rathod's parents, mother Gopi and father Ramji Panwar, had come to live with her in the village of Son Wadhona after the death of her husband, Atmaram. He was 35 years old when he had killed himself in September 2013, a year before I first interviewed the family. The compensation given by the government, as per rule, had come in two parts—Rs 29,500 was given to the widow in cash and Rs 70,500 was held in a fixed deposit in her name.[1]

According to her parents, Manjubai had spent the money in repaying debts and on household expenses. They said Atmaram had an outstanding loan from the bank, and about Rs 30,000 as an informal loan from a relative on Manjubai's side of the family. He had struggled to repay the debts for years and finally taken the ultimate step of committing suicide by consuming poison. The official record was more precise, although less conclusive. The report,[2] submitted by the SDO to the district administration, summed up the observations, comments, and statements on the suicide. It had stated that at the time of his death, Atmaram had pending loans taken in his own name in 2008 and another in the name of his mother, Subbibai, from the same lending agencies. The payable amount had grown to Rs 91,462.

After the death of her husband, Manjubai worked for daily wages to support her family. On the day of the first interview in 2014, she was away working in the fields as wage labour; her parents and daughter Priyanka were at home. As this was not a village of the 1990s or even the early 2000s, and as everyone carried a cell phone, the neighbours offered to call Manjubai home for the interview. But, as she would have lost precious hours at work and in wages, this suggestion was ruled out. At the time when Atmaram died, Manjubai was 34 years old and her children, Prashant and Priyanka, were 12 and 11, respectively.* Their grandparents said that Prashant studied in Class 8 in a 'good school' in Yavatmal. The school had waived his fee as a concession to his father's death. Prashant was a bright student and even the neighbours in the

* As in 2013.

village seemed proud of his academic performance. For a moment, as they spoke about the young boy's bright future, it seemed as if they all collectively willed him to succeed in life. They had seen the family suffer and Manjubai's struggles to make ends meet.

FIGURE 9   Priyanka, Manjubai Rathod's daughter, August 2016
Source: Author

Priyanka silently heard her grandparents speak; she had just returned from the village school where she studied in Class 7, and was still in her dark-blue-and-white school uniform, which was dusty and uncared for. Her face was unwashed; her thick, wavy hair pleated indifferently. Her large, expressive eyes held a complaint as she heard the questions concerning her father's death. She refused to speak at first and her grandparents answered the questions directed at her. Then, reluctantly, she began to talk, 'I like to study. I like going to school.' She spoke in a low, hesitant voice, barely audible over the others' conversation. Until then, the desolation of the premises appeared almost like an imagined thing, as if the knowledge of loss had seeped into the observation of it. It was Priyanka's voice that materialized the various absences of the place, those that came to life with the death of her father. The most felt was the absence of affection. She was forlorn: 'My father was a very kind man. He never lost his temper with me. He was very good to me.' Her simple words explained the complaint in her eyes. 'I know he killed himself because there was no money. He had to borrow from a relative and it bothered him that he couldn't repay.'

The one year since his death had done nothing to fade her father's memory—or his words—from Priyanka's mind. Her eyes quickly welled up as she recalled, 'He used to always insist that I get educated; he told me that I must go to school regularly.' That was another absence, the absence of the advice of someone who loved the children. Priyanka's tears did not stop and her silence spoke for the rest of the interview. She was hurt deeply by the death of her father and was not convinced about the causes that would drive him to take his own life. Perhaps she thought, it was unfair that her father should have left them, and held him responsible for the current state of their life. Perhaps she was angry with him for giving in to his troubles. It appeared as though she had lost someone who inspired her, someone who meant the world to her.

FIGURE 10   Manjubai, Atmaram Rathod's widow, January 2015
Source: Author

At the second visit in 2015, Manjubai was available for an interview. She was a thin woman whose face was lined beyond her age, so much that her dark hair appeared out of place. She worked for a daily wage of Rs 100 and found work through the week during harvest time. But there were also months without any work and she found those difficult to survive. According to official reports,[3] she had said that Atmaram had consumed pesticide on 26 September 2013, due to which he died two days later. Her statement was quoted in the SDO's report that her husband was worried over the loss of the soybean crop from lack of irrigation. He then lost the jowar crop because of an attack by wild pigs. He was concerned that he would be unable to repay the loan that year again, which led him to commit suicide. She recollected, 'That year, soybean was destroyed by pests and it became clear to all of us that we could not expect to earn anything from the field.' She spoke about the day before Atmaram's death. 'That entire day, we were both busy with our chores and our work. We did not even get to speak with each other. That night, we talked about the failed crop and how it would affect our life. We thought about what we needed to do to deal with this crisis. In a way, it was like any other night. I slept, and I thought he, too, had gone to sleep. But he consumed poison and we had to rush him to the hospital. He died after two days.'

According to the post-mortem report,[4] Atmaram died on the night of 28 September at 3 a.m. at a hospital in Yavatmal. The post-mortem began at 12.10 p.m. the same day and continued for one hour. The report stated that '50ml of pale reddish fluid with abnormal smell [was] perceived'[5] in the stomach and the probable cause of death was poisoning. The police and the administration certified[6] his character and stated that he had no addictions, and that his mental condition and social status were good. Such investigation pointed to the suspicion among the administration that he might have killed himself for reasons other than the ones stated by his family. It pointed to the possibility that Manjubai might not have been completely honest when she stated that he had committed suicide because of crop failure and his inability to repay outstanding loans. The state did not have any right to judge Manjubai's statement, except for the fact that it dispensed compensation for death. Considering that it could deny the compensation if the death did not meet the criteria, the investigation by the administration should have been transparent and accessible to public scrutiny. Many farmers' families do not even have a copy of the investigation conducted by the administration and were unaware of how their statements had been interpreted by officials.

The 43-question form[7] that was required to be filled out for every suicide confirmed that Atmaram grew cotton, soybean, tur, and jowar, but did not register his struggle with cultivating different crops to repay the debts. The questions dug deep into the life of the deceased farmer, but the intention behind doing so was not very clear. For instance, Question 18 asked whether the children of the farmer were married. Questions 20 and 21 were about how many animals the farmer had and how many of them were young. The next series of questions, from Questions 22 to 24, were about whether the farmer had sold cotton to the federation or to private buyers. The attempt seemed to be to discover additional sources of the farmer's income. However, that was already explained by his widow's statement. The sheer number of officials involved in the investigation was also perplexing, and included the panchayat sarpanch, deputy sarpanch, police patil, civil surgeon, SDO, agriculture officer, tehsildar, as well as the district collector. The elaborate chain of officials appeared to create an alibi for the state as it recognized the circumstances of a farmer's death.

The state's suspicion seemed to be further aroused by the fact that Atmaram's family did not have a ration card, which was required for BPL[8] families to avail welfare. Manjubai had to file an additional declaration that the family did not, indeed, have a ration card. The troubles that the long-winded and seemingly transparent procedures inflicted upon the potential beneficiaries were often too difficult to be put into words. Yet, the procedure only partially explained why Atmaram, whose 'mental condition and social status were good',[9] committed suicide in a little dark village of this nation. The compensation was awarded after various officers of the administration decided that Atmaram was 'eligible'[10] for it. Of the total Rs 1 lakh awarded, the tehsildar decided that the fixed deposit should be made in the name of the children; the family had no say in it. It appeared like a positive intervention by the administration to ensure that the compensation amount was not used up to repay private loans, and the family would get a monthly interest till the amount matured. Atmaram's death certificate[11] helped get a concession for Prashant at his school in Yavatmal. The house was in Manjubai's name and the land was in the name of her mother-in-law, Subbibai. 'It was never transferred to my name after my husband's death. It is being cultivated but I do not get any benefit from it,' she pointed out, but had no complaints. 'There are, after all, other family members who depend on the crops of that land. They too have children like I do.'

The family had never sought welfare provided by the government. There seemed to be distrust about getting any such assistance and even Manjubai had never thought of applying for any welfare schemes. She did, however, receive the ration card and BPL card she had applied for after the investigation in August 2015. There were other more immediate concerns that bothered her: 'The electricity bill for the single bulb in the house costs from Rs 100 to Rs 200, and the water bill is Rs 60 per month. I can pay only if I manage to get work as farm labour.' Then there were the private loans that did not go away easily; she had to clear Rs 40,000 of a Rs 1 lakh loan taken from a *shahukar* (private moneylender). 'It is impossible now to repay anything anymore,' she concluded anxiously. There was a good reason for her to worry; private moneylenders were not very conciliatory towards those who delayed repayment. It was not a matter of choice but an absence of it—there was no money and no one to help her. The government had done its job—it recognized that her husband had committed suicide and compensated her. Now, even the government was absent from her life.

Manjubai's son, Prashant, was old enough to understand scarcity. When asked what he wanted to do in life, he said he hated agriculture; his face turned stormy as he explained why. 'I remember my father telling me to study well and become some-one worthwhile in life. He did not want me to become a farmer. He wanted me to be someone everyone respected.' He did not smile, and spoke precisely. He had a focus far too advanced for his years. Unlike his sister, he seemed to realize that their father's memory would not help them any further.

Prashant said, 'My father wanted me to be a *thanedar* [offi-cer in-charge at a police station]. That was his thinking, his way of giving me a respectable life. He had studied until Class 5 in school. I think differently. I would like to be an engineer and I think it would give me more respect.' The answer hurt Manjubai, who said in a subdued tone, 'I have no idea how to make his dreams come true because I have nothing and I cannot keep beg-ging people for help.' She paused, desperate, realizing that she had to explain this to her son. 'Everyone has responsibilities and it is not easy for anyone to constantly take money out of their pockets and give it to me instead.' But Prashant was a keen child who had something of the determination that could be seen in his father's photograph on the bank passbook. Perhaps Manjubai saw the same grit that characterized Atmaram, who had struggled hard to be a farmer, in his son who struggled hard not be one. But the realities that tied her to her circumstances prompted her next remark. 'How can my child dream?' she rued, and fell silent. There was so much left unsaid in those words that she could not speak for a moment. Then asked, 'How can a child in this situa-tion even have a future?'

Priyanka looked forlorn and Prashant's young face was set seri-ously as his mother spoke the truth. 'My son is a witness to our situation. He knows there is no money. He may dream of a bright future, but it will all be impossible.' Prashant heard her in absolute silence as she continued, 'There is no answer to the question of what he would like to be in life. It is not in his hands. His fate is already sealed by our poverty.'

Those from the administration who had made Manjubai answer questions just a few days after her husband's death should have been there in that ramshackle house that afternoon. Those who found Atmaram 'eligible' through the condescension of the bureaucratic procedure should have tried answering some of her questions instead. But the administration was absent there, like everything else.

★★★

By July 2017, Manjubai had lost both her parents from the complications of old age, and she was once again left alone with her troubles.

The next interview with Manjubai was held in August 2016 on a balmy evening. The village had been a busy place with the children just returning from schools and rushing for their tuitions. Shruti, a young villager, had kindly accompanied me to the Rathod house, and on the way, explained in English why she wanted to be a post-graduate. That evening Son Wadhona was a place of hope and dreams of the children. Prashant and Priyanka Rathod had grown taller; they had just celebrated Rakshabandhan.[12] Prashant was in Class 10[13] in a school in Uttar Wadhona and he walked with his sister, who was in Class 9, every day to the school, which took them 15 minutes. Prashant took tuitions for English and Geometry for a monthly fee of Rs 400. He said he would like to travel to far-away countries. 'That is why I want to be an engineer; then I can travel to the US and Europe,' he explained. Priyanka wore red bangles and did not speak much. Manjubai was the same, her patient brown eyes fatigued. When asked whether

FIGURE 11   Gopi and Ramji Panwar, Manjubai Rathod's parents, January 2015
Source: Author

she felt that her circumstances had changed in the past two years, she said that they were the same. She was right; she still worked as farm labour for daily wages and the family expenses were still too high for her to meet. Her voice was heavy as she said, 'I am facing the toughest times of my life. Will I ever see better days?' The answer was yet another thing absent from her life.

Speaking in 2017, Manjubai said the trauma of witnessing the hardships of her life may have claimed the lives of her parents. 'Why am I so unfortunate?' she asked. 'First I lose my husband, and now, my parents. There seems to be no end to loss in my life.' Her parents, Gopi and Ramji Panwar, had been intensely affected by their daughter's life and had stood by her as she recovered from her husband's death. She grappled with her circumstances on the one hand, and the energy and enthusiasm of her children on the other. 'How do I provide for the dreams of my children with my earnings as a wage labour on farm lands?' Manjubai asked.

It was difficult to speak to her about hope; she survived despite its absence, an absence that summed up all the others.

⌘

Notes

1. Monthly Income Scheme (MIS) account of Manjubai Rathod under the Post Office Saving Schemes, for a sum of Rs 70,500, on 22 February 2014.
2. Letter from the SDO to the district collector of Yavatmal (Farmer Suicide Department), on 11 November 2013.
3. Statement of Manjubai Rathod recorded and presented to the district administration of Yavatmal by the talathi of the Son Wadhona village.
4. Memorandum of the post-mortem examination of Atmaram Rathod held at Dispensary Hospital, Yavatmal on 28 September 2013.
5. Memorandum of the post-mortem examination of Atmaram Rathod.
6. Statement of police constable (*patil*) of the Son Wadhona village recorded and presented to the district administration of Yavatmal by the tehsildar of Ner, in which the village of Son Wadhona is situated.
7. Statement from the 43-question form for suicide procedure, signed by the talathi of Son Wadhona and the tehsildar of Ner.
8. The Below Poverty Line (BPL) yardstick has been used by the Indian government as a tool to decide the economic status of a poor person. Those earning less than Rs 32 a day in a rural area or less than Rs 47 a day in an urban area fall under the BPL line. 'Report of the Expert Group to Review the Methodology for Measurement of Poverty', Planning Commission, Government of India, 2014, available at www.planningcommission.nic.in and

'New Poverty Line: Rs 32 in villages, Rs 47 in cities', *Times of India*, 7 July 2014, available at www.timesofindia.indiatimes. com/india/New-poverty-line-Rs-32-in-villages-Rs-47-in-cities/articleshow/37920441.cms?from=mdr, last accessed 12 December 2017.

Broadly, the debates over the BPL and APL (Above Poverty Line) are that it is difficult to qualify for BPL benefits, as 74.52 per cent of the rural population lives on a household income of less than Rs 5,000 per month (see 'Social Economic and Caste Census 2011', Government of India, available at: www.secc.gov.in, last accessed 12 December 2017); that the international standards set to measure poverty are unfair to developing countries (see Sanjay Reddy and Thomas Pogge, *How Not to Count the Poor, 2005,* available at www. papers.ssrn.com, accessed 6 July 2017); and that large-scale corruption, government irregularities, and bureaucratic malpractices were affecting the issuing of BPL cards. Therefore, the BPL list failed to capture ground realities of the poor, as also observed in the 18 cases in this book.

9. Statement of police constable (*patil*) of Son Wadhona village.
10. Letter from SDO to the district collector of Yavatmal (Farmer Suicide Department), on 11 November 2013.
11. Death certificate of Atmaram Rathod, on 30 September 2013.
12. A Hindu festival where the sister ties a sacred thread on her brother's wrist as a mark of affection and the brother promises to protect her.
13. The Indian school education system consists of two national board examinations in Class 10 and 12, administered either by the central or state boards.

CHAPTER THREE

The Happy Ever After

Mira Dike, Dhabdi Village, Arni Tehsil, Yavatmal District

A Widow Since 18 November 2005

There were two entrances to the house in Dhabdi, a village in the Arni tehsil of Yavatmal whose population of about 2,500 was entirely dependent on growing cotton. The starkly empty house demonstrated how people could live without possessions, without things that marked their comfort, identity, memory, sentiments, or achievements. It was as if everything was equalized, and nothing required preservation. There were, however, signs of resistance: the façade was painted sunlight yellow as if to battle the darkness inside and the doors were adorned with cheerful, traditional motifs. There were two worlds in that house, one that was visible to everyone and another that was visible only through a haze of tears. Mira Dike seemed to exist in the twilight between the two.

In 2014, Mira affectionately held the framed photograph of her late husband Dilip, one of the few things she had managed to preserve. Dilip had committed suicide in 2005 following crop failure from a severe attack of the red bug pest (locally known as '*lalya*'), which routinely devastated the cotton crop in Yavatmal. Dilip had been the sole breadwinner in the family and cultivated the 4-acre, rain-fed land that produced low yields of cotton and tur. His suicide report stated that in the year he committed suicide, he had planted the same crops by taking a loan of Rs 45,000 from a lending agency. He already had a 15-year-old unpaid loan of Rs 22,000 from another lending agency. He had hoped that the crop yield in 2005 would help him clear his previous debts and allow him to start afresh. But that year, the crop plunged Dilip deeper into debt and desperation. A Marathi newspaper, while reporting his death, had carried a photograph of Mira and their two children. The children were still in their school uniform, as if no one had the time amid the tragedy to help them change. Eleven-year-old Sneha looked angry and sad, and eight-year-old Aniket looked perplexed. Mira's sense of loss, so evident in the

FIGURE 12 Mira Dike (left) with her son, Aniket, and daughter, Sneha, September 2014
Source: Author

newspaper photograph, had only deepened with time and turned into the indifference that engulfed the house like the winter mist.

Loan recovery agents, a much-dreaded breed in these parts, had come knocking on Dilip's door assuming that he could repay them despite the destroyed crop. With his financial situation in decline, Dilip feared he might fail to provide for his children. 'His heart was broken and he was very worried about how the household would survive,' Mira recalled, her eyes forlorn. On the day of his suicide, she had been working on the farm and the children had been at school. She found him dead when she returned home late in the afternoon; he had hung himself from the rafters in one of the rooms.

FIGURE 13   The rafter in Dilip Dike's house from where he hung himself
Source: Author

The room, though locked now, was diligently kept clean. 'No one goes into that room,' Mira explained briefly. It was a sparse space with sundry items stacked in a corner. The tin ceiling overhead was supported with wooden beams, a white cloth was tied on the rafter to mark the spot where Dilip had hung the noose. The months before his death had been particularly difficult. 'It cost us too much to cultivate cotton. After paying the farm suppliers, the labour, and household expenses, there was never any money to repay the banks. It was the same story every year and to take a bank loan was a gamble with the rain.'

That gamble failed in 2005. Two years after Dilip's death, the family constructed a well to irrigate the field in which the water was found at 40 feet. Yet, the crop yield continued to remain low due to diseases. Mira reflected, 'Life has only got tougher since my husband's death. Sometimes, when I get desperate, I wonder if his decision was right. I would like to do the same; give up my life and escape. Then I realize I cannot do that as I am bound by my love for my children. I am worried about what might happen to them.' In 2014, Aniket was still a beneficiary under the Bal Sangopan Yojana (scheme)[1] of the state, which gave him Rs 5,000 per year, according to Mira. While it did not cover his entire educational expenses, it did allow planning for his schooling after Class 12. It hurt Mira that the scheme did not support Sneha's education. 'Such a grant must be given to both children. I should not have to choose as to who should and should not get the benefit of education. I want both my children to study, but I cannot afford it.' It was Sneha's personal decision to stop her education after Class 12 examinations; she decided against spending the meagre earnings of the family. Mira also believed that the government should support education after high school, so that students were encouraged to pursue graduation. The Bal Sangopan Yojana (scheme) was scheduled to end when Aniket turned 18 and Mira feared that, like Sneha, even Aniket might have to give up his education.

Two families survived on the same 4-acre land, which was now in the name of Dilip's brother, Vinod, whose family also shared the house. In 2012, he had sown the cotton crop thrice to ensure it survived and the yield was between 10–12 quintals for the entire land. He explained the odds. 'We put in every effort, invest every penny and face every risk, only to earn back what we spend on the farm. There is nothing left to save for any emergencies. As a farmer, I have no option but to focus on agriculture; that is what I do. But I do not want the next generation to be without choices like I have been,' he said. While the yield of cotton had remained almost the same as it had been during Dilip's time a decade ago, the cost of cotton cultivation has steeply escalated. In January 2015, the cotton was picked thrice to yield 10–12 quintals. For the harvest, 10 labourers were employed at the rate of Rs 100 each for picking 20 kg of cotton. The cotton was sold at Rs 3,750 per quintal, and the total estimated earnings from the crop were between Rs 37,500 and Rs 45,000 until January 2015. According to Mira, the ideal price for cotton should be Rs 5,000 per quintal to recover the cost of cultivation. It would have then fetched them between Rs 50,000 and Rs 60,000. But even at enhanced rates, the earning remained low due to low soil productivity. There had been no formal loan taken by the family for cultivation in that year, but Mira expected to take a loan to sow cotton in the next season.

Vinod wanted Aniket to study well and find a good job in the city. Mira's disconnection was in stark contrast to the impatience of her brother-in-law. Neither of them had to remind Aniket of his role; he carried the knowledge of his father's death like a weight on his shoulders. He was acutely aware that he had to excel at his studies because he knew what his education cost the household. In the case of Sneha, who was 20 years old in 2014, the burden was more than that of money. Her brown eyes, set in a round face, smiled perfunctorily in another rendition of Mira's indifference. She had reconciled to the end of her education after Class 12 to be married, but had not yet made peace with the death of her father. 'People face troubles all the time, life is full of problems. But people should stand and fight when they face challenges. My father did not. He just left us in the middle of everything,' she said, her words unambiguous as if she had thought of them several times before speaking. And yet, they brought tears to her eyes. 'He could have told us he was troubled, that he was contemplating suicide. He did not imagine how his death would affect us, because he would not have left us if he had known what would happen to us without him.'

No one spoke in that room after her words. Then, gathering herself, Sneha went on, 'That is why I hate agriculture. No good can ever come of it. The faster we leave cultivating crops, the safer we all will be.' She had learnt about agriculture by working on the crops with her father. 'He knew the risk of depending on agriculture. We had no irrigation in our land and it must rain for the crops to prosper. Nothing was in our hands.' Her memory of her father was vivid, as if she lived through the details often. He used to call her Neha. 'He was very affectionate towards me and told me never to be dependent on anyone in life for anything. He wanted me to study well and be financially self-reliant. It had always been important to him that I should not have to be supported by another individual.' There was a loss in her voice that was beyond the grief she expressed; it was as if she had not just lost a father but the entire direction of her life. That also seemed the reason for her reconciliation; there was nothing left to live up to or for—no one had big hopes from her anymore.

In 2015, as she prepared for the final examinations for Class 12, she was confident of her subjects. Sneha had the rigour of the discipline seen in a good student, but knew it was the last examination she would ever take. Beneath the compromise, there was simmering anger. She said, 'A loan has to be taken every time the crop is sown. There is never any profit, there is never anything to save, and that itself should stop us from indulging in agriculture.' But, as her own family members reiterated, it was the only thing that farmers were trained to do. 'It will change. For instance, I will never do agriculture in my life. Someday, if I can, I might study for a B. Ed. [Bachelor of Education] because I would like to be a teacher. I am good with history, but not very good with economics,' she said with grim humour. 'That has narrowed down the choice of my job.' Although she spoke lightly, it was as if with the knowledge of the impossibility of her dreams.

The government had paid a compensation of Rs 1 lakh after Dilip's death. Of the compensation amount, Rs 30,000 was handed to Mira and the rest was put in a bank, as per rules, in her name. According to Vinod and Mira, Aniket's education expenses were paid from the Rs 30,000. Mira saved the rest of the compensation of Rs 70,000 for Sneha's marriage. Even after 10 years, the government's compensation for her husband's death was still the only thing Mira could count on. For Sneha, however, that money came with painful memories of her father's death. It was possible that she recalled the prolonged and harsh investigation conducted by the administration into the reasons of his death.

In 2015, the search for a suitable groom for Sneha was in full swing—her relatives were exploring eligible (and affordable) marriage partners for her. She was confident that she would be engaged within that year. The famous Sri Omkareshwar temple of Lord Shiva would be the venue. Sneha was aware that the compensation money would be required for the marriage, not just for the ceremony, but also for dowry.[2] The winter sunlight reflected in her angry eyes as she said, 'I don't like it, but can I change the system? The dowry must be paid, as if it is owed to the groom's side, even if we cannot afford it.' Going against the system was a risk that her mother could not take. Sneha knew that Mira saw only one chance of happiness for her child and she did not want to fritter it away in idealistic experiments. 'The average dowry to be given to the bridegroom by the bride's family depends on the quality of the match, whether it is good or bad,' she said, wryly. A good match was a graduate with a government job or a post in a firm of repute; a bad match was a farmer. In most cases, the wedding ceremony and attendant gifts are borne by the bride's household, and the feasts and even the choice of food are stipulated by the groom's family. In other words, the bridegroom's family did not spend on the event, while the bride's family incurred severe expenses. This unjust tradition often led poor families to consider a daughter an economic burden, and a son as an advantage. But it continued mainly because parents of sons were often reluctant to give up on the dowry, which they considered their right. Usually, even education or good employment made no impact on the bridegroom's desire for dowry. As Sneha explained, 'For a good match the dowry is highest, at about Rs 5 lakh, and the bride's family bears all additional costs of a reasonably lavish wedding, which generally works out between Rs 1 to Rs 1.5 lakh. For an average match, the dowry is Rs 2.5 lakh with an expenditure of Rs 1 lakh on marriage ceremonies. For a bad match, the dowry expectation is Rs 50,000 to Rs 1 lakh.'

It seemed futile to enquire if the grooms sought dowry from the poor and whether even educated young men were willing to let the burden of expenses fall entirely on the bride's side. 'Good people do not accept dowry because they can see it is unjust. But some see it as an opportunity to make money,' Sneha said. It hurt her that her future husband might accept the compensation money for her father's suicide as dowry. Such insensitivity pained her and, as a young woman who was confident and educated enough to take care of herself, she found no reason to submit to this arrangement except to bring solace to her mother. 'The idea does not evoke any interest in me. It is possible that I too might end up like my mother, and struggle to bring up my children alone and helpless, is it not? My husband could also commit suicide just like my father did, could he not?' That brought quick tears to Mira's eyes and Sneha apologized. Then said in a lighter tone, 'I keep telling my mother that she is going to lose me if I get married, and also all the money she has.' Mira composed herself with effort and said, 'I will lose everything.' Realizing her words had saddened her mother, Sneha joked, 'I will find a job and earn that money back for you. You will not lose anything.' That made Mira smile reluctantly.

Mira's son, Aniket, was a quiet teenager without the fashionable inattention of the usual 17-year-old.* Instead, he had a sense of determination, as if it was a commitment to himself. His uncle spoke about his wishes for his nephew, 'I want him to be serious about his goals. If he wants to change his destiny, this is the time for it.' Aniket knew what that meant; he would be a farmer if he failed to get a good education and employment. He said, 'I want to either qualify for professional courses and become an engineer or work for the government.' This was not optimism; he was good at his studies and passed Class 10 with 74 per cent marks. In the next visit in 2015, Aniket was away from home, studying for his exams and Sneha continued to have high expectations of her brother. 'He should take tuitions but he cannot afford it. He needs books to prepare for competitive exams but he cannot buy them. We heard from someone who visited him recently that he borrowed notes from friends who took coaching classes to get through competitive examinations. He is really doing everything he can to succeed. He knows what it would mean for our family.'

It was, however, Mira's burden to watch her children leave her side to walk on their chosen paths in life. Apart from working as farm labour on daily wages, she also found employment temporarily as an anganwadi worker,[3] having undergone training in 2007, a few years after Dilip's death, for implementing the government's Integrated Child Development Services (ICDS) Scheme.

The year 2015 would decide many things for Mira and her family, including the marriage of her daughter and the future of her son. Amid all the anxiety, Mira appeared distant and detached as always, a still-life figure amid the sunlight that streamed in through the two entrances of the house.

★★★

* As in 2014.

Earlier in 2016, there was a silence at the Dike residence, which had not been there before. Mira washed a white shirt in the backyard under a tap; it was just after 9 a.m., an hour before she had to report to work for farm labour. She constantly glanced at the clock as she sat down for the interview. It was the centre of her life, as she went about her busy day, earning whatever she could to pay for Aniket's education. A calendar for 2015 still hung on the wall in the front room; perhaps, because it was from the panchayat samiti in Arni that described the various government schemes available for poor farmers. The walls were a fading yellow, the doors were now painted blue, the front door, pink from the time of Sneha's marriage celebration. She now had a baby boy, Shivansh.

Sneha was married in 2015 to Nikhil Raut of Karanja town who was a farmer with 8 acres of land. The wedding had taken place as planned in the Shri Omkareshwar temple at a total expense of Rs 2 lakh. Mira said routinely that she was relieved her daughter was in a happy marriage, but her eyes filled up nevertheless. The Dike family had taken a new loan of Rs 40,000 from the bank but had not borrowed from private moneylenders. Aniket had begun his graduate studies in computer application in Amravati and was home for a few days; he was no longer a beneficiary of any government scheme that covered the expenses of his education. It cost Mira Rs 50,000 annually to put her son through the course; he had already given up a seat in an engineering college in Pune, which he could not afford. Aniket said, 'I missed my father when I filled up the form for the graduation course, where it said father's name and signature. I wish he had been around when I entered college.'

Sneha's son, Shivansh, was almost one year old in July 2017. She was happy in her new life and, for the moment, content to be a housewife. However, she still missed her father. 'It's a loss I shall never overcome,' she said, speaking on phone from her new home. 'If he had been alive, I would have continued my studies and my mother wouldn't have struggled so much.' Deep down, there is a fire in her heart that makes her add, 'I am waiting for my child to grow up and begin school. I shall take up some work then. I shall not sit idly at home.' There is promise in her laughter, as well as preparation. 'I believe this is just the beginning,' she said. 'There is so much more to be done in life.'

For Mira, and for her children, there was no such thing as absolute happiness. It took courage to live the everyday destiny with the memories of a farmer long gone, and dream of the happy ever after. It took courage to believe in the future despite the past.

～

Notes

1. According to the Government of Maharashtra's Women and Child Development Department's website, the Bal Sangopan Yojana (scheme) provides assistance to children whose parents are not able to take care of them owing to difficult circumstances. See www. womenchild.maharashtra.gov.in

2. Although criticized socially as well as being illegal, the tradition of accepting dowry and gifts from the bride's side continues in India. Education, especially among girls, has been an important factor in reversing the trend of dowry.

3. The Integrated Child Development Services (ICDS) describes an anganwadi worker as a community based worker chosen from the local community to work for the ICDS programme. She is expected to mobilize support for the care of young children, girls, and women. See www.icds-wcd.nic.in

CHAPTER
FOUR

Death amid Doubt and Denial

Pushpabai Raut, Akpuri Village, Yavatmal Tehsil, Yavatmal District

A Widow Since 14 April 2014

For the state, the life of the farmer has always been a grey area, with few legitimate supporting witnesses or documents. As it intervened rarely in his life, the state was left with little knowledge about the farmer after his death. So when the state had to establish farmer suicides, it developed extensive paperwork to investigate the claims made by farmers' families and friends. Elaborate statements were recorded on the lines of an inquest to ascertain whether the farmer had committed suicide owing to unpaid farm debt or for other reasons. It was the duty of state representatives to follow procedure and provide compensation as relief to the bereaved family. And yet, the claims were examined as if the dead farmer had been guilty of cheating unless proven innocent, especially if he was poor and unable to repay debts. At the heart of this attitude of the state representatives was a dismissal of democracy and the belief that the policy of relief was mere populism designed for votes. That would also partially explain the state's negligence to connect with the farmers until they were forced to. This battle between the faceless state and the faceless poor went on, until someone came along to represent the truth. Such a person made the paperwork redundant and questioned the basis of the mistrust, elitism, and entitlement that the state displayed. Sixty-five-year-old Janardhan Raut represented the truth of the farmers—dead and alive—and all those who suffered, not just in the Yavatmal district but throughout the country. Janardhan, a farmer, visited the collectorate to meet the district collector on 24 March 2014. Before he left his house, he informed his family that he would request for some relief for the consecutive crop failures in his 2-acre field, which was the main source of livelihood for his family. The family saw him leave in the morning from his home in Yavatmal's Akpuri village and expected him to return with a positive response. Instead, they received the news that Janardhan had consumed poison and attempted suicide. He was rushed to a government hospital, and died 22 days later, on 14 April 2014.

This incident again brought the issue of farmer suicides out of the grey and made the state confront it. And yet, it took two months and two days for the same administration to decree, in the manner of patrons, that it had recognized Janardhan's death as an eligible suicide[1] and that his wife would be compensated with a relief of Rs 1 lakh. It would appear that the state's suspicion of the poor had been so institutionalized that it could not believe in them even if the state itself was the witness. This ubiquitous sense of denial could not be more established than when the district administration's farmer suicide wing repeatedly wrote in the letters summarizing Janardhan's death, that he had committed suicide on the premises. Despite that, there was no investigation about *why* he committed suicide, even when the family stated that he had not planned to kill himself. The state machinery could not have been more directly complicit in this case, and more conspicuously involved. But it was starkly evident that the state would remain guiltless, like a silent but partisan observer of a game. It coldly followed the laid-down procedure, which was to ascertain whether Janardhan told the truth about the circumstances that led to his suicide. Eventually, it was established that he had—in life and in death.

His story seemed to live on in Ghatanji, where the family stayed after the incident. Six months later, in September 2014, his presence seemed to be reinforced through every word of the story retold by his son, Vikas. Janardhan's 60-year-old wife, Pushpabai, was not well and wasn't at home. Her ill health added another expense that remained unrecorded in her husband's official file. Like most widows of Vidarbha, she was acknowledged for a brief moment as the wife of a farmer who had committed suicide, but rendered invisible once the compensation was granted. Twenty-seven-year-old Vikas knew why it was unjust for the state to ignore the farmers during their lifetime, only recognizing them in death so as to award compensation. Vikas carried the burden of that most elusive of all closures—justice. The anger in his eyes seemed to be on the verge of action. 'My father had always fought

Figure 14   Vikas, Pushpabai Raut's son, September 2014
Source: Author

against the odds. He did not win all the time but that did not stop him from fighting,' he explained, and added with a sense of irreconcilable disbelief, 'It seemed he lost the will to fight.' There are never enough words to explain the loss of a parent, and he discovered that as he spoke of losing his mentor and guide.

In the earlier season of 2013–14, cotton had to be sown twice in their 2 acres of land due to heavy rainfall, but still perished. The family had said so in their statement, and yet, the tehsildar of Yavatmal[2] had to once again confirm it in a letter to the district collector, quoting the agricultural officer[3] that from 2011 to 2013–14, the yields of cotton, soybean and tur had indeed been medium to low. Similarly, it was also known that the tehsil had a very high incidence of suicides by farmers who had planted these very crops, and the district witnessed 3,589 suicides from January 2001 to August 2016, according to official figures.[4] In her statement,[5] Pushpabai said her husband had been worried about the lack of yield, and had constantly pondered over how to repay the loans he had taken for farming. She also said that the family was left with nothing to survive on. The statement had a flat and distant tone, as if it was recorded by a hand habituated to writing official documents. Her statement also noted that Janardhan had left home on 24 March 2014, and consumed poison at the district collectorate office. This line was repeated in every document in Janardhan's file, and there appeared to be a consensus on how to address his death. It was, therefore, no surprise that Pushpabai's statement had this line too and that the writing of the statement did not match her signature at the end.

Vikas recalled the dark months of the winter of 2013–14: 'We had lost all our investment in the crops, including the very expensive seeds.' The seeds sold for Rs 930 for 400 gm in 2015 and usually one or two bags, at around Rs 1,800 per acre, were required. Deciding not to continue the gamble with cotton in that season, Janardhan had sown pulses, but lost the crop once again to heavy rains. Vikas explained, 'That was why my father went to the district collectorate—to appeal for relief.' But he stated that his father had not intended to commit suicide. 'He left home that day saying he would ask the collector for help. He did not mention anything about killing himself; he did not even carry the poison he had consumed later. His hands were empty when he left home. So what happened at the collectorate that he decided to take this step? What drove him to get the poison from someplace and consume it there?'

Vikas appeared to be the kind of man who would not have let questions like this linger without being answered. 'I think someone might have said something to him and he could not stand it,' he said, but stopped without elaboration. It seemed that Janardhan might have been mistreated when he had gone to request for relief for his failed crops. Out of anger and humiliation, Janardhan had probably decided to commit suicide at the office itself and avenge the words spoken to him. But all this was without evidence or witnesses, despite the fact that the district collectorate was a busy place. It was, however, also a place where state patronage was distributed. It was difficult to find witnesses there to a poor farmer's suicide attempt, a mark of protest against the state's indolence.

Janardhan was rushed to the hospital in Yavatmal where he was admitted to the intensive care unit and kept on external life support. Two bottles of blood were also administered, but to no avail. The post-mortem report[6] stated that he had developed bed sores with advanced sloughs that reflected the poor standard of the medical care provided to him. The terminal step he had taken, however, had made news and drew people to his bedside at the hospital. Even the district collector visited Janardhan, and it appeared that the state, stunned by his move, was ready to act in any way possible to help him. It was a good story for the media, which made space for a poor farmer on its pages. All this attention came at a price; he made a poignant picture of a suicide victim hanging on to life by a thread. Then he died. The spotlight was switched off and the farmers' community was once again abandoned to the grey unknown. According to Vikas, his father had not said a word or made a statement while he was in hospital. But then, he had not expected him to. 'My father never used to burden anyone with the troubles of his life. He sheltered me and I did not get to know how serious the crisis was until he gave up,' he said, his brown eyes tormented and sad. 'For instance, he never told me that he had taken a loan to repair the house.'

The families of the farmers who committed suicide discovered another facet to the unequal relationship between the state and the poor, which was not always evident to everyone. Unlike the state that never forgave the poor for their lack of paperwork—ration cards, identity cards, and other documentation—and punished them with delays, the poor had to forgive the state for everything. The poor had to be fair to the state. Vikas said he could have complained against the district administration, but he had not. 'People said that as the incident had taken place at the collectorate, I should ask for a job in the government as compensation,' he said, the hurt from the advice still evident. 'I did not, of course.'

There was much investigation into Janardhan's loans, to ascertain whether he had, in fact, committed suicide owing to debt burden. The state, of course, did not just go by Pushpabai's statement that Janardhan was anxious about the unpaid loans, and had hated that he could not repay the debts. The loan details provided by the lending agency[7] showed that Janardhan had taken a farm loan in 2009 that had amounted to Rs 43,625 at the time of his death in 2014. Vikas stated there were other loans of over Rs 1 lakh, but these had not been mentioned in the file of enquiry or substantiated by paperwork. Private loans did not figure in official documents and, therefore, could not be considered as debt burden on the farmer. However, the state's dismissal of private loans did not diminish their importance and had to be repaid by any means, even with the compensation money that the widow received. Pushpabai did exactly that.

Meeting Pushpabai in 2015 was an extraordinary experience. Her grief for Janardhan had an existence of its own, almost like an alternate identity. She kept the true depth of her grief to herself and portrayed a normalcy that had a debilitating effect on her. 'He never told me things that he knew would trouble me,' she said. 'I used to get stressed at his struggle and I used to fall ill,' she said. She cooked as she spoke, as if that allowed her time to select the information to be shared with others. The kitchen was in a corner of the room in which they lived and slept. There was a bed in the opposite corner and a few chairs. Containers of different kinds occupied the space around her, mostly filled with groceries but there were medicines as well. Most plastic containers were recycled and had carried something else when they were bought; there were no new objects in that kitchen. The steel utensils had lost their sheen; some had been soldered and repaired several times. Her hands seemed to carry the imprint of the times, the past and the present kneaded into the dough for her family. Her medical bills were up to Rs 300 per month, an expense that Vikas

FIGURE 15   Pushpabai, Janardhan Raut's widow, January 2015
Source: Author

had to budget for. She worked with a certain speed and the gas cylinder next to the stove explained it; at Rs 400, this was another inevitable expenditure, and Pushpabai ensured that the cylinder lasted longer with the speed of her cooking.

'There was never enough yield from the field,' Pushpabai recalled. 'We barely got between 15 and 16 quintals of cotton from our 2 acres. The best yield had been between 20 and 25 quintals, but that was a long time ago,' she paused, as if to check her memory. And as if it failed her, she returned to the present. 'It was the same problem with soybean and my husband worked hard to earn some profit from the crops. He did everything there was to do, but without irrigation, we were helpless. Then it rained so heavily in 2013–14 that we lost every crop we sowed. That loss was unbearable for him,' she stopped abruptly and spoke no more on this issue.

The problems continued even after Janardhan's death. 'The banks still bother us for the loan repayments. We told them my father had died and even submitted documents of the death. We have no money to repay the loan', Vikas said with helpless finality. There was nothing to repay the banks with; of the total compensation of Rs 1 lakh, Rs 70,500 was kept in the bank in Pushpabai's name and the rest was given to her in cash. It was mentioned in the file that the family did not have a Below Poverty Line (BPL)[8] but had an Above Poverty Line (APL) card. Pushpabai explained that they never used that card because of the bad-quality subsidized grain they were issued. 'The 4–5 kg of grain we get is not good enough to eat,' Pushpabai said. They submitted the forms for a BPL card, which, at the time, was yet to be issued.

The money that had come in compensation for Janardhan's death seemed to perplex her. 'They gave me Rs 29,500 in cash and Rs 70,500 in fixed deposit, and it went towards paying private loans taken from the shahukar,' she paused, and the silence raised an important question. How did the state fix compensation for farmer suicides? Pushpabai seemed to wonder about the inadequacy and the pointlessness of the amount she had got. When asked why they paid the shahukar with the relief money, Vikas intervened, 'We can get a loan from the shahukar at any time we want. A moneylender is not like the banks that do not lend to us if we default. A moneylender will always lend money to us, even in emergencies, although at a high interest rate. That's why we repaid the moneylender.'

In 2014, Vikas had rented 10 acres of land at Rs 1 lakh for a year to try his hand at agriculture and repay the debts. On why he was confident that this gamble would pay off, he had said, 'This land is irrigated, unlike our family land. There is a well in this field and electricity too.' He believed that the problem with agriculture was the adverse conditions under which it was done, and with a fertile land for the high-paying cotton crop, he could earn enough to clear all his debts. However, in 2015, Vikas changed his opinion when agriculture failed on the 10 acres. This was especially tough for him, as he had rented the land with loaned money. The yield from the land had been 60 quintals and the total cost, including loans, had been Rs 6 lakhs. A quintal sold for Rs 3,800 to Rs 4,000 in 2014–2015. 'I did not earn even half of what I put into the field. It did not work out,' he said, dejected.

He had now understood why his father kept fighting despite the odds. 'It is that hope of a single good year that keeps the farmers going through all hardships and debts. It is the hope that one good crop will take care of all the bad crops of the past. But that is no longer happening; we do not have that good year and that good crop anymore,' he said. Cotton used to be the crop that made good every bad debt, every lost crop. 'Farmers should not sow cotton anymore, we will only default on our loans,' he said. 'I had to sow the seeds four times because of crop loss caused by rain. I am done with agriculture. I have moved on to a job this year.'

In 2015, Vikas was working at a krishi kendra on a salary of Rs 60,000 per year. It was the steady source of income that agriculture could never provide. But he was not happy. He was, perhaps, the last of the generation that believed they could take over agriculture from their parents. He was not educated beyond Class 12 and had not learnt any other skill. 'I had never even applied anywhere for a job,' Vikas said, explaining the choices he had to make. 'I know nothing else but farming, which my father taught me. And now I cannot be a farmer,' he said. Ironically, as farms were not passed on to daughters, his 33-year-old married sister,[*] Arpita, had to be a good student and was now a qualified teacher. He was aware of the difference between them, and was proud of the better life she led.

After the brief break that he had taken from work for the interview, Vikas headed back to his job. Pushpabai seemed to be lost in her corner. There was a palpable vacancy in the house in the space Janardhan should have occupied. It could only be filled if the state had been accountable to the farmer's family and answerable for his death. That seemed as impossible to expect as it was to think Janardhan would return from the dead.

★★★

The situation changed only slightly in 2017 for the family; Vikas was now married to Komal on May 14. She hailed from across the state borders, from Adilabad district of Telengana. He had once again taken 15 acres of land on lease and sowed cotton in 2017.

Earlier in 2016, 62-year-old Pushpabai's eyes had welled up as she remembered her husband. 'I still cannot believe he is no more. Even to this day, it feels unreal,' she said. She appeared even frailer, even more burdened by the loss that she did not share. The three faded red bangles in the right hand and the four on her left were equally fragile. A shelf in the room held different medicines and an oil for pain relief. She appeared unchanged but Pushpabai was not the same within. It showed in her anger at the way the world treated her son. 'He works every minute of the

[*] As in 2016.

day, and yet there are loans that remain to be paid. No one helped him, no one rewarded him for the way he had handled the death of his father. Does that not show character? Shouldn't he have been supported in some manner for not blaming the administration? But nothing has happened; it is as if we do not exist.'

Twenty nine-year-old Vikas did not contradict his mother's candid speech. It was doubtful if he would have accepted a job from the collectorate where his father had died. While the administration could have employed his services in areas where it lacked insight—like the plight of the farmers who committed suicide—that was not how the state thought. The state was focused on moving on, counting on the amnesia of the people. It hoped Janardhan's tragic death would be forgotten and did not require Vikas inside the system to remind it of its failure.

Vikas had inherited the 2-acre land after his father's death, but he transferred it to his mother's name. He explained, 'I put the land in her name because who knows what might happen in the future. I just want to make sure that there was something in her name to support her.' They kept their house locked in Akpuri and lived in Ghatanji because the community held Janardhan's suicide as a mark of weakness, refusing to give a bride for Vikas. It was unfortunate that the community did not recognize the effort Vikas had made to survive on his own, as he continued to do a job and cultivated the land with a new bank loan of Rs 52,000.

In comparison to 2014–15, there was a further decline of hope in the Raut family in 2016, except that Vikas looked forward to his married life. They had applied for Niradhar Scheme[9] for Pushpabai but were yet to get it. It was as if the unhelpful state and community had forced the anger of the family to be replaced with reconciliation, and choice to be replaced with compromise. That was how farmer suicides were remembered in Vidarbha. And forgotten.

1. Letter from the SDO to the district collector of Yavatmal (Farmer Suicide Department), on 16 June 2014.
2. Letter from the tehsildar, through the SDO, to the district collector of Yavatmal (Farmer Suicide Department), on 14 June 2014.
3. Letter from the tehsildar, through the SDO, to the district collector of Yavatmal (Farmer Suicide Department), on 14 June 2014.
4. Information given by the Department of Land Resettlement and Rehabilitation situated in the District Collectorate Office of Amravati District.
5. Statement of Pushpabai Raut, on 22 April 2014, recorded and presented to the district administration of Yavatmal by the tehsildar of Yavatmal, in which the village of Akpuri is situated.
6. Memorandum of post-mortem examination of Janardhan Raut held at the Dispensary Hospital, Yavatmal, on 14 April 2014.
7. Letter from the tehsildar, through the SDO, to the district collector of Yavatmal (Farmer Suicide Department), on 14 June 2014.
8. The Below Poverty Line (BPL) yardstick has been used by the Indian government as a tool to decide the economic status of a poor person. Those earning less than Rs 32 a day in a rural area or less than Rs 47 a day in an urban area fall under the BPL line. 'Report of the Expert Group to Review the Methodology for Measurement of Poverty', Planning Commission, Government of India, 2014, available at www.planningcommission.nic.in and 'New Poverty Line: Rs 32 in villages, Rs 47 in cities', *Times of India*, 7 July 2014, available at www.timesofindia.indiatimes.com/india/New-poverty-line-Rs-32-in-villages-Rs-47-in-cities/articleshow/37920441. cms?from=mdr, last accessed 12 December 2017.

   Broadly, the debates over the BPL and APL (Above Poverty Line) are; that it is difficult to qualify for BPL benefits, as 74.52 per cent of the rural population lives on a household income of less than Rs 5,000 per month (see 'Social Economic and Caste Census 2011', Government of India, available at: www.secc.gov.in, last accessed 12 December 2017); that the international standards set to measure poverty are unfair to developing countries (see Sanjay Reddy and Thomas Pogge, *How Not to Count the Poor, 2005,* available at www. papers.ssrn.com, accessed 6 July 2017); and that large-scale corruption, government irregularities, and bureaucratic malpractices were affecting the issuing of BPL cards. Therefore, the BPL list failed to capture ground realities of the poor, as also observed in the 18 cases in this book.

9. The Sanjay Gandhi Niradhar Anudan Yojana provides financial assistance to oppressed and marginalized citizens, such as, specially enabled persons, orphans, widows, the destitute, women who were freed from human trafficking, and more recently, transgenders. The scheme is also applicable for the people aged 65 years and above, whose annual income is less than Rs 21,000 per annum. Under the scheme, the beneficiary receives Rs 600 per month and, in case of a single family having more than one beneficiary, the amount increases to Rs 900 per month. The benefits continue till the children of the beneficiary get employment or reach 25 years of age. In case the beneficiary has only daughters, the assistance continues even after the daughters reach 25 years of age or get married. See www.mumbaisuburban.gov.in; www.amravati.nic.in

CHAPTER FIVE

How to Count the Dead

Savita Ade, Borgaon Village, Arni Tehsil, Yavatmal District

A Widow Since 11 September 2012

Farmers, according to the state in case of death, are those 'who own and work on [the] field (cultivators) as well as those who employ/hire workers for field work/farming activities. It excludes agricultural labourers'.[1] In Vidarbha, the definition of a farmer was most significant because it decided whether a deceased farmer's family deserved state compensation. It was a narrow definition that did not include several circumstances of farm crisis that the state constantly encountered through its enquiry of farmer suicides. The definition of farmers in Vidarbha must include the state of the irrigation facilities in their farms, the productivity of crop, and the requirements of the children and the elderly. The state definition ignored loans borrowed from private moneylenders on the basis that these could not be ascertained and there was no record. The definition did not consider the position of the widow, her education, and her ability to survive after the farmer's suicide. The definition also did not consider those who lived on daily wages as farm labour and did not have land of their own. Such oversights seem deliberate as these factors were known to the state when it decided whether a farmer's suicide made his family eligible for compensation or not. And yet, the elected governments and administration sought to limit the definition of a farmer. As a result, when cases failed to fulfil the criteria, the official numbers of farmer suicides remained low, and the farm crisis that spread across the region remained understated. Functionally, for the administration, it meant less work had to be undertaken to complete the investigation into each suicide, and less pressure from the political hierarchy that was answerable to the voters.

In a scathing comment on this method, P Sainath, journalist and author, stated:

> So the number of suicides keeps mounting—but the number of farm suicides keeps falling! If accepted at face value, this jugglery would imply that only farmers are doing well. Everybody else is sinking in Vidarbha. Read more seriously, the region specific data—viewed against the national and state figures—suggest that Vidarbha is today the worst place in the nation to be a farmer.[2]

The political leadership in the government was wary of backlash from the opposition on the high numbers of farmer suicides. But even the opposition aimed only at discomfiting the government without any real commitment to change, as was evident under the different political parties and coalitions that had been in power in Maharashtra.[3] Political parties sought to avoid the perception of being anti-farmer or of neglecting agrarian crisis, which could be detrimental to them electorally. As a result, those with the authority to make the framework for farmer suicides less stringent had no inclination to do so. Predictably, farmer suicides that did not fit the narrow definition were routinely dismissed as suicides that had nothing to do with agricultural distress. There was no redressal of this decision, no reinterpretation of the facts in favour of the dead farmers, no scope for appeal; the democratic government acted like an absolute power when it dealt with its poor. The fact that successive governments and administrations continued with patronizing words such as eligible (*patra*) or ineligible (*apatra*) to describe farmer suicides showed how much the state believed in its particular individuality as a benefactor and not as an impartial mechanism of delivery.

Among the criteria to officially recognize farmer suicides were the requirements that the dead farmer had to own agricultural land and should have unpaid farm loans from banks in his name.[4] Without these, a farmer suicide would not turn into an official number and his wife, who was considered a mere bystander in this situation, would not get the compensation. These were some reasons why the unofficial farmer suicides in Yavatmal district remained high, as did the number of widows who were refused compensation by the state. In a way, the farmer who was not even a number when he was alive fought to become one when he was dead. Only the tyranny of a welfare state gone wrong could make its citizens feel more valued as a statistic than as a life.

The lines that differentiated one death from another were not drawn in public; they were written down in official documents kept in closed files. Even when death did fit into the narrow definition of a farmer suicide, the state enquiry seemed to consider the farmers and their families guilty of misrepresentation until proven innocent. Those who made the rules must have known that a farmer need not always own land, cultivate it, or owe money in his name to the bank. It was unlikely that those with the authority to decide the fate of a dead farmer were so unusually blind to his life and his nature. A farmer could be so true to his word that he hated unpaid debts; he could be so righteous that he killed himself rather than face humiliation; and, he could be so proud as to only depend on honest means of livelihood. The case of Vijay Ade of Anji village proved that the administration had to reach beyond rules that declared him ineligible and go by the man people knew him to be. His case also explained why, in the suicide enquiry files, there were no columns to be filled for honesty, righteousness, and truth. For then, every farmer's suicide would have to be acknowledged as the failure of the state and the government. Even the intermittent loan waivers had failed in Vijay's case. In February 2008, as part of the financial budget proposals, the central government proposed waiving loans worth Rs 71,680 crore,[5] as part of an effort to alleviate the burden of debt on farmers who had taken money between the period of 1 April 1997 and 31 March 2007. However, according to the audit, only Rs 52,516 crores of loans were waived upto 2012.[6]

Vijay Ade attempted suicide on 2 September 2012, and died 10 days later on 11 September 2012 at a hospital in Yavatmal. It was not a straightforward case of a farmer's death due to unpaid debt, because the 5.63 acres of land and the loan were not in his name but in the name of his mother, Yamunabai. An agricultural loan taken in 2010 amounted to Rs 55,044[7] after interest in March 2012, a few months before Vijay died. However, the district administration did not care that Vijay's mother was too old to work on her field and repay the debts, or that Vijay might have taken the responsibility on himself. He might have never even considered the question of ownership of the land while he struggled to make his failing crops survive. Perhaps he had already tried everything he could to repay the loan—and when he finally realized that he could not honour his debts, had ended his life out of frustration and helplessness. Apart from the virtues of humanity, the official files also lacked the columns to record desperation and despair. They were, however, able to declare farmers who had committed suicide but did not have land or loan in their names as ineligible for compensation.

Accordingly, the tehsildar of Arni declared that Vijay's family as ineligible or apatra[8] for getting the state compensation of Rs 1 lakh. The tehsildar's report was the most crucial recommendation in the investigation because (s)he had access to all details regarding the resident of the tehsil, which in this case, was Arni. The tehsildar was closest to ground reality and her/his observations were taken as final on all information regarding the villages of the tehsil and, in this case, the village of Borgaon. The report was a comprehensive exploration of Vijay's life, which was easily accessible to officers of the state. The tehsildar could take a exhaustive look at the loan documents, bank records, land records, and any other document without addressing concerns of privacy or giving explanation to the family. The officer could also use such information as he or she deemed fit for the report, and reach conclusions about farmers like Vijay that would be rarely challenged by higher officials. The general public would never get to see the tehsildar's words or opinions about Vijay, or have access to the documents that he or she had referred to, unless they followed the procedure and asked for them. So, making use of this lopsided privilege, the tehsildar of Arni had written to the SDO in September, the very month that Vijay had committed suicide, that his family was ineligible for the state compensation.[9] He listed various reasons for his decision, presumably all based on the exercise of his exclusive powers in the tehsil to gather information required for reaching such conclusions: First, it was found that the land belonged to Vijay's mother and that she had a pending loan of approximately Rs 50,000. Second, though his family members stated that he might have committed suicide because of the pending loans, there seemed to be no solid reason for Vijay's suicide. Third, the agriculture officer of the tehsil stated that from 2010–11 to 2012–13, the rainfall and the crop yields had generally been good in the tehsil, particularly, for cotton, pulses, and soybean. Fourth, the local officers of the village and the block stated that there was no harassment about loan repayment from any bank to have prompted the suicide.

To sum up, the case was ineligible for compensation as it did not satisfy the requirements of a farmer suicide due to agricultural distress. It was possible that the official documents had misinterpreted the honesty and shock of Vijay's family as their doubt instead. They had all mentioned in their statements that the loan was the main reason for Vijay's anxiety about repayment and possible suicide, but Vijay had not spoken to them about his intention to kill himself and they mentioned it to the authorities truthfully. It was ironic that the state, which devised checks to ensure that the family of the farmer should not lie, might have used their truth against them.

Vijay's father, Kishan Ade, said in his statement[10] that he had taken his son to the general hospital where he had died after 10 days of treatment. He confirmed that the land was in the name of his wife, Yamunabai, but his son took care of the farm and repayment of the loans. Kishan had felt that his son had committed suicide due to the stress of non-repayment of loans. Vijay's mother, Yamunabai, was asked to provide a statement[11] about his death. She, too, confirmed that he took care of the farm and that the crop yield was inadequate. She felt that the pressure of unpaid loans had led Vijay to commit suicide. Vijay's cousin, Pandurang Ade, spoke about the events of that fatal morning on 2 September 2012 in his statement.[12] Pandurang's field was next to Vijay's and they met daily while working. Around 10 a.m. that day, he heard screams and went to Vijay's field to investigate. He found that Vijay had consumed the poison and rushed him to the hospital. The sarpanch[13] and the police officer[14] of the village noted in their respective statements that when they enquired why Vijay might have consumed poison that morning, Kishan had mentioned the pressures of loan repayment.

Savita Ade, Vijay's widow, was a mute witness to the claims and counter-claims on whether Vijay's death qualified as a farmer suicide. In her statement,[15] she spoke of things that had little meaning to the administration; she remembered him as never being insincere, dishonest, or irresponsible. She spoke about his hard work and his optimism, and the qualities that made her husband not only anxious about repaying the loans, but also weakened him when he failed. She remembered him as a happy person and said that their life together was blissful, as he never quarrelled over any issue or created strife. About the loan, she said Vijay planned constantly on how to generate profits from the crops to repay the debt. She felt that the failed crop that year had driven Vijay to his death.

Even in 2015, three years after his death, Savita was still not reconciled to the loss of the man who had loved her and dedicated his life to the well-being of his family. 'No one thought he would kill himself,' she said, 'because he was optimistic and thought of solutions. His parents used to always worry about the accumulated debt with interest. The house needed repairs and they had reminded him often. He just quietly worked towards fulfilling all these demands, but never spoke about suicide or showed any tendency like that.' It might have been this disbelief, shared by everyone who knew Vijay, which the administration conveniently interpreted as doubt. The police and administrative officers of the village also got another fact wrong in their report; there had been harassment from the moneylenders and even the bank for repayment of the loans. Savita revealed, 'The banks kept sending reminder letters, which created tension for my husband. The shahukars also bothered us about settling the debts. But my husband got only about 5 quintals of cotton from the land. It was just not enough.' So much for the agricultural officer's statement that generalized the crop yield as good in the tehsil.

The agriculture officer had, however, been right when he reported that there was adequate rain that year. It was the same rain that had devastated Vijay's last crop and plunged him much deeper into debt than ever before. The report had also been wrong when it stated that all family members, including Vijay's parents, worked on the farm. As Savita explained, the farm was Vijay's sole responsibility. These inconsistencies might have led to the administration's eventual decision of changing Vijay's case from ineligible to eligible. Evident in this case was the selective negligence on the part of the administration to report the truth behind the suicide.

FIGURE 16   Savita, Vijay Ade's widow, August 2016
Source: Author

Savita and Vijay had two children—Bhushan and Roshan. Vijay was a loving father and enjoyed their company. In 2015, nine-year-old Bhushan, the older son, was living with his grand-mother in Borgaon, while seven-year-old Roshan lived with his mother in Anji. Roshan was an avid reader, and throughout the interview, stayed next to his school bag so that he could read whenever he got the chance. He also wrote and, for reasons of his own, doodled the alphabet on my notebook. Savita said she would ensure that he would not grow up to become a farmer. 'The land is leased, so we do not do agriculture anymore. However, to support the family, I work as a daily wager,' she said. This paid the fee for Roshan's education at a private school. 'It is English medium,' she pointed out. Savita missed her elder son, but could not afford to take care of him financially. 'Bhushan is in Class 3 in the zila parishad school where education is free,' she said, as if reconciled to this incompleteness as well.

It was understandable that Savita had not gone to the hospital to identify Vijay when he died in Yavatmal at 8.30 a.m. on 11

September 2012. Vijay's post-mortem report[16] found that the death had been due to poisoning. That would have reassured people who doubted whether farmers who might have died from other causes were made to look like suicides due to debt. A farmer's struggle did not end with his life, as he still had to establish his integrity and character even after his death. On the other hand, the state did not investigate why a 30-year-old man with his entire future ahead of him lost faith in his destiny and in his life.[17] There were no equations to ascertain the loss of hope in a nation.

FIGURE 17   Roshan, Savita Ade's younger son, August 2015
Source: Author

At the end, however, there was some glimmer of justice. Vijay died on 11 September 2012. On 1 October 2012, the SDO wrote to the district collector[18] that Vijay's case was ineligible for compensation as he had neither land nor a loan in his name, and the agricultural conditions had been good in the tehsil of Arni. This went against every statement made by his family, friends, and even the sarpanch of Borgaon, the village where Vijay had lived. However, on 17 October, the district administration declared the case eligible for compensation.[19] It was a vindication of the kind of person Vijay had been in life that even the state could not cheat him in death.

★★★

Even in July 2017, there was no improvement in the Ade family's situation, and they were still struggling against the same odds. Both of Savita's sons now stayed with her, which made her happy, but this was layered with the sorrow that she could not afford their education.

Earlier, in August 2016, the premises of the Ade house in Borgaon were filled with the warm fragrance of the wet earth of the monsoons. The thatched hut stood shakily on its wooden support, as if ready to collapse under the weight of the rain. Savita seemed withdrawn and listless as she sat next to her father, Bhopidas Rathod. She had undergone a foot surgery, which had left a permanent scar. Part of the compensation, Rs 30,000, was

FIGURE 18 Bhopidas Rathod, Savita Ade's father, August 2016
Source: Author

spent on the children, while the rest was deposited in the bank. She did not get support from the anganwadi scheme or benefit from any other welfare programme; there was no new bank loan taken but there was a new shahukar loan of Rs 1.5 lakh.

Bhopidas spoke about his daughter's life. 'I could not afford her education and I regret that now. Her younger sister, Sangita, studied up to Class 12, which has stood her in good stead. Education would have supported Savita today in these difficult times,' he said. He had been fond of Vijay, who had always respected him as a father-in-law. He looked back at life with sadness. 'If only I knew he was under so much stress about the loan, perhaps we all could have suggested some solution. But I knew nothing about the situation.' Speaking of solutions to improve agriculture, Bhopidas mentioned irrigation facilities, bullocks, and repairs to the houses, none of which he could afford.

At that time in 2016, Savita's two children still lived separately, in Borgaon and Anji. I noticed how Roshan's handwriting had improved markedly as he once again scribbled the letters of the alphabet in my notebook. His curious face, free of all worry, was the only bright thing at the Ade residence. Everything else seemed poised for decline and disappearance.

༺༻

Notes

1. 'Accidental Deaths and Suicides in India, 2014', National Crime Records Bureau, Ministry of Home Affairs, Government of India, Chapter-2A, p. 266.
2. P. Sainath, 'Maharashtra: Graveyard of Farmers', *The Hindu,* 14 November 2007. Available at www.thehindu.com/todays-paper/tp-opinion/Maharashtra-lsquograveyard-of-farmersrsquo/article14874806.ece, accessed 5 July 2017.
3. Bhavika Jain, 'Farmers' Suicide in Maharashtra: Opposition Slams State Govt for Doing Little', *The Times of India,* 6 April 2017. Available at www.timesofindia.indiatimes.com/india/farmers-sui-

cide-in-maharashtra-opposition-slams-state-govt-for-doing-little/
articleshow/58051662.cms, accessed 3 July 2017.

4. Based on the information shared by the district administration of
   Yavatmal.

5. In February 2008, the Government of India announced loan waiver
   for farmers called 'Agricultural Debt Waiver and Debt Relief
   Scheme, 2008' (ADWDRS). According to a report by the Public
   Account Committee, 2013–14, the scheme sought to assist farmers
   who had outstanding loans taken between 1 April 1997 and 31
   March 2007. The beneficiaries were divided into three categories;
   farmers with land up to 2.5 acres qualified as 'marginal farmers';
   those with up to 5 acres qualified as 'small farmers'; and those with
   more than 5 acres qualified as 'other farmers'. The scheme was estimated to cover 3.69 crore small or marginal farmers and 0.60 crore
   other farmers. All the loan taken by a marginal or a small farmer was
   waived off, while 25 per cent of the loan was waived off for other
   farmers if they gave an undertaking to pay the remaining 75 per cent
   by June 2008. See 'Implementation of Agricultural Debt Waiver
   and Debt Relief Scheme, 2008', Ministry of Finance, Government
   of India, Report by Public Accounts Committee (PAC) 2013–14.

   However, the Comptroller and Auditor General of India (CAG)
   Report of 2013 observed that the scheme did not achieve its
   intended goals for reasons such as corruption and malpractices like
   errors of inclusion and exclusion of beneficiaries, poor documentation, tempering of records, non-issuing of benefits in many cases.
   See www.cag.gov.in

6. 'Report of the Comptroller and Auditor General of India on
   Implementation of Agricultural Debt Waiver and Debt Relief
   Scheme, 2008', Report No. 3 of 2013 (Performance Audit), Union
   Government, Ministry of Finance, Delhi, p. 8. The audit was to
   assess the implementation of the scheme, and the CAG report was
   submitted to, and presented in the Parliament, on 5 March 2013.

7. Letter from the SDO to the district collector of Yavatmal (Farmer
   Suicide Department), on 1 October 2012. It merely states that the
   loan was in the name of the mother of the deceased farmer, without
   enquiring into the reasons.

8. Letter from the tehsildar to the SDO of Yavatmal, on 26 September
   2012.

9. Letter from the tehsildar to the SDO of Yavatmal, on 26 September 2012.

10. Statement of Kishan Ade, recorded and presented to the district administration of Yavatmal by the talathi of Borgaon village which is situated in the tehsil of Arni, in Yavatmal district.

11. Statement of Yamunabai Ade, recorded and presented to the district administration of Yavatmal by the talathi of Borgaon village.

12. Statement of Pandurang Ade, recorded and presented to the district administration of Yavatmal by the talathi of Borgaon.

13. Statement of the sarpanch, recorded and presented to the district administration of Yavatmal by the talathi of Borgaon.

14. Statement of the police officer, recorded and presented to the district administration of Yavatmal by the talathi of Borgaon.

15. Statement of Savita Ade, recorded and presented to the district administration of Yavatmal by the talathi of Borgaon.

16. Memorandum of a post-mortem examination of Vijay Ade held at the Dispensary Hospital, Yavatmal, on 11 September 2012.

17. Pranali Chindarkar, 'Alarming Increase in Young Farmers' Suicide Rate', *DNA*, 25 October 2015. Available at www.dnaindia.com/mumbai/report-alarming-increase-in-young-farmers-suicide-rate-2138208, accessed 1 July 2017.

18. Letter from the SDO to the district collector of Yavatmal, on 1 October 2012.

19. Summary of the case, district administration of Yavatmal, on 17 October 2012.

CHAPTER
SIX

The Life and Death
of a Sentiment

Anita Nandagawli, Adgaon Village, Ner Tehsil, Yavatmal District

A Widow Since 1 September 2007

The house in Adgaon was easy to reach; it was at the end of a narrow path and under the shade of an imposing banyan tree, which was a village landmark. An entrance led to the front room of the house, which clearly enjoyed a special status; it had two electrical bulbs that were switched on for a few hours at night, and there was the air cooler in the corner, received as dowry in a marriage, but not yet connected to electrical supply. The room also had a cot, placed strategically to let a person rest undisturbed even if the door remained open, while a wooden chair sat in the corner. A nearby door led directly into the open yard in the middle of the house where a wood stove burned under a thatched roof. Many rural households still used the wood stove despite its drawbacks because a cylinder usually cost about Rs 800* on an average and

---

* Rates may vary.

served for a month or two, depending on the size of the family.
Wood, on the other hand, was free.

Cotton fields skirted the house of late Devanand Nandagawli on one side. The deficient monsoon rain of September 2014 fell indifferently on the waiting plants. The sun set behind the cement-and-brick house, and there was the faint outline of a television dish on the terrace. Cattle in the front yard shifted slowly, as if feeling the dusk's approach. Devanand's photograph was on a wall that was the colour of the evening outside, framed by a garland of unfading plastic flowers. He had consumed poison on 1 September 2007, exactly seven years ago. The eldest of three brothers who were all dependent on the 9-acre field, he had committed suicide when the cotton crop failed that year.

Devanand left behind his wife, Anita, and their two children. Thirty-year-old Anita was thin, her frame sparse—a feature common among women in Indian villages. Data shows[1] that women in rural India do not get the benefit of proper nutrition in their

FIGURE 19   Anita, Devanand Nandagawli's widow, September 2014
Source: Author

formative years or even throughout their life. She worked in peoples' fields for a wage, tended cattle, and took care of household chores. Despite everything, it was easy to get drawn to Anita's bright smile, which filled the small room with light and hope.

'Did I show you all the documents I have?' she asked, speaking about the death of her husband. Her attitude was diligent, her expression earnest as she checked the small plastic pouch in which the documents were preserved and laminated to prevent damage. This was clearly one of her most important possessions, the tangible proof of her husband's struggle. The post-mortem report[2] was painfully elaborate and Anita knew every detail of it: 'Provisional opinion as to cause of death: Poisoning, however, viscera preserved for chemical analysis.' Anita did not need the post-mortem report to tell her that Devanand died of poisoning. But a government document has sanctity like nothing else in rural India and has the power to grant or deny recognition of a farmer's suicide in Vidarbha. No one, and especially no farm widow, is negligent of official documents; least of all someone as focused and meticulous as Anita. It was as if her husband's absence had forced her to be doubly aware of the world and given her an extra pair of eyes, along with an immense patience to repeat the circumstances of her husband's death. 'There was no money...' She stopped, standing up from the chair for a male member of the family who entered the room. 'There was a bank loan of Rs 60,000, which was unpaid for years. We could only clear a part of it through the Rs 30,000 cash compensation we received; the Rs 70,000 was deposited in the bank.'

The family had an APL card and it had not been easy to get a BPL one, which provided more food grain. Anita's name was not on the ration card, although she had applied for its inclusion. The family had not sought welfare under any government scheme, and they had not been able to respond in time for the schemes that the government had offered. About a year ago, in August 2013, Anita had to undergo a surgery. There were documents for this as well, a biopsy report[3] and a discharge summary from a private hospital in Yavatmal. 'It cost me Rs 20,000 for one day,' she said regretfully. The histopathology report of the lump that was surgically removed showed 'multiple granulomas'[4] and the advice was to 'investigate for Koch's disease'.[5] When asked if she had gone through any follow-up medical treatment, Anita explained that it had become impossible after the bills for the surgery; she did not want to incur any more expenses.

Anita had another document of importance; a letter issued in 2013 from the Women and Child Development Department[6] of the administration asking her to submit relevant papers to enrol in a scheme that ensured her two sons would get monetary support every month for their education. Eight-year-old Gaurav was in Class 3 and seven-year-old Shourav was in Class 2.[†] They were still in their white-and-khaki school uniform, too involved in the conversation to change. 'A lot of things are free and that's why we can afford their education,' Anita said, adding, 'Their school fees, books, uniforms, mid-day meals. Of course, the free toys have long gone!' Anita herself had studied until Class 7, while working on the farms. She watched as one of her sons opened an English exercise book, her gaze ensuring he handled the pages with respect. Both children grimly listened to her; despite their age, they already knew that their difficult financial situation made their education unaffordable. The monthly expense for the family was Rs 6,000 and the yearly bill for electricity at the house was Rs 1,500; there was no bill for electricity at the farm because there was no water to draw from the well. The requirements were increasing; a basic cell phone was necessary and its monthly bill was Rs 100. Further, the family had to sell two cows to fund her father-in-law, Suryabhan's treatment, who had been unwell.

They missed the deadline to submit the documents to the Women and Child Development Department because the family

---

[†] This was in 2014.

had been away from home, when the letter came in 2013. The letter also asked her to be present in person at the time of submission of documents, which meant Anita would have had to take a day off from work. She could not communicate to the officials who summoned her that she could not detach herself from her world even for a day. Instead, it should have been easier for the government to reach out to her, or perhaps, the government was far busier than Anita, widow of Devanand Nandagawli, mother of two, a farmer and a daily wage earner.

The house looked almost the same in 2015; the sun rose from behind the cow-pen in the front yard, and the light reached deep into the house as if to check the time on the clock in the front room. The façade had been painted; it had been just a few days since Sankranti, the festival of happy farmers preparing for a new season and new harvests. The room was still blue, and the air cooler still sat in the corner, as if it remained clueless about its function. Someone had thoughtfully placed a shawl over it, considering the winter. Suryabhan was dressed in a fresh white cotton dhoti and tunic, the traditional attire for men in villages while indoors. However, his son, Avinash, wore track pants and a T-shirt. Suryabhan said, 'I will continue doing agriculture on my 9 acres of land, whether any of my sons are interested or not.' He missed the son he had lost. Devanand had shared his burden and his debts until they crushed him to death. There was a catch in his voice as he said, 'I constantly remember my son, and I miss him every time we are all together as a family. He is always in my thoughts.' There was stillness in the room as he continued, 'Yes, my son committed suicide. And yes, it was because of crop failure and debt. But I cannot give up on agriculture or my land. My son died because of crops that failed due to lack of irrigation, it wouldn't have happened if we had irrigation in my field. We are dependent on rain and when the rains fail, we face severe hardships.' But the option of selling the land or moving away from agriculture did not appeal to him. 'This is a 30-year-old land. I paid Rs 20,000 in cash for 6 acres, and then bought 3 acres more for Rs 10,000. There never were any irrigation facilities in the field,' he explained. 'If we sell, we will get Rs 1 lakh per acre,' he paused, as if even the thought of it required strength for him to endure. Then said, 'There is no way I will sell this land. Ever.'

Like Suryabhan's 9-acre, rain-fed field, most of Vidarbha's farms lacked irrigation facilities, which caused low yields and agricultural distress. Suryabhan was very aware of the problems of agriculture, especially those that beset small and marginal farmers. He believed it was tough for traditional farmers to survive on agriculture alone. But he also had the spirit of a farmer, of someone who had seen both the anger and benevolence of nature, the bad and good harvest, and the rainclouds at the end of every drought. 'There are many difficulties we face as farmers,' he continued, 'but if we sell our lands then we will never find our way out of our problems.'

It seemed a difficult argument to accept, considering that the untenable conditions led many farmers to end their lives. In fact, Devanand's brothers had themselves been unable to reconcile themselves with farming after his death and seemed to have broken the tenuous link with the land that had supported generations of their family. Sentiment for agriculture, like with any other sentiment in Vidarbha, sounded risky and ominous. Suryabhan, however, felt quite the opposite. 'Even if we make losses, we need to continue working the fields, and I'll tell you why. I have learnt through my experience that like in anything else in life, only perseverance and hope can lead to success. I farm in the hope of a better harvest and in the hope that it may rain.' There was a hint of revenge in his determination, a burden of loss on his squared shoulders. 'As long as I have the strength in my ageing arms,' Suryabhan said, 'I shall continue tilling this land.'

The region remained rain-fed despite the obvious problems of irrigation and the farmer suicides. In the absence of accessible canal irrigation, wells were facilitated by the government, but only for fields smaller than 5 acres. Suryabhan's 9 acres, of course, did not meet this criterion. He needed the water for the crops so badly that he even came up with a drastic solution. 'If I divide my 9 acres equally between my two sons and me, then each part will get 3 acres. That way, we'd be eligible for a well.' Perhaps, knowing his desperation, the local official of the village sought a special cost for cutting up and re-registering the land. 'I paid because there was no choice; I needed that well. But this plan did not materialize— the official died in a road accident.' Suryabhan lost his money and his urgent solution awaited the pleasure of the next village official. Without the documents of registration that would have shown 3 acres each in the name of his two sons and Suryabhan, it was impossible to get the well. That meant another year of waiting for the rains, and the clock ticked on at a steep cost.

That year, in 2014–15, Suryabhan had sown soybean. The yield, as usual, was low. He was disappointed. 'The cost of culti-vation has been around Rs 55,000 including inputs, labour, and other costs. The total earning was about Rs 12,000 from 6 quin-tals of soybean at Rs 2,000 per quintal. This was not the yield I expected.' They had not taken any loan that year, either from banks or private moneylenders. But that did not mean there was no debt. 'We borrowed most of the inputs for the crop from the sellers, and we need to repay them with interest.' He had a single-page receipt crowded with figures from an agricultural agency in Darwha, a nearby town. For every input taken, there was an interest levied. The equation showed that, at one point, the total amount due for inputs for soybean was Rs 30,150, of which Rs 25,000 had been repaid. The remaining Rs 5,150 had incurred an interest of Rs 1,050. Along with cost of pesticides and further inputs, Suryabhan owed over Rs 10,990 to the input provider. They had recently cleared Rs 3,000 of this amount, leaving Rs 7,990 in unpaid debt. Suryabhan needed to repay this to be able to buy inputs for future crops. The longer he took to repay, the higher would be the interest.

Anita, meanwhile, visited the Women and Child Development Department in Yavatmal in December 2014 to submit the documents to get the benefit of the Bal Sangopan Yojana (scheme).[7] To the credit of the department officials, they did not mind the almost one-year delay in her visit and accepted Anita's application. However, the cheque for her children only came once, for Rs 1,800. The payment was expected to take care of the expenses of the children, get them proper nutrition, and pay their medical bills. It did not support Anita if she planned to enrol them for a computer course or enter them in talent quests or even take them on an education trip to, for instance, the nearby Sewagram.[8] The amount fixed by the state for the welfare of children seemed to assume that they would never require anything more than food and clothing. The state paid the children of the poor to live, not to dream.

But Anita wanted her children to have the best she could provide and for that, she did farm labour at daily wages of Rs 100 for eight hours. She was joined in her efforts by her mother-in-law and her brother-in-law, Avinash. Together they worked in others' fields, picked cotton, harvested tur, or sowed wheat. This seasonal work was not available during summers. From whatever they earned, the family had to feed itself, take care of the children, and also repay the dues so that the next crop could be sown, even if it sunk them deeper into debt. Lessons of the past ensured that Suryabhan did not consider cotton farming. He explained, 'The variety of Bt cotton that is available in the market requires considerable irrigation, which we don't have, and higher quantities of pesticides, which we cannot afford.' He remembered a time when cotton used to thrive. 'The seeds of cotton about 15 years ago used to produce plants that did not require much irrigation. We used to do fine before the seeds changed and now we have no choice but to plant the Bt seeds. It is too risky for my field, which doesn't even have a well.'

As a democracy was expected to address such problems of the common people, the farmers frequently took their grievances to the elected representatives. The village of around 800 houses had one polling station, with approximately 1,400 voters. Promises of irrigation were made during every election campaign but were never kept. Suryabhan now had developed a deep mistrust of politics and its intent to change the condition of the farmers. 'I have heard irrigation facilities being promised to us since my youth,' he said. 'We vote for those who promise us what we need desperately, and we appreciate the fact that they at least know our problems. But we also know they will forget us once they are elected. And they always have.'

At 26, Avinash did not have the length of experience to form such a final opinion, but he was beginning to. 'We applied for a BPL card, which we need to be eligible for almost every government scheme for welfare,' he explained. 'After we completed the process, which is done according to the convenience of the government departments, we have been told that we need to wait until after the panchayat elections in the villages. That is what elections do with the lives of common farmers in villages. We can think of other things only if we have earned our wages for the day and know we can survive tomorrow.' Avinash had tried to get government support for the failed soybean crop. He argued, 'The size of the land at 9 acres means we cannot get the relief for crop failure that is only given for less-than-5-acre fields. We never benefitted from a loan waiver for the same reason, as the sarpanch of the village told us our land was too large to qualify for such schemes. Everyone in the village knows our problems are because of lack of irrigation, but they can't change government rules.'

There was a difference between Suryabhan, who thought of dividing the land to qualify for a well, and Avinash who could discern the injustice behind the criterion for such schemes. 'My brother died because of unpaid loan, yes; but there were other aspects to it as well. He had borrowed Rs 60,000 from the bank to cultivate groundnut. But the crop failed entirely from lack of rains, and he lost everything. There was no money for anything;

the harvest was so meagre that we could not even collect it and take it to the market. He owed Rs 7,000 for the labour that had worked on the farms, and they were poor people like us who needed the wages. He was deeply hurt that he couldn't pay them.'

Suryabhan listened to his son in pained silence and Anita's smile was lost. It was a memory they had all worked very hard to forget. And they needed their forgetting, because they could not afford anger—after all, they lived the same life and walked the same path that had killed Devanand. Avinash, however, wanted to be angry. He cultivated his anger with desperation, as if it was his last chance for survival and the only way he could break out of this circle of hopelessness. He said, 'I want to find a job. I am done with agriculture. I have given the exams for my second year of B A; I will be a graduate in one more year. I will find a job in Pune and bring my family out of these difficult times.'

Avinash hoped to join his younger brother, Vasanta, in Pune where he had obtained technical training. But Avinash was aware that he would leave his father alone in the middle of the farm crisis. He argued defensively, as if against himself, 'I refuse to work on the farm, even if it had supported us all these years, because we are constantly waiting for rains that are never enough. But if I go to Pune, I will return in June for the sowing of the crop and help my father. It would still be useless, I know we cannot make profit but I will return to help my father.'

The real reason for Suryabhan's resolve became clear now. 'I know my grandchildren will not work in the fields. But I must hope for that one good harvest.' It was this same hope that had killed Devanand. Suryabhan had released his other sons from the hope that had kept him tied to his land, waiting for that one good crop, that one good monsoon, or that one last failure.

★★★

The future came in its usual merciless way. Anita's father-in-law died in 2017 after six months' treatment in a Nagpur hospital.

On an earlier visit in 2016, there had been no one at the house in Adgaon until Anita returned from working on the fields as a wage labourer that late afternoon. She was thinner this time, and looked weaker. She explained it was from the increased number of hours she had been working; she was the only one in the family who did. Suryabhan had been away in hospital for two months in Nagpur and Avinash had stayed with him. Her father-in-law had developed a swelling on the head that had deteriorated over the last few years. His condition brought tears to Anita's eyes; he had been the person who had ensured she got her due in the family after Devanand's death. There was apprehension in her tone, as Anita said, 'I don't know what will happen to me if he goes away. I may no longer have a place in this house or get any part of the land.' She had paid the medical bills with the money she had got as compensation for her husband's death. The BPL card was yet to be issued, and the children were yet to get the next Bal Sangopan grant. Without any support, a new loan of Rs 1 lakh had to be taken from private moneylenders at a steep interest. 'I will have to continue working as a wage labour for the rest of my life. I help people, but will anyone remember that? Will anyone help me? I was expecting my second child when my husband had committed suicide. I survived the past with the guidance of my father-in-law.' She asked, 'How will I survive the future?'

Anita had survived, tenaciously clinging to the semblance of a life, working in the fields of others and paying her children's school fees. She was capable of raising her children and supporting herself single-handedly, and yet, was grateful that she was sheltered against the unknown world outside. That was the life of the shadows of Vidarbha.

☙

Notes

1. According to the National Family Health Survey, 26.7% of rural women have a Body Mass Index (BMI) which is below normal

(BMI < 18.5 kg/m^2), National Family Health Survey-4, 2015–16, Ministry of Health and Family Welfare, Government of India, Delhi, p. 6, available at www.rchiips.org, accessed 30 November 2017.

2. Provisional post-mortem report of Devanand Nandagawli, on 1 September 2007.
3. Histopathology report of Anita Nandagawli, on 26 August 2013.
4. Histopathology report of Anita Nandagawli.
5. Histopathology report of Anita Nandagawli.
6. Letter from the District Women and Child Development Department, Yavatmal, October 2013.
7. According to the Government of Maharashtra's Women and Child Development Department's website, the Bal Sangopan Yojana (scheme) provides assistance to children whose parents are not able to take care of them owing to difficult circumstances. See www.womenchild.maharashtra.gov.in
8. Sewagram is a village in Wardha district in Maharashtra where Mahatma Gandhi and his wife Kasturba had lived for a while. It was a centre of the national movement for Independence from 1936 onwards.

CHAPTER
SEVEN

The Harvest of Time

Sunita Dhale, Chincholi Village, Ghatanji Tehsil, Yavatmal District

A Widow Since 1 May 2012

There was something permanent about Vidarbha, where the trees recounted history and the sunlight judged choices. The soil short-changed the farmer by harvesting time from his life in return for quintals of cotton that were never enough. This loss accumulated like weight around the shoulders of every farmer as if to convince him that eventually, it would all be futile. There was nothing permanent about Vidarbha.

Ramdas Dhale was a man who had refused to believe in loss; he was like millions of farmers in India who fought their desperation with an undying hope in agriculture. It was not easy, Ramdas must have known. The unpaid debts his family had incurred in cotton cultivation proved that failure was more certain than success. But he had not given up like others in his district; and he certainly must have been aware of the suicides by farmers like him. He had carried the burden of his family with the kind of strength found only among those who sought to change destiny. He fought until he discovered that, like debt and loss, destiny too was one of the permanent things in Vidarbha. Ramdas committed suicide on 1 May 2012, at his residence in Chincholi village of Ghatanji tehsil.

Ramdas must have known the consequences; that there would be no one to cultivate his land except for his ageing father; that his family would suffer without his support and guidance; and that the government compensation would not be enough to repay the outstanding debts. There must have been a reason why he wished this upon his own family when he planned his own death. There had been no suicide note to explain any of this, and yet, there were no questions in the expressive brown eyes of Sunita Dhale about why her husband had committed suicide. She had been 36 years old when Ramdas died, a mother of three children. The tragic event had taken place at the residence of the Dhale family, where the middle room was now half-filled with harvested cotton. In May 2012, the same room must have been empty after Ramdas had sold all the harvest. The earnings must have felt light in his hands, and the troubles, heavy. Standing in that room, it

FIGURE 20   Sunita, Ramdas Dhale's widow, September 2014
Source: Author

was difficult to imagine what could have revived the will to fight the odds. A mirror that hung on the wall next to the heap of cotton perhaps still held memories of his face as he took one last glance at himself and met his determined eyes.

FIGURE 21   Room full of cotton produce in Sunita Dhale's house, January 2015
Source: Author

It was a simple house that candidly revealed the efforts to construct it and the places where the money had run out. The courtyard was shared with another house and the narrow porch was painted with grey and white squares, much like a waiting chessboard. On the day in 2012, Sunita was woken up at 4 a.m. by the anguished screams of her husband. He had just consumed the pesticide meant for the cotton in his field. Ramdas must have wanted to keep his plan a secret, which was why he took the step in the early hours when his family slept peacefully. But he could not have helped crying out in agony as the pungent chemical burnt through him and destroyed every internal organ it reached. He was rushed to the district government hospital in Yavatmal where he died two-and-half hours later at 6.40 a.m. He was 43 years of age.

Ramdas' mother, Laxmi, was 60 years old at that time and his father Kishan was 65. They had no doubts about why their only son had committed suicide. Kishan had taken a farm loan in 2008 that had amounted to Rs 44,371, to be repaid on 2 September 2011, as mentioned in Ramdas' suicide file.[1] The loan was transferred to Ramdas as he took over the responsibilities of agriculture from his father. In his statement, Kishan said that his son had tried his best but failed to meet the basic expenses of the family and the medical bills for his mother's treatment. There was a consensus about the cause of his suicide even among the village panchayat members, who said in their statements that the family had not benefitted from the loan-waiver scheme even though they had applied for it. In the last few years of his life, Ramdas had tried to repay the debt through a good yield of cotton.

After his death, this long struggle was encapsulated in a six-line official certificate or *pramana patra*[2] in his suicide file that explained how the crop had failed for two to three years. It had also recommended that Rs 1 lakh be given as compensation to the family, Rs 30,000 in cash and the rest deposited in a bank. The compensation was the state's way of sharing the widow's burden, but it failed to make any impact on Sunita. The cash was spent on the much-required expenses of the family, and the financial assistance of the state withered away quickly.

Sunita worked as a supervisor at an anganwadi school[3] and had been appreciated by the Women and Child Development Department for being the best teacher in the district. She earned Rs 5,000 per month, an amount that she found inadequate but could not afford to forego without finding another job. She did not qualify for the Niradhar scheme[4] because she was an anganwadi worker. The family had a BPL card made in 2002 that provided them rice at Rs 3 per kg and wheat at Rs 2/kg,[5] the quantity of grain not revised since 2002. To augment her income,

Sunita had applied for a sewing machine that the local panchayat was yet to approve.

In September 2014, nearly two years since the death of her husband, Sunita still grappled with the aftermath. The faint smile vanished from her face as she remembered Ramdas. 'We need money for everything,' she said, with the disappointment of one used to living in communities where money was not everything. Villages had been such places before the needs of people changed and agriculture became unsustainable. 'We can manage to grow the food for our survival, but I just hope the children are taken care of somehow,' she said.

It was not surprising that among the portraits of gods in the Dhale house, prominence was given to Saraswati, the goddess of learning and knowledge. There was awareness about the importance of discipline and the need for focus among Sunita's children, as if they knew time could be taken away from them, like with their father. They were witness to the harvest of time; now there was an impatience for change among them, an impatience with losing time.

Payal was 17 years old, Vaishnavi was 14, and Om was 10 in 2014. The constant sadness in Sunita's eyes melted a little when she heard her children speak. Payal was a determined, clear-headed girl whose face brightened with revolutionary thoughts. She was old enough to register the impact her father's suicide had on her mother. A widow still faced the hurdles of tradition as she lived in the house of her husband, brought up children, and took care of his parents. For instance, there existed the notion that widowhood came to a woman due to her own misfortune. Sunita did not speak of encountering such an attitude, but Payal raised pertinent questions. 'In earlier times, it used to be said that the best death for a woman is to die before her husband,' she said, without glancing at her mother. 'Why is that the best death? Why should women die first?' This was a question that was met with absolute silence from her grandparents, who belonged to the earlier times Payal referred to. 'What sin have we women committed that we must die first?' she demanded. It was clear that Payal would not allow custom to dictate her life or the impending end of her education to weigh her down. She argued, 'The family of a girl insists that she should not leave home, even if she follows every rule they set. It is because of such families that I wish I had been a boy.' On whether she planned to conform to the invisibility awaiting her, she said, 'I will fight, because I want to be free.'

FIGURE 22   Payal, Sunita Dhale's elder daughter, September 2014
Source: Author

On whether she believed agriculture killed her father, she asked, 'If no one does farming, how will everyone else survive?' Perhaps, she was merely repeating a justification she had heard about agriculture or her father's suicide. But she seemed reconciled to the fairness of the argument. Payal stayed at a relative's home to study, a partial victory against her family's reservations. In 2014, due to her good grades, Payal had opted for Science as her subject in Class 11 in the government school in Ghatanji town, and said that it could take up to Rs 40,000 in tuitions and other fees to continue studying the subject. Instead, she was contemplating studying Law, which would cost much less. In the meanwhile, she excelled at speeches, essays, and poetry in the school. She gathered praise from her family for her achievements and the prizes she won. Like with her mother, her smile did not last long in her eyes either. But unlike her mother, it was replaced not by patience, but by anger.

Vaishnavi was quieter, with speaking dark eyes that observed life like an artist, intimately, yet from a distance. She was good at her studies and had won awards in school at the district level. She was in Class 10 in 2015 at a nearby school and her favourite subject was Mathematics. The fee for her school was about Rs 30–40 per month, while her books cost up to Rs 5,000 per year.

As compared to Payal's determination to find answers, there was less of the unresolved about Vaishnavi. It was as if any anger or complaint that Vaishnavi had, was settled by choosing memory and ignoring the parts that were painful. The life of the sisters was different from that of the brother, because Om's destiny seemed to have been set by tradition: He was being groomed to step into his father's shoes and had a different battle ahead in his life. While his sisters fought to acquire an identity, Om would have to fight against the one he was born with.

In 2015, he was in Class 6 and his favourite subject was Marathi. It was certain that he would inherit the agricultural land that had kept the family in penury and failed to save his father's life. It was less certain, however, whether he would also inherit the hope that had made his father invest in the dream of the elusive one good crop of cotton. His grandfather, Kishan, said, 'We can sell the land and get some money. But what will we do then? What will our children do? Without land, the private moneylenders do not give loans. We need loans for the marriage of my granddaughters. The land is kept for Om.' But Kishan knew that unless the land was provided with irrigation facilities, nothing could change. In 2015, he had applied for a well to be commissioned by the panchayat through the Mahatma Gandhi National Rural Employment Guarantee Act (2005) and expected it to be approved soon. A similar well had been sanctioned in the village in 2014.

The land had been in the family for more than 70 years, from the time before Independence. Kishan and his brother had 5 acres each, now slightly reduced to 4.5 acres in his share. Clearly, the financial state of the family had not changed enough for anyone to have expanded their holdings. Dressed in traditional white cotton clothes, Kishan explained that in the early years, jowar was extensively cultivated on the land. 'Cotton came much later and used to produce low yields of just 2 to 3 quintals for the entire field. In those days, if the production was low, the cost of cultivation was also low. Comparatively, now the productivity is quite high and so is the cost,' he reasoned.

The crops cultivated by the Dhale family in 2010–12 when they had outstanding loans, according to the agriculture office for Ghatanji tehsil,[6] were cotton and tur. In 2010–11, they harvested nine quintals of cotton and 60 quintals of tur, while in 2011–12, they got 8 quintals of cotton and 48 quintals of tur. It was clear from the records that the production of both crops had progressively decreased, eventually leading to Ramdas' suicide. Kishan said that the cost of cultivation in 2015 was between Rs 1 and Rs 1.5 lakh for a yield of 15 quintals. The crop was bought that year by a private cotton mill at the rate of Rs 4,000 per quintal, and Kishan estimated that unless one quintal sold at a minimum of Rs 5,200, there could be no profit in cotton cultivation. 'To begin with, the expensive Bt cotton seeds cost Rs 930 per 450 gm. For 4.5 acres, we must use seven packets. In 2015, we had to sow the seeds thrice because of the failure of rains, once in June, then twice again afterwards. We usually spray pesticides five to six times for the crop. Our bill for the water pump in the field comes to about Rs 1,000 to Rs 1,200 per year.' In 2014–15, Kishan's health issues had cost the family an additional Rs 1,000 in medical bills.

The previous year had been when the general elections were fought;[*] there had been an intense campaign mounted by the opposition, and it had eventually won the election. The results made no difference to Sunita as no party had spoken about problems of farmers like her. 'Politicians make familiar promises and we vote because we are supposed to. It does not matter who we vote for, or who wins the election. We want solutions; I have young children who cannot work in the fields, and I have an anganwadi job from which I cannot get time off to do farming. My father-in-law or mother-in-law cannot till the fields at their age. How are we to survive on my meagre salary? What happens to the farm?' Sunita asked these desperate questions in a calm, even tone. 'If we employ labour, we must pay them Rs 100 per day per person if it is a woman and Rs 200 in case of a man or for every 40–50 kg of cotton they pick. If we cultivate cotton, we must employ at least six women for the harvest. How do I save any money from agriculture when I must spend so much on it?'

Kishan was brief. 'We welcome loan waivers and but it is only a temporary solution. My land will never give a good yield without irrigation facilities. Politicians promise us big things, but they do not help us get the loans. Bank officials do not clear our pending loans despite knowing our condition. We are always at the mercy of the local moneylender and that will never change.' Kishan's assessment had to be true; he had seen three generations of his family suffer because of agriculture. There was nothing left to lose, except time.

Kishan's words explained what the children inherited. While the boys inherited land and desperation from their fathers, the girls inherited invisibility and loss from their mothers. It was best summed up in Payal's poems as she searched for a different kind of harvest. She sought justice and hoped that those who wielded power experienced the loss felt when a farmer kills himself.

[*] The general elections of 2014.

Perhaps that's why she would be denied visibility; for how could the family, the community, or the state answer her?

***

By July 2017, Payal and Vaishnavi had left home to study in Ghatanji town, taking a stand against the invisibility that awaited them.

Earlier, in 2016, the plentiful monsoons had a visible impact on the Vidarbha farmers, and a constant smile lingered on their faces. 'I am expecting a good yield this year, about 30 quintals from the land,' Sunita said. Still the only working member of the family, she continued to be employed as an anganwadi worker. She had paid her husband's loan of Rs 35,000 with the help of a shahukar loan, which was repaid with half of a bank loan. She explained, 'There had been legal notice for the repayment of the loan on 12 December 2015, asking for a way of ending the loan default. I had earlier paid Rs 4,000 and then Rs 28,000.' This was part of the original loan of Rs 44,000, which was restructured at Rs 36,000. 'That loan is now nil,' Sunita said with relief. Through the last one year, she had repaid a loan of Rs 1 lakh, along with paying every other expense, including her children's tuition fees of Rs 6,000 per year. She argued, 'My children will have nothing to do with agriculture and that was what their father had also wished. He wanted Om to be well educated and find his place in the world. My daughters never ask for anything, but I want to do the best I can for them.'

Time had wrought many changes in the Dhales: Kishan Dhale looked older and more fragile. He explained that while Om would continue with agriculture, he would not work on the field but visit it the way an owner would, to oversee the work of the labourers. The children had changed too; Om was more confident, and studious, Vaishnavi more creative, but the rebellious Payal had inexplicably fallen silent. 'What is the point in planning a future? I want to study Law, but I know I will not be able to.

I want to help my family by getting a job. I do not care much about my dreams. I have to fight against so many odds; no books, no tuition, no classes.' The girl, who was prepared to take on the world just a year ago, now asked, 'What is the point in nuturing dreams?' There would be no answer, and Payal knew it.

అన్

Notes

1. Report of Ramdas Dhale's debt, signed by the officer in-charge, on 9 May 2012.
2. Certificate signed by the tehsildar of Ghatanji and the SDO of Kelapur, on 9 May 2012.
3. The Integrated Child Development Services (ICDS) describes an anganwadi worker as a community-based worker chosen from the local community to work for the ICDS programme. She is expected to mobilize support for care of young children, girls and women. See www.icds-wcd.nic.in.
4. The Sanjay Gandhi Niradhar Anudan Yojana provides financial assistance to oppressed and marginalized citizens such as specially enabled people, orphans, widows, the destitute, women who were freed from human trafficking, and more recently, transgenders. The scheme is also applicable for people aged 65 years and above, whose annual income is less than Rs 21,000 per annum. Under the scheme, the beneficiary receives Rs 600 per month and in the case of a single family having more than one beneficiary, the amount increases to Rs 900 per month. The benefits continue until the children of the beneficiary get employment or reach 25 years of age. In case the beneficiary has only daughters, the assistance continues even after the daughters reach 25 years of age or get married. See www.mumbaisuburban.gov.in; www.amravati.nic.in
5. Figures taken from the official website of the Department of Food and Public Distribution, Ministry of Consumer Affairs, Food and Public Distribution, Government of India. See www.dfpd.nic.in/public-distribution.htm.
6. Certificate signed by the tehsil agricultural officer of Ghatanji tehsil and others.

CHAPTER EIGHT

A Home of Death and Memories

Babarao Zhambre, Sonkhas Village, Ner Tehsil, Yavatmal District

Lost His Brother Keshavrao, in May 2011, and His Widow, Gayabai, in August 2014

Death lived at some addresses as if it now owned space as well as time. These places spilled over with emptiness despite being crowded with incomplete lives, and resounded with silence despite the echoes of lost voices. A fog of tragedy surrounded such a house in Sonkhas village, and it crept all the way up the narrow lane to meet visitors on the main road. The desolation enveloping the house was inexplicable, illogical, and possibly even imagined. The village itself was vibrant and busy, like most villages in Vidarbha, with no scope for the timeless darkness that tenaciously followed the traveller to Babarao Zhambre's house. The ownership of that address had been wrested from the mortal hands of his family, five of 10 of whom had perished from various causes, three dying in quick succession in less than three years.[*]

---

[*] His brother Keshavrao had lost two daughters earlier because of their ill health.

It had all begun with the death of Keshavrao, who committed suicide in 2011 owing to his inability to repay farm debt.

When I first met him for an interview in the late morning on 5 September 2014, Babarao was about to leave the village to sell milk. Two large plastic canisters with green and white stripes were strapped to his bicycle, and he walked carefully over the unpaved path that connected the village to the main road. He could not ride the bicycle until he was on the dark tar road, as the milk would have spilled out of the canisters. He did not turn his bicycle round to return home for the interview and, instead, left it on the side of the lane, trusting the village to guard it for him. It took five minutes to his house by that lane, which was fringed by greenery; it remained verdant through my three visits between 2014 and 2016.

Babarao was a grim, silent man who answered questions with brief replies. His was not the silence of someone lost in thought; it was the silence of one who was through with all conversation, all discussion about possibilities. There was nothing left to speak about. When Babarao did answer questions, it was with the patience of someone who knew his life would be difficult for others to understand. Somehow, this was even more evident at the house he had shared with his brother and his family. The premises contained several structures in a spacious courtyard whose thick hedge perimeter seemed to demarcate the sadness that emanated from the premises.

At the entrance, a quiet transaction took place between a hawker and a young girl. The girl carried books in a plastic basket, much like dirty laundry, and dealt with them in similar fashion. After their acquisition, the hawker dropped the books in a metal container on his bicycle to protect them from the rain that threatened to pour at any moment. When I asked Sushma Zhambre, Babarao's 17-year-old-daughter, if she found the books useless, the young girl clarified that she had passed the examination; these were schoolbooks. 'I failed at my first attempt at passing the Class

12 examinations,'[1] she added with candour, 'in Economics and English. But I managed to pass the re-examination.' She was, as Babarao explained later, attempting to seek something rarely achieved in his family of cattle-rearers—an education. Selling old books was a good way of funding her next class, especially when there was very little hope that the used books would be required for any other child in the family.

Babarao and Keshavrao had dreamt of a life together, built homes next to each other, worked together on their 8-acre land, and reared a large herd of milch cattle that gave them good profits. But those dreams had died, and Babarao now lived not only with the absence of his brother, but half of his brother's family. He had overseen the last rites of Keshavrao's wife and daughter as well, and there was now a lock on the door of that house of death. Babarao pointed to it in silence, as if the house would tell the rest of the story. In a way, it did.

FIGURE 23 The roof of Keshavrao Zhambre's house, from where he hung himself
Source: Author

Keshavrao had lived in that house with his wife Gayabai, his unmarried daughter Sunita, and three sons, Uttam, Ravindra, and Mangesh. His other two daughters, Lalita and Vanita, were married and lived away. Babarao recalled those times with an intense look in his eyes, as if he hoped that if he looked hard enough, the dead would come alive again. Keshavrao had killed himself in 2011 by hanging from the rafters of his house. Sunita died a year later from a heart disease, at a hospital in Amravati. They were barely recovering from this loss when Gayabai was diagnosed with cancer. The family had lost her just 15 days before I met them in 2014. Babarao's eyes were narrowed in grief as he said, 'I sold the buffalos every time a medical bill had to be paid.' The elaborate buffalo pens pointed to a much larger herd at one time, and now there were about a dozen cattle left. 'It cost so much, but I did it out of hope of saving the lives of my brother's family. It did not help.'

There was an embattled fatigue about him. 'My brother died because there was no money to educate our children, marry them off well, or further their future in any way. He defaulted on his debt only for two years but he could not get any new loans from the bank. And the krishi kendra[2] refused to lend him any more farm material,' Babarao said, and he knew that the problem was not about the amount or the time. 'It was about how nothing ever changed,' he said. As compensation, the government had offered Rs 1 lakh to Gayabai, of which Rs 29,500 was given directly and the rest was kept in a fixed deposit in a bank.

In 2011, Keshavrao had 4.94 acres of land in his name and a pending loan of Rs 56,042 taken in 2009. The SDO,[3] in charge of the Farmer Suicide Department, had recommended to the district collector that Keshavrao's death was a farmer suicide caused due to debt and that his family was eligible for compensation. The state's approach, while considering whether Keshavrao's suicide met the criteria for compensation, seemed one of indifference, as proved from several instances where it had stopped short of an actual assessment of Keshavrao's situation. First, the bank had confirmed that the pending loan and the amount were accurate.[4] As it was common knowledge that farmers took private loans more often than formal loans, to restrict focus on the latter reflected the reluctance of the administration to investigate further and identify borrowings from moneylenders. And in Keshvrao's case, the futility of this approach was particularly stark, because he had been taking private loans since 2009, as he was a defaulter and hence denied loans by the banks. Secondly, the administration explored the reasons he failed to repay the loan. The state reviewed whether a farmer suicide was eligible for compensation based on criteria like land ownership, unpaid formal loan, and the general trend of crop yields. These, however, did not cover the range of circumstances of a farmer who committed suicide. This was evident from the fact that farmer suicides did not occur due to non-payment of loans after a period of a single year or even two years. In many cases, these occurred after several stressful years, pointing to the efforts of farmers who consistently try to repay their loans, but fail.

Thirdly, the administration found that Keshavrao's land had been low yielding since 2009 and the list of crops that the family used to cultivate, as provided in the letter of the agriculture officer,[5] was long and diverse. They had cultivated soybean, cotton, tur, and other pulses. The administration, however, did not give any reason as to why the various crops had failed. Fourthly, the investigation revealed that Keshavrao's yearly income was Rs 15,000 and yet he did not have a BPL card,[6] which got cancelled after the 2001 census. The administration, once again, did not explain as to how this came to be.[7] As mentioned before, facts were discovered and presented indifferently, and without an attempt to either explain their circumstances or its impact on the farmer.

On 31 May 2011, 60-year-old Keshavrao, who had been trying to collect money to buy seeds to sow the new crop of cotton that season, hanged himself in his house. He died instantaneously according to the post-mortem report.[8] At the time of his death,

Gayabai had taken Sunita for a check-up for her heart condition. When Gayabai returned home, she opened the doors of the house and went looking for her husband, only to discover him hanging from the rafters. Her sons, who had returned from working in the fields and were resting in the courtyard, rushed into the house hearing her cries. Gayabai, who was 55 years of age at that time, had been married to him for three decades. She never recovered from the shock, succumbing to her disease within three years of Keshavrao's death.

While recording her statement in 2011,[9] however, Gayabai was not asked about how devastated she felt; instead, she was questioned closely about what she believed to be the cause of her husband's death. Within a fortnight of Keshavrao's demise, Gayabai was expected to evaluate his social, financial, agricultural, and mental condition so that she could qualify for the state compensation. As with any other widow of a farmer who must answer the questions of the administration at its convenience, she had little choice but to set aside her grief and her anxiety about the responsibilities that were now hers. And like most widows, Gayabai showed strength that the administration neither recorded in their lengthy reports nor, perhaps, even noticed. She stated[10] that Keshavrao had been worried about loan repayment and, especially during that season, he was troubled that he would not have the money to even buy seeds for the new crop. He failed to borrow from banks, friends, and even relatives. He had mentioned often in the days preceding his suicide that only death could end his troubles. The family reassured him and hoped that some way could be found for the work to continue. Hope, however, was not the solution; Gayabai understood why Keshavrao was worried—the consistently low yields had shown no signs of improvement.

In his statement,[11] his son Ravindra had said that he had found his father constantly anxious about the new crop as it was impossible to get a new loan without clearing the old ones. Ravindra stated that his father would sit alone, brooding and distraught, to figure out ways of getting the funds for the new crop. This fact was supported by the village sarpanch as well. It was possible, although not mentioned, that on that fateful day Keshavrao had gone to raise funds to buy seeds for the new crop and had once again failed; this time, for the last time.

Babarao seemed to live as if he had lost an important part of his life and the house he kept bolted contained more than mere death and shadows. The explanation was hidden in Babarao's statement[12] to the administration taken after his brother's death. Babarao knew Keshavrao's problems closely and was also aware of his anxieties. He had been in the fields working when he heard of his brother's death. In his statement, he highlighted the fact that his brother was agitated that the banks had refused him a loan, as did his relatives. Babarao himself faced troubles—the low crop yields could not support them. He too had a pending loan[13] and stated that he could not help his brother with money. But this was not as

FIGURE 24   Babarao Zhambre, Keshavrao's younger brother, September 2014
Source: Author

simple a statement as it appeared. It hid the guilt of a brother, the helplessness of poverty, and the despair of being a mute spectator to a tragedy. Babarao would never be the same again.

Babarao said he had taken a private loan of Rs 50,000 to plant cotton in his field; the amount, with interest, was Rs 2 lakh in 2014 but he was still unable to repay. Private moneylenders were reluctant to issue new loans if their old debts remained unpaid; besides, new loans usually meant higher interest rates. However, there was no other choice for farmers who were declared defaulters by banks. The crop of cotton yielded between 5 and 10 quintals per acre when the rains were on time. The rains were not on time in 2014 and the crop had to be sown twice. That had already cost Babarao Rs 40,000 and the season had only just begun. There was spraying to be done several times, fertilizers to be applied, and labour to be paid. The Bt cotton crop was neither completely pest-resistant nor well yielding. As a result, the earning from the crop was barely enough to run the household, let alone repay the debts. 'The central government had promised *karza maafi*, to waive loans for poor farmers. We had hoped that our unpaid debts would be finally cleared because of the loan waiver. But the loan waiver applied only to farmers who owned land of 5 acres or less. Although we have 8 acres, our condition is no better, but we still didn't meet the government criterion.' Babarao struggled with such problems and knew he would continue to do so; he saw no other alternative to agriculture. 'Farming is what we do. This is all we know. We rear cattle and we till the soil. That's how we live,' he said.

The villages were changing; they now had electricity, internet, cell phones, and cable. Change made the youth wish for something better than agriculture, which kept them alive in poverty but killed their dreams. Educated young men and women struggled to find jobs, but if they failed, their only alternative was agriculture. That was what Babarao had meant; without education and skills, the next generation would have to do agriculture not as a choice but as a compromise. While people from the village and others in Babarao's acquaintance had migrated to the cities in search of a better livelihood, he did not believe that to be a solution for himself. 'What will I do in a city?' he asked. 'I cannot leave my home and farm, which give us shelter and take care of our basic needs. Who will take care of that in a city?'

Despite his financial burdens and untenable circumstances, Babarao had tried his best to educate his two sons, Satish and Bhaskar, and daughter, Sushma. The sons, who had been in school at the height of the crisis at home, had to give up their education: Satish, had studied up to matriculation but failed the examination. The daughter, however, was more diligent and was even awarded a scholarship of Rs 1,000 in school. Her parents were proud of that fact, and it was the only time Babarao smiled. 'I want her to study as much as possible. I am in no hurry to get her married,' he said. His wife, Indubai, observed dryly at this point, 'We have no money to get her married anyway. So she might as well study for as long as we can afford it.'

That suited Sushma just fine. 'I want to study further; I want to be a medical nurse. I know it takes money to get an education, but I will do it somehow. It is a three-year course and it will cost us Rs 50,000. Then there is the expense of going to Yavatmal to do the course.' Sushma spoke about her plans as she stood leaning to the door of her home. Her parents sat in the porch and heard her affectionately. There was something about her dreams that brought hope to the family. Many a son had failed at what Sushma was attempting to do—find an alternative to the life they led in that village. This could be a solution for every son and daughter who would come later. This was no time to discriminate against the girl; no argument could work against the only one among half-a-dozen children who managed to pass a Class 12 examination. She was the one who got the chairs for the guests, she was the one who made the tea, and she was the one who collected the empty cups for washing. But she was also the one who listened to the story of her uncle's death, her face sad, but her eyes, resolved. The death of Keshavrao and what happened to his family thereafter seemed to serve as a reminder of a tragedy that could never be repeated. Babarao had not yet planned on how to support her education but appeared to reconcile with pinning his hopes on a few cattle and some acres. Sushma listened to him in respectful silence, quietly determined to make her own destiny, her own way.

★★★

By July 2017, Sushma was married and lived in nearby Sonkhas village.

Earlier in August 2016, it had rained for eight days continuously and the monsoon had washed away the young crop of cotton. The Zhambre family grappled with another loan that might never be repaid. Satish still worked as farm labour for daily wages, but could not afford to employ labour in their own field. 'We harvested 10 quintals of cotton in the 2015–16 season, and we expect the yield to be even less this year,' he said. The cotton sold at the minimum support price of Rs 3,800 but the prices could go up to Rs 4,200 in the open market. As the banks denied fresh loans, he would have to borrow from private moneylenders. Every article of value was on its way to being lost in this struggle for survival; most articles were already pawned. 'We borrow money by pawning the gold ornaments of the women of the family. For a *mangalsutra*,[14] we could get Rs 10,000, and out of that, we must give Rs 2,000 to the moneylender. The interest rate could be anything between 3 and 5 per cent, depending on how the moneylender perceives our ability to repay.' When a private loan was taken against the land of the farmer, the process was far more irreversible and weighed in favour of the moneylender. The farmer had to pledge the land to the moneylender with photographs on a sworn affidavit. Satish felt it was a final step for a farmer; there was nothing left to fight for when the land was pledged for loans. 'We are slaves of the moneylender the moment he lends us money. He begins to dictate our life and gives us a date on which we must pay the debt,' he said. Two of Keshavrao's three sons, Ravindra and Mangesh, tilled the 8-acre land that they shared with Satish. The sons of the two brothers replayed the life of their fathers, hoping for different results. The only difference was that Ravindra and Mangesh did not stay in their father's house but lived in a nearby village in the same tehsil, while their other brother, Uttam, lived in another district. Kesavrao's daughters, Lalita and Vanita lived in Wardha district. Speaking in 2016 over the telephone, Lalita blamed the state of agriculture for the death of her father, and her brother Ravindra echoed the sentiment.

Sushma Zhambre was changed in 2016; she was no longer the determined, promising girl from just two years ago. She appeared listless and angry, and for good reason. After passing her Class 12 examination, her family did not allow her to study further as it would have entailed travelling just 3 km each day within the tehsil of Ner. Instead, she worked on the sewing machine they got from

FIGURE 25 Sushma, Babarao Zhambre's daughter, August 2016
Source: Author

the panchayat, repairing torn clothes or stitching new ones for the villagers, and earned Rs 500–600 per month. It felt like a weak excuse to her. 'I can adapt myself to the conditions because I have the ambition to study further. But how do I change the mindset of my family?' she asked. Her parents and brother, Satish, planned her marriage in a year's time and repeatedly pointed out that the next time I visited, Sushma might be already gone. The silence with which Sushma bore these statements, designed to convey that her days at her home were numbered, seemed to only alienate her and make her feel she was alone in her battles.

Sushma was prepared to chase her dreams and struggle without asking for help, but such resolve was to no avail. 'The administration has organized a camp for briefing children of farmers, who had committed suicide, about how to become a qualified nurse. I am all set to go, but my family says I must not,' she said. Ironically, her mother and her brother, Satish, strenuously argued that they could not support her dreams any futher, when perhaps Sushma needed their support the most. That was in 2016.

Speaking on phone two months after her marriage in 2017, she said she had not visited her home even once. It takes time to adjust to the new life, she said, in a tone of reconciliation that was unusual for her. Even the sewing machine, the only thing that her parents allowed her, did not travel with her to her new home. She could be forced into the usual invisibility imposed by marriage in such circumstances, and exchange her dreams for the shadows that awaited her. For, only the shadows belonged to the women in Vidarbha.

প্র

Notes

1. The Indian school education system consists of two national board examinations in Classes 10 and 12, administered either by the central board or the state boards. The school is followed by college and university education.

2. Krishi kendra or kisan kendra: Agricultural input shops that provide farm requirements, sometimes on loan in lieu of produce.

3. Letter from the SDO to the district collector of Yavatmal (Farmer Suicide Department), on 6 July 2011.

4. Letter from the SDO to the district collector of Yavatmal (Farmer Suicide Department).

5. Letter from tehsil's agricultural officer to the tehsildar of Ner, on 29 June 2011.

6. The Below Poverty Line (BPL) yardstick has been used by the Indian government as a tool to decide the economic status of a poor person. Those earning less than Rs 32 a day in a rural area or less than Rs 47 a day in an urban area fall under the BPL line. 'Report of the Expert Group to Review the Methodology for Measurement of Poverty', Planning Commission, Government of India, 2014, available at www.planningcommission.nic.in and 'New Poverty Line: Rs 32 in villages, Rs 47 in cities', *Times of India*, 7 July 2014, available at www.timesofindia.indiatimes. com/india/New-poverty-line-Rs-32-in-villages-Rs-47-in-cities/ articleshow/37920441.cms?from=mdr, last accessed 12 December 2017.

   Broadly, the debates over the BPL and APL (Above Poverty Line) are that it is difficult to qualify for BPL benefits, as 74.52 per cent of the rural population lives on a household income of less than Rs 5,000 per month (see 'Social Economic and Caste Census 2011', Government of India, available at: www.secc.gov.in, last accessed 12 December 2017); that the international standards set to measure poverty are unfair to developing countries (see Sanjay Reddy and Thomas Pogge, *How Not to Count the Poor, 2005,* available at www. papers.ssrn.com, accessed 6 July 2017); and that large-scale corruption, government irregularities, and bureaucratic malpractices were affecting the issuing of BPL cards. Therefore, the BPL list failed to capture ground realities of the poor, as also observed in the 18 cases in this book.

7. Question 41 from the 43-question form.

8. Memorandum of a postmortem examination held at Dispensary Hospital, Yavatmal, on 1 June 2011.

9. Statement of Gayabai Zhambre, recorded and presented to the district administration of Yavatmal by the tehsildar of Ner, where the village of Sonkhas is situated, on 17 June 2011.

10. Statement of Gayabai Zhambre, recorded and presented to the district administration of Yavatmal by the tehsildar of Ner, where the village of Sonkhas is situated, on 17 June 2011.

11. Statement of Ravindra Zhambre, recorded and presented to the district administration of Yavatmal by the tehsildar of Ner, where the village of Sonkhas is situated, on 15 June 2011.

12. Statement of Babarao Zhambre, recorded and presented to the district administration of Yavatmal by the tehsildar of Ner, where the village of Sonkhas is situated, on 15 June 2011.

13. Statement of Babarao Zhambre, recorded and presented to the district administration of Yavatmal by the tehsildar of Ner, where the village of Sonkhas is situated, on 15 June 2011.

14. The sacred thread is a symbol of Hindu marriage usually worn by women with gold embellishments.

CHAPTER
NINE

A Museum of the Possible

Jayashri Sawankar, Sirasgoan Village, Ner Tehsil, Yavatmal District

A Widow Since 2 May 2002

Shelves on the blue-green walls of that room were stacked with objects that hummed with life; these were much-read school books, well-posed photographs, dolls wrapped in time, and gods covered in ancient glory. It was as if these were chosen carefully from the daily mortal stream of life and immortalized, like pebbles for posterity. It was a home aware of the fragility of everything, and more so of the short distance that life always was from death. This was not the home Ganesh Sawankar had left behind when he committed suicide by consuming poison at the age of 28 in 2002. It was the home of Jayashri, Ganesh's wife, who had to turn overnight from being a sheltered, home-bound housewife to a heavily indebted farmer and an unemployed mother of two young girls. She had spent the last 12 years[*] trying to ensure that the sudden, drastic change had no impact on the lives of her children. The

[*] As in 2014.

fatigue was evident in her dark eyes that never smiled, and in her sense of resignation about everything.

FIGURE 26 Jayashri, Ganesh Sawankar's widow, August 2016
Source: Author

The death certificate[1] issued by the tehsil office at Ner on 14 March 2008 stated that Ganesh Sawankar had committed suicide by consuming pesticide on 2 May 2002. Ganesh had been unable to repay a debt of Rs 50,000 to a bank, and other loans to private moneylenders, because of a failing cotton crop on his 3-acre land. Jayashri recalled, 'After he died, the moneylenders asked me to repay the loan. I told them I had no idea about it because my husband never shared such information with me. They refused to believe me and threatened to take action. I asked them to go ahead, because I had no money to repay.'

That had not dissuaded the moneylenders, but in time, they realized she was telling the truth, as the entire village was witness to her struggle for survival. 'People suggested that I should remarry, but that was impossible. I could never think of another man, or forget my husband's affection for me. I could not have lived without those memories. Everyone said that my two daughters would only be a burden on me, whereas a son would have taken care of me.' She smiled faintly. 'I wonder if a son would have been strong enough to face what my daughters had to face; I wonder if he too would not have committed suicide like my husband had. Men seem unable to deal with the hard life and, perhaps, it takes a woman to survive the tough times. Women are different. We do not accept defeat.'

Time had let Jayashri reconcile with Ganesh's suicide, but there was still a sense of betrayal at his surrender. Without choice, she had to measure her every success against his defeat, and she did not like it. When she spoke of her strengths as a woman, there was emphasis on her survival rather than any victory. As a testimony to her resolve, Jayashri never borrowed from the moneylenders who had harassed her husband. She had leased out the 3 acres at the rate of Rs 5,000 a year, even though it meant giving up on whatever little farm output there was. Having passed out of school, she worked as a part-time attendant at a dispensary and earned Rs 1,200 per month. She had benefitted from welfare schemes, mostly through her own awareness and through long-drawn battles with the state to be identified under categories of unsupported women, single mothers, and widows with children, etc. But she did not count the Rs 1 lakh compensation she received for the suicide of her husband as state support. It seemed to have a different meaning for Jayashri, as if the government had awarded her husband for the brave fight he had put up against his fate and his eventual martyrdom. In her museum of possible things, there was no place for the deposit slip[2] for Rs 70,000 that was folded and tucked away in a plastic cover.

Apart from her job, she acquired a sewing machine through a scheme implemented by the local panchayat and added that to her income through stitching and mending clothes. Jayashri had also obtained training in cattle management and milk production technology in 2008 in a study course organized by the district administration. But none of this would have facilitated the education of the two children, she said. 'It would have been impossible to put my children through school but for the state support under the Bal Sangopan Yojana (scheme).'[3] The scheme had paid for the education of her elder daughter Vaishnavi, until she turned 18 years. The letter[4] informing her of the scheme had come to Jayashri in 2011–12, nine years after the death of her husband. It said that the money would be granted for the upbringing and education of the children of farmers who had committed suicide and to support the widow. Jayashri was summoned at 11 a.m. sharp on 30 June 2012, a Saturday, at the office of district administration's Department of Women and Child Development in Yavatmal. She was also asked to carry with her a photo identification card, bank pass book, certificate from the school principal of the child to ascertain she was a student, and her mark sheets. Jayashri was given 15 days to put together all the documents and present them before the department officials. The manner in which the state delivered the welfare made it look more like a dole than a grant, especially because Jayashri needed it. These were not things that a sensitive and strong woman like Jayashri or her elder daughter Vaishnavi would have missed.

Then the scheme stopped when Vaishnavi had needed it the most. Jayashri explained, 'Children over 18 years of age cease to benefit from the Bal Sangopan Yojana (scheme). I find that strange, because parents and school-going children are already incentivized through fee waivers or free books, etc., in schools. It is the education after school that many parents cannot afford and children are forced to look for full-time employment or work on the farms.' In 2014, Vaishnavi studied at the school in Ner, the tehsil headquarters, which was about 18 km away from the village, incurring a cost of Rs 600 per month just for daily transport. The only option was to let her stay at a hostel in Ner, which Jayashri would not allow. Eventually, however, she did. Jayashri explained, 'Vaishnavi told me that we find the world the way we see it. She said that if she was good, the world would be good to her.' Vaishnavi called home every night. Though Jayashri had not wanted her affection to come in the way of her daughter's life, she had hoped that there was still time before letting Vaishnavi go. She said, 'Vaishnavi is a very independent person, she can live away and alone. It is I who cannot live without her.'

Vaishnavi, like her younger sister Sakshi now, had studied in the zila parishad high school of Sirasgaon. Her exam results for Class 10 showed she was good with languages and social sciences. She was also good at sports, and Jayashri fondly recalled an instance when her teachers had wanted Vaishnavi to participate in a race but she did not have running shoes. 'She wanted to run in that race so badly, and her teachers promised that if she won the race, she would be gifted running shoes. So she ran barefoot. I still remember the state of her feet when she returned home. But she had won the race,' Jayashri said, her eyes tearful. 'Sometimes I feel sad that I am unable to provide my children the things they really need.'

There was a hint of the vehemence of a woman who had to often face the argument that she might need a man's help to succeed. She said, 'I do not think I would have done any better if I had been a man. I believe I am able to do all that I can because I am a woman. I cannot afford to give up, it is not an option. I know I am the only support for my children. I cannot escape and I do not want to escape.'

Vaishnavi listened to her mother in silence and did not speak immediately. Then she said, 'Once I finish school in 2015, I want to do a short course in something that will get me a job. My mother has already done enough and I want to support my sister's education by finding a paying job.' Nursing was an option that could get her a job fairly immediately to support her own further education. There was a sense of urgency in her decision, born from the awareness that she might have already wasted time in chasing impossible dreams. Vaishnavi had only been a child when

FIGURE 27 Jayashri Sawankar (centre) with her daughters Vaishnavi (left) and Sakshi, January 2015
Source: Author

Ganesh committed suicide, but she had come to learn from her elders that the inquest had not been conducted satisfactorily by the police. Instead of resentment, this knowledge had inspired her to think of joining the police force. She said, 'I do not want someone else like me, a daughter who barely knew her father, to grow up thinking that the police could have done a better job in their investigation.' She had a fascination for firearms, which she discovered from a distant relative who was in the Indian Army. 'I loved the army rifle. It gave me a sense of responsibility, as if I could stand guard against anything,' she said. Vaishnavi felt that her accomplishments in athletics and karate would help her when she joined the police force. More importantly, this was one way to ensure that the money that her mother had spent on her extra-curricular activities would not go waste. 'It is my dream to be a policewoman, like the people I see standing outside the police station in Ner as I drive by in the bus. I want to be like them one day. But it can wait,' she said. She specialized in Commerce in

Class 12, but was worried about how her education after schooling would be funded. The look of concern was out of place on her young face, but it was part of her decisions, part of her life. When she spoke about things she could not afford, which was often, there wasn't ever any bitterness in her.

Her education pattern provided an insight into the futility of learning important subjects like Science, Mathematics, and Social Sciences in regional languages in Indian schools. She gave up Science after Class 10, and might have to give up Commerce after Class 12. Vaishnavi was educated in a medium called 'semi-English,' which was an equal mixture of English and Marathi. 'I would have had to take English tuitions if I had continued with Science, but that would have been an extra expense every month. I could not afford to learn Science and what I had learnt in school was virtually useless because it was not in English.' This partial education was unfair to children who could barely afford it. Even sports were expensive and Vaishnavi had to give up karate. 'I have not gone to the classes for the last three months,' she said in January 2015. The fee was Rs 150 per month, and they said I may have to pay more to get a black belt. I like to learn karate but I cannot afford it.' Both Vaishnavi and Sakshi scored over 70 per cent in their studies, and the promising mark sheets were a testament to their determination.

The major expense in Sakshi's case, who was in Class 9, was tuitions for Geometry, Algebra, Mathematics, and English. She borrowed books from her sister and others; these books had been passed on from one student to another and were carefully preserved without the usual underlining or remarks of any kind. After Sakshi, her books would travel to another family, another child who was determined to study despite poverty. The expense of the children's education could not have been trimmed any further without affecting the quality of their learning. But this was still beyond the capacity of Jayashri, who worked every minute of her day. However, it was not an isolated story; there were other women in the same village who struggled to meet the expense of their children's education. Together they had formed a self-help group (SHG) of 11 women and opened an account in a national bank a year ago. This helped them save for the money needed for their children's education, which would otherwise have remained unaffordable for each family. Every member contributed Rs 100 per month to this account and it was loaned back to the members depending on their requirements. It was through a brief loan from this SHG that Vaishnavi could travel to Amravati to participate in a competition in 2014; the other component of Jayashri's expenditure was Vaishnavi's sports activities, which included athletics and kabaddi. Once again, there was no ownership of the materials required for sports, like shoes, uniforms, and tracksuits. Like books, these too belonged to everyone. Vaishnavi, therefore, was not worried that she could not afford the sports material. She said, 'I borrow and play whenever I can. I get shoes and tracksuits of other sportspersons when they are not playing. Only sometimes, when other children participate in a tournament at the same time, I do not get access to the equipment. But that is all right. I will have my own stuff someday.'

Sakshi, who was 14, had a simple plan. 'I want to be a schoolteacher when I grow up. I think that is something I can achieve easily because I am good at studies. I would like to teach Mathematics and Science at my own school. Teachers do not teach well in our school and often wipe clean the blackboard before the students get a chance to copy in their notebooks. It cannot go on like this.' Sakshi liked to participate in dramatics at district-level competitions. She was quietly proud of her achievements and strictly followed a timetable for her Class 10, which was pasted on the neatly painted wall of the front room. After much searching—and gentle scolding from her sister—Sakshi finally produced a certificate for coming first in a district-level folk dance competition and an acting competition in 2013 held in Yavatmal.

She did indeed have a nice stage voice. 'Besides acting, I love to draw. You will find that most of my drawings are sketches without colours, unlike my sister's paintings. That is because my sister does not let me use the colours as I mix them up.' Like Vaishnavi, Sakshi too was good at debates, which was borne out by the fact that she argued her point in every conversation. Recently, she was commended in school for her debating prowess on a topic that was rather ticklish. 'The debate was on whether we should watch television programmes or not,' she explained gravely. Vaishnavi quipped. 'You can guess which side she took.' Sakshi continued excitedly, 'Yes, I supported watching television. There were arguments that television should not be allowed in homes as it had a negative impact on young minds. But I countered that we also get to learn from television programmes. It is entirely up to us whether to watch or not to watch television. The television itself does not force us to watch now, does it?'

Vaishnavi, too, had participated in a debate on the prime minister's nation-wide Swachh Bharat Abhiyan and argued that campaigns did not help if people's mindset remained unchanged. She also kept a diary in which she wrote everything that happened in a day. But the ordinary 200-page notebooks cost Rs 40, an expense that Vaishnavi was aware she could not afford as she wrote on the pages. As a result, no word was wasted, no corner of the book left unfilled.

Jayashri preserved every little memory of her children; she knew how transient childhood was. She was diagnosed with diabetes two years ago, the medicines for which cost Rs 250 per month. 'I worry about what would happen to my children if I fall ill. This thought ensures that I am very careful with my medication and diet,' she said. Her plans for herself were all similarly tempered. There were requests that Jayashri should contest the panchayat elections in January 2015, but she had refused. She explained, 'People do not understand my situation; I cannot contest because I cannot antagonize anyone in the village. There is no telling when I might need someone's help.' She was pragmatic about her dependence. 'Even as part of an election campaign, if I oppose someone who is important, I won't be able to survive in the village. But I hope things will change by the time my children grow up.' The village had between 2,000 and 2,500 voters and over 500 houses. 'Women vote for women in this village and that was the reason for the suggestion that I should contest. In a big election, where there are a number of contenders and different issues, people tend to take things in their stride. But in a small election, like a panchayat election, people will remember things forever.' She added with her typical calmness, 'Politics is not for me; not because I am afraid I may lose, but because I am sure I will win.'

***

By 2017, Vaishnavi had been working as a part-time nurse for a few months in Ner and was earning Rs 2,000.

Earlier in August 2016, she had been away from home to study a course in Nursing in Latur. She was pursuing a graduate degree in Commerce as well and her education was no longer supported by the state. Back home in Sirasgaon, her paintings on the green walls and her photographs, made up little for her absence. It was for such times that Jayashri had preserved this museum. Her three acres of land were still on lease. She had been recently awarded Rs 15,000 by the administration under a new campaign[5] for independently supporting two children, a recognition that was publicized in the media. She had qualified for schemes under the campaign but had refused to apply. 'There were women at the meeting who deserved the welfare much more than I did,' Jayashri explained simply.

Sakshi had grown tall and now she wanted to be a farmer. Since 2014, her future plans had included becoming a teacher, an actor, a policewoman, and a sarpanch, among others. She explained her change of heart, 'I like working on the farm, but it would be good if I can get a tractor. I do not want our land to be on lease; it belongs to my father and I will cultivate it.' There was a well in the field that was acquired through a government scheme, and water was available at 40 feet depth. The crops grown were usually pulses and the cost was shared between Jayashri and the lessee; in 2016, her share of the cost had been Rs 25,000. Jayashri noted, 'If the state had supported my husband with Rs 1 lakh that they paid after his death, he would not have committed suicide. It is not the farm that lets us down.'

Notes

1. Certificate of death issued by the tehsildar of Ner, on 14 March 2008.
2. Jayashri Sawankar's deposit slip from a lending agency, of Rs 70,000, on 27 September 2014.
3. According to the Government of Maharashtra's Women and Child Development Department's website, the Bal Sangopan Yojana (scheme) provides assistance to children whose parents are not able to take care of them owing to difficult circumstances. See www.womenchild.maharashtra.gov.in
4. Letter from District Women and Child Development Office, Yavatmal, on 15 June 2012.
5. Baliraja Chetna Abhiyan, according to the documents provided by the Yavatmal District Collectorate in 2016, was a scheme approved by the Government of Maharashtra in 2015. It was proposed to run for three years on a fund of Rs 32 crore annually. Every village would be given Rs 1 lakh to spend on libraries; distressed farmers; public festivals; loans of up to Rs 20,000 without interest for two or three months for sowing and for medical treatment. At the village level, a committee was to be formed with the sarpanch as president, gram sevak as the secretary, and members who included the agricultural assistant, an anganwadi worker, prominent men and women of the village, a police officer and a retired lawyer, doctor, or ex-servicemen from the village.

SECTION II
Amravati

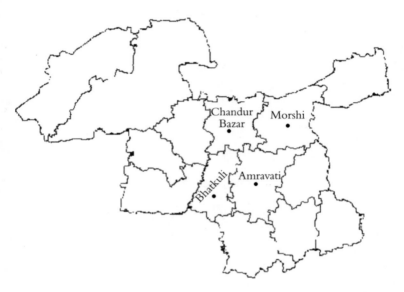

FIGURE 28   Map of Amravati district
Source: Amravati district website[1]

*T*he Amravati district of Maharashtra state has an area of 12,210 sq km. The total population of the district is 28,88,445; of this, the rural population of 18,51,158 lives in 1,997 villages, according to the District Census Handbook Amravati, 2011.[2] At 87.4 per cent,[3] Amravati's literacy rate is higher than the 82.34 per cent[4] for the state of Maharashtra and 72.99 per cent[5] for India. The district has one of the highest sex ratios for the state at 951.[6] Agriculture is rain-fed and employs 70.1 per cent[7] of the total workforce. While there are 2 lakh farmers in the district, thrice the number are employed as farm labour. As found in this research, many farmers worked as farm labour owing to the unsustainability of agriculture on their own fields.

The district is divided into 14 administrative units, called tehsils. Of these, three tehsils of Bhatkuli, Chandur Bazar, and Morshi were selected for the present research, as explained in the methodology in the Introduction. According to the District Census Handbook, the largest total population among the three chosen tehsils is in Chandur Bazar, followed by Morshi and then Bhatkuli. Chandur Bazar has a total area of 684.19 sq km and a total population of 1,77,499[8] across its 169 villages. Morshi has an area of 786.80 sq km and a total population of 1,45,151[9] spread across 166 villages. Bhatkuli's 137 villages are spread across 581. 23 sq km and have a total population of 1,13,109.[10]

Farmer suicides in the three tehsils from different years between 2001 and 2014 were chosen for an in-depth study. The earliest case of suicide was in 2003 in Borala and the latest was in 2014. Most farmers featuring in this book are small and marginal, while most widows have not studied beyond Class 12. Just like in Yavatmal, the daughters of many of these farmers in Amravati excelled at their studies, but were forced to think of marriage; many sons did not want to be farmers, but could not rely on the half-hearted education offered at schools.

And just like Yavatmal, in Amravati too, no two stories were the same.

ॐ

Notes

1. Available at: www.amravati.nic.in, accessed 4 July 2017.
2. District Census Handbook Amravati, Maharashtra, Series–28, Part XII-B, Directorate of Census Operations, Maharashtra, 2011, p. 12, available at www.censusindia.gov.in, accessed 9 December 2017.
3. District Census Handbook Amravati, Maharashtra, Series–28, Part XII-B, Directorate of Census Operations, Maharashtra, 2011, p. 11, available at www.censusindia.gov.in, accessed 9 December 2017.
4. Census of India, 2011, Office of the Registrar General & Census Commissioner, India, available at www.censusindia.gov.in, accessed 9 December 2017.
5. Census of India, 2011, Office of the Registrar General & Census Commissioner, India, available at www.censusindia.gov.in, accessed 9 December 2017.
6. Number of females per 1,000 males.
7. District Census Handbook Amravati, Maharashtra, Series–28, Part XII-B, Directorate of Census Operations, Maharashtra, 2011, p. 11, availabale at www.censusindia.gov.in, accessed 9 December 2017.
8. District Census Handbook Amravati, Maharashtra, Series–28, Part XII-B, Directorate of Census Operations, Maharashtra, 2011, p. 22, available at www.censusindia.gov.in, accessed 9 December 2017.
9. District Census Handbook Amravati, Maharashtra, Series–28, Part XII-B, Directorate of Census Operations, Maharashtra, 2011, p. 22, available at www.censusindia.gov.in, accessed 9 December 2017.
10. District Census Handbook Amravati, Maharashtra, Series–28, Part XII-B, Directorate of Census Operations, Maharashtra, 2011, p. 22, available at www.censusindia.gov.in, accessed 9 December 2017.

CHAPTER
TEN

Once Upon a Time a Farmer

Jyoti Bhumbar, Ashtgaon Village, Morshi Tehsil, Amravati District

A Widow since 13 December 2007

The story of Praveen Bhumbar was a cautionary tale across the well-laid-out village of Ashtgaon in Morshi tehsil of Amravati. It was a story that had unfolded slowly and painfully before the eyes of the entire village. Praveen was a hard-working farmer who struggled to make his 3.5-acre land yield enough to sustain his family, which included his father, wife, three children, and brother. He had cultivated cotton, which used to produce enough profits for the family to set some savings aside; that was how they had rented a tea stall on the road. But the outstanding loans proved to be too much of a burden for Praveen, who burnt himself with kerosene on 12 November 2007, and died about a month later, on 13 December. He was 35 years old at the time of his death and had a loan of Rs 36,863 from a lending agency in his name, including interest, which had been outstanding since 2005. His wife Jyoti had been 31 years old, his son Sachin was 5, while the twins Gauri and Gaurav were 4.

FIGURE 29   Jyoti, Praveen Bhumbar's widow, January 2015
Source: Author

In the letter[1] written by the tehsildar of Morshi to the district
collector of Amravati, it was stated that the loan was taken by
Praveen, an important fact in the state's investigation into farmer
suicide due to farm debt. There were other loans[2] taken by his
father, Shaligram, the sole burden of which was on Praveen as
his father's old age and deteriorating health did not allow him to
work towards their repayment. Their farm was rain-fed and even
though there was a well, the water was never enough, especially
if the rainfall was deficient in a season. Besides cotton, the family
tried to grow tur on the field, which was mainly for household
consumption. The small size of the land meant that cultivation
was limited and so was the yield, which was usually too little to be
sold in the market. In 2015, eight years after Praveen's death, the
state of agriculture and the family's financial situation remained
unchanged. There was, however, a change in the importance the
family gave to agriculture in their life. Praveen's wife, Jyoti, no
longer cultivated their land but now worked as farm labour on

daily wages, while Rajesh, his brother, ran the tea stall they had opened together 15 years ago on the main road from the tehsil capital of Morshi town. The days of surviving on the farm were over for the Bhumbar family; agriculture had cost them not just money and time, but also the life of a loved one.

Rajesh had studied up to Class 12,[3] which he had failed, and dropped out of school. Higher education was a luxury that the small farmers of Vidarbha can rarely afford, and the children are often witness to the effort it takes for their families to pay for their studies. Sensitive and aware of the difficult times, the children work hard to pass school, but if they fail in a class, they usually discontinue their education. The end of their education also spells the end of an opportunity for these children who cannot wait too long for employment and usually join their family in working as farm labour for daily wages to add to their household income. It is on these crowded fields under the scorching sun that the dreams of the educated wither under the gaze of the wealthy landlord and the self-assured state. There is no scope for anger; in fact, no time for it.

Rajesh explained, 'I wanted to study further and go to college. But when I reached Class 8, I realized there was no money to support my education any further. Then my mother's brother in Chandur Bazar offered assistance and funded my education until Class 12. But when I failed in that examination, I dropped out of the school.' As with many things in the lives of the Vidarbha farmers, the options available to them are conditional and time-bound. Nothing waits for those who cultivate the land; they have to wait for all things to come to them, including the benevolence of rain and the kindness of men. That is also the reason behind the usual silence of the widows in these villages; there is nothing to express, protest, or argue about. She can only wait.

Jyoti sat in a small plastic chair, with a palpable sense of detachment from everything around her. She seemed to be the kind of person who looked for purpose in life and found it in the affection for others, which gave her the energy to work. With her husband gone, she seemed not just alone, but lost. Her children now were her primary concern, and she did what she could for them. 'I work as a farm labour for a daily wage of Rs 100 and manage to contribute to the running of the household,' Jyoti said, and added without conviction, 'I save whatever money I can for the children and hope it will help them in their life.' She could not save much, and with the given funds, there was only so far that her children could study. What was worse, there were no other avenues to earn from or hope for. It was as if a way of life had come to an end, but she was still trying to resuscitate it. The time she had spent with Praveen was now a faded memory, something she remembered as if it was a story from a book. The happiness of those early times was overshadowed by the stark difficulties of the present, which began in the dark period preceding Praveen's suicide. The farm loan that Praveen had been unable to pay tormented him in the days before he killed himself. Jyoti recalled, 'My husband never spoke about the loan, but we all knew he was under immense pressure. He was a proud man and ensured discipline in the household; he believed that hard work paid off, and chose only the right path to earn a livelihood. But the financial situation of the family worsened and he began to lose hope. He was saddened that he had plunged the family into debt from which there would be no recovery. He felt it was his responsibility to find a solution, and did not burden any one of us with his troubles.'

That day in November of 2007 had started normally for Jyoti; she had left for work on the farm. But she returned home late in the afternoon to discover that Praveen had set himself on fire using kerosene. She understood why her husband had killed himself. 'He was that kind of a man. He just could not bear the fact that the basic necessities of the household were not being met. He was seriously worried about the simple sustainability of life.' Apart from the loan from a lending agency, Praveen had also borrowed agricultural inputs from a krishi kendra[4] and taken a loan from a private moneylender, which together amounted to between Rs 60,000 and Rs 70,000. These loans were not written off or rescheduled like formal loans when the farmer died; they had to be repaid by the family. 'Life has only become tougher for us after his death,' Jyoti said.

In 2015, the twins Gaurav and Gauri were 12 years old studying in Class 7, while 13 year-old Sachin studied in Class 9. Gaurav lived in Chandur Bazar with the same relative who had helped Rajesh with his education. The family had to be dispersed so that the children could be supported; Jyoti had reconciled to this distance but missed her son constantly. There was no fee to be paid for the two children in the zila parishad school, and Gauri even got the school uniform free. 'I cannot send them to good schools; I cannot afford to give them an English education in a convent. It is way too expensive for a poor farmer's child. I do my best but it still does not prepare my children for a better future,' she said, her frail shoulders burdened by the problems left behind by her husband and those that life had added since his death. She was aware of the escape Praveen had opted for, but justified it as the act of a sensitive and honest man. She did not hold him responsible for the present state of her life. 'I work as labour now, something I never imagined I would do in my life,' she said and paused. 'I never worked as labour when my husband was alive. We had responsibilities even then, but we faced them together. I miss him so much.'

Rajesh ran the tea stall alone and supported the family. Like most farmers in these villages, the monthly expenses were a constant source of worry for him. 'The electricity bill for the month is about Rs 700–800, water bill is Rs 700 annually. These are bills that have to be paid, and then there are medical expenses and those for the children. Money is required for these necessities and none of them can be compromised upon. This tea stall and farm labour are the main sources of income, aside from the farm where agriculture is a gamble.'

Ashtgaon, a village of 1,500 people, knew of the hardships of the Bhumbar family. The tea stall was on the district road that connected the village with Morshi, which was a moderately busy route. The state transport buses stopped close by to drop passengers, and there were a few other shops that mainly dealt in repairs of farm equipment. The tea stall stood under the shade of a thick banyan tree and had a few chairs for people to sit. Most of the villagers stopped there for a cup of tea, cookies, or toast before heading their way. Invariably, they asked about the well-being of the family and whether there was any trouble. Rajesh liked the support of the community and was inspired to keep on with his struggle.

Ever since his father Shaligram, who suffered from asthma, had fallen ill, Praveen had taken care of the family. Rajesh remembered his brother with respect, 'My brother used to be my guide. He was strict but also affectionate. I still remember the way he used to discipline me if I returned home late. He wanted me to become someone important in life, and not remain a poor farmer.

FIGURE 30   Rajesh, Praveen Bhumbar's brother, at his tea stall, January 2015
Source: Author

I wish I could do a job and build myself a career.' The earnings from the tea stall were enough to run the household, but there was not enough left to save. 'We do not have extra money to do anything else. Every member of the family works and contributes to the expenses that we all know must be paid. We work hard every minute of the day to just survive. Where is the chance for us to aspire for anything more or be anyone better?' he asked.

Even eight years after his death Praveen was deeply missed by his wife and brother. A loan and a crop had killed him, like most other farmers who commit suicide in Vidarbha. A chapter seemed to be closed and it brought an end to the dependence on agriculture, to the constant wait for rains, and to a life regimented by nature. Now, Rajesh made tea for a living and Jyoti worked as farm labour. The compensation she had received for Praveen's suicide seemed to be the last tribute to the fight they had all put up to remain farmers. And lost.

★★★

Jyoti's father-in-law Shaligram Bhumbar had died in Ashtgaon in 2016 from complications arising out of asthma, just four days before my next visit. He had been 74 years old and the treatment had cost the family Rs 50,000. In 2015, he had participated in the interview, mostly listening to the conversation without comment. His smile was sorely missed on that visit to the Bhumbars, who continued their struggle to survive. Rajesh was sad, yet reconciled; his usually hopeful eyes were fatigued. 'I am all alone now,' he said simply, summing up his life after the death of his brother and now his father. All the money that had come as compensation after his brother's death had been spent in the running of the household and to meet various expenses. 'Two of my brother's children attend school at an expense of Rs 40,000 per year. We manage these expenses with profits from the tea stall and earnings from the daily wages.' The earlier loan taken by his brother had been restructured but still remained unpaid; there was no extra money to clear the old loans. In addition, there were new loans to think about, along with a pending private loan of about Rs 50,000. There had been two cows with the family at one time, which were sold. And yet, Rajesh tried to be optimistic about the situation. 'The situation has not got better, but it has not worsened either,' he said, sitting in front of his tea stall, which was shut to mourn Shaligram. 'I had hoped there would be some change, even a little, so that I would see some improvement in life. Unfortunately, there is absolutely no difference in the scope of our troubles and if it continues in this manner, I will have to commit suicide,' he said desperately. Rajesh repented immediately, recalling the loss he had felt when his brother had died. He said that he had considered taking up additional work. 'I have a licence to drive commercial vehicles and I have been wondering if I should take that up again. It will considerably add to the income of the family,' he said. The crop he cultivated this year was cotton and tur, but knew that the yield would not be much. 'We have no irrigation in the field except for a well and it is not good enough for sustainable productivity of the crops,' he said. His main source of income remained the shop, from which he earned about Rs 9,000 a month in 2016. But even the shop required repairs; a ceiling had collapsed from heavy rains, and Rajesh had kept that project on hold for lack of funds. Jyoti continued to work as a daily wager at Rs 100 per day and received support from the Niradhar welfare scheme[5] of the government. She had also applied for the anganwadi welfare scheme[6] but did not get the job. On that day, she had already left for the fields to work and could not participate in the interview.

Rajesh had been married for a few years now, and he and his wife were trying for a child. His in-laws had even paid for their daughter's fertility treatment. He was fond of children and smiled as Gaurav joined the discussion. Gaurav had come visiting from Chandur Bazar in the wake of his grandfather's death. He was an intense child of 13 years who was determined to make a mark in life. There were towering expectations from him and he was already aware that failure was not an option. He recited the commandments he had been made to memorize by the family, especially his mother. 'One should never lie, never cheat, never drink, never gamble, never waste time, never watch too much television ...' The list was long. All the instructions were designed to keep his focus on studies and ensure he did not fall in with bad company. These were possibly based on the fears of a mother who had sent a young child away to live and study. Gaurav's life in Chandur Bazar was not easy, but he did not complain even once while speaking about it. He lived with a relative's family and took care of their 36-year-old son who was confined to the bed due to a medical condition. Gaurav shared the details of his daily schedule of work and study. 'I wake up at 6.30 a.m., have a bath, clean the house, help their son get ready, and leave for school between 7 and 7.30 a.m. The school ends at 2 p.m. and it takes

FIGURE 31   Gaurav, Jyoti Bhumbar's son, August 2016
Source: Author

me 15 minutes to walk back home. Then I have a bath again,' he explained. 'This time I offer prayers to god, wear the *tilak*[7] on my forehead and sit down to study from 3 to 5 p.m. Then I go out to play between 5 p.m. and 7 p.m. and return home. I have dinner and study until 10 p.m. My favourite subjects are History and Geography. And I want to be a policeman.' After much inter- rogation about the choice of the specific profession, he said that it was considered a respectable job.

Gaurav could not be drawn into critiquing his siblings' educa- tion and summarily announced that his brother and sister studied well. 'My mother told me that my father wanted all of us to study well, so we all do our best in school. He had specifically left a message for me not to waste time with vices and not to get diverted from my task. I do like to play cricket and kabaddi but only when I have finished my studies.' Gaurav spent his every waking hour either working or studying, with just two hours a day set aside for playing. There was little chance of his attention getting diverted from his goal. Rajesh was proud of the boy and clearly had been instrumental in teaching him the discipline that Gaurav displayed. In that moment when Rajesh and Gaurav were together, it was clear that their relationship filled the absence in each other's life—of a father and of a child. These were the lega- cies that would build the future and bring about the change that Rajesh so desperately waited and hoped for.

❧

Notes

1. Letter written by the tehsildar of Morshi tehsil submitted to the district collector of Amravati, on 15 December 2007.
2. Report of debt by Sehakari Society, on 23 December 2007.
3. The Indian school education system consists of two national board examinations in Class 10 and 12, administered either by the central or state boards. The school is followed by college and university education.

4. Krishi kendra or kisan kendra are agricultural input shops that provide farm requirements, sometimes on loan in lieu of produce.

5. The Sanjay Gandhi Niradhar Anudan Yojana provides financial assistance to oppressed and marginalized citizens such as specially enabled persons, the destitute, orphans, widows, women who were freed from human trafficking, and more recently, transgenders. The scheme is also applicable for the people aged 65 years and above whose annual income is less than Rs 21,000 per annum. Under the scheme, the beneficiary receives Rs 600 per month and, in the case of a single family having more than one beneficiary, the amount increases to Rs 900 per month. The benefits continue till the children of the beneficiary get employment or reach 25 years of age. In case the beneficiary has only daughters, the assistance continues even after the daughters reach 25 years of age or get married. See www.mumbaisuburban.gov.in; and, www.amravati.nic.in

6. The Integrated Child Development Services (ICDS) describes an anganwadi worker as a community based worker chosen from the local community to work for the ICDS programme. She is expected to mobilize support for care of young children, girls and women. See www.icds-wcd.nic.in

7. The tilak is a mark worn by a Hindu on the forehead after prayer and worship, and also as an ornament or a symbol.

CHAPTER
ELEVEN

Those that Money Can't Buy

Tarabai Vyavhare, Prahaladpur Village, Chandur Bazar Tehsil,
Amravati District

A Widow Since 25 February 2014

Great importance is often placed on symbols of achievement that
are seen as milestones in the journey of life. A personal residence
is one such symbol; it proves that one has built on the legacy of
the past and improved prospects for future generations. A house is
seen as something to be proud of, not a thatched hut or a make-
shift structure, but a brick and concrete building that will not fall
victim to the vagaries of nature. Such symbols are rare among the
farmers of Vidarbha, who constantly struggle even to survive from
one season to the next. That was the reason it was all the more
special that Namdev Vyavhare, a farmer, had such a house in the
village of Prahaladpur in the Chandur Bazar tehsil. His life's aim
was fulfilled when the house was built, and he dedicated it to his
wife, Tarabai. He had succeeded in fulfilling promises of a good
life to his family; he now had a stature that signified his hard work
and intelligence. Namdev had been reborn as a respectable man
with a promising future in whom people could trust.

However, this was precisely what brought him trouble. Farmers of Vidarbha, especially poor farmers, could not afford such signs of dignity. They are expected to live in the darkness and hopelessness of their corners of the countryside. They are supposed to take loans and repay them with interest, even if their crops fail. Most farmers in Vidarbha, like those elsewhere in the country, took loans for agriculture. While some of these loans were taken from banks, others were from private moneylenders at a very high rate of interest. Both lending sources were brutal when it came to recovery of loans, and while the banks left an official trail of paperwork, private moneylenders employed more informal means of recovery. Both lending sources, however, seemed certain that the farmers should miraculously generate thousands of rupees that they had lost in agriculture to repay the loans. It was as if undeclared wealth was somewhere hidden in their sparse huts and skeletal homes. It was insinuated that they lied about their income so that they could delay repaying loans. It was never expected that the farmer was telling the truth, that he would never default on a loan if he could repay. He would rather die, as Namdev did.

Namdev killed himself at the age of 63. There was a garland of marigold around his photograph which hung from a wall in his home; his family remembered him with respect and affection. He looked like a traditional man who must have taken great pride in his hard work and enjoyed the success that came with it. Faced with the prospect of an unchanging future, Namdev rebelled against the mediocre and sought a better life for his children than what the villages offered. His achievements were due to this stead-fast resolve and belief in himself, which caught the attention of the community and also earned him admiration. A big part of his dream was building a house for his family, one that would work as a stepping stone for future generations. That vision, however, was not acceptable to those who supported a poor man to rise but did not allow him to be an equal. The vendors of dignity in this society draw invisible lines to divide the level playing field so that farmers like Namdev never make it to the finish line. He had nothing but his self-belief and agriculture to support him, and that was no substitute for money. The banks and moneylenders who harassed a self-respecting farmer for loan repayment on his house should have known money was not a shortcut to dignity. They might have possibly discovered that after Namdev ended his life when he could not repay the loan on the house.

It was a 150 sq m, single-storey house that had been constructed incrementally over a period of time. In 2015, the exposed brickwork still had to be cemented from the outside and the terrace was unfinished. Two of his sons and their families lived with Namdev and Tarabai; the other three sons and daughter lived elsewhere. It was a small house strewn with toys, books, and things that signified life and movement; that was what Namdev had meant it to be.

Namdev had only two sources of income—agriculture and agricultural labour. Generations before him had failed to create what he had made and perished with their hopes unrealized. The administration, while investigating the circumstances of his suicide, identified his limited sources of income[1] and also stated that there had been no bank notices for recovery of the loan.[2] Significantly, attached elsewhere in the slim file were copies of the various bank notices that were issued at regular intervals demanding that Namdev repay the loan he had taken for the house in 2010 along with an agricultural loan, which together added up to Rs 2,41,931. His 4 acres of land had produced low yields of crop for the past few years, which made it impossible for Namdev to repay his debt. But then, the crop yields of every village were known to the administration, and could not have been hidden from the bank either. And yet, there were notices for repayment in November 2012, and in February, March, and November 2013. The letter sent in February 2013[3] requested Namdev to repay the outstanding loan within seven days, failing which, information about him along with his photograph would be published in various newspapers. The notice also stated that any mental stress created due to this recovery motion was entirely because of him and the bank was not responsible.

The tone of the bank letters remained the same as they threatened to dishonour Namdev in different ways and aimed at humiliation by making public his unpaid loans. This was part of the usual system in which respect was assured only through one's solvency or the availability of adequate funds. To ensure that society works on such a system is most suitable for lending agencies that depend on profits and interest. But in such a system, poverty is unacceptable and the inability to repay loans is an insult. The practice of defaming defaulters is rooted in the belief that the worth of a human being is assessed by the banks. As lenders, and therefore, those with capital, the banks were above assessment by those without. Namdev, for instance, could not have questioned the manner in which the letters were written from the bank about the loan repayment. The only way he could have replied to the letters was by making the payment, and if he failed to, there would be more letters of the same kind. In this process, the bank was assisted by the law and the rules weighed heavily against farmers like Namdev. In a notice sent on 1 March 2013,[4] the bank stated that it could take any action legal or otherwise to recover the loan, and that the house for which the loan was taken could not be leased, transferred, sold or bought, etc. In effect, the bank had decided that Namdev's house did not belong to him technically. What was left with Namdev was the physical possession of the house, even as its seizure was the next step planned by the bank. In August 2013, the bank issued a possession notice for the house and attempted to seize it.

This followed a period of turmoil for the family and soon the bank sent another letter[5] for recovery of the crop loan that Namdev had taken. Once again the bank ominously stated that it was not responsible for the various actions it could take in the matter. The investigation of the administration had discovered through its officials that the income from agriculture for Namdev for a period of three years from 2011 to 2014 had been less than Rs 1 lakh.[6] This revealed the exact cause behind Namdev's inability to repay the loan, and was one of the reasons why the administration decided the suicide was eligible for compensation. Availability of this information with the bank might have prevented Namdev from being cornered with no hope of an escape. Even the location of the agricultural land, next to a canal that overflowed during the rains, pointed to the problems Namdev faced in cultivation. His son Jai Prakash had been through every step of the process with his father while he was alive. 'People representing the bank used to employ bad language and threaten to throw us out of the house,' he said in 2015, less than one year after his father's death. 'But we had nothing to repay the loan with; we lost the soybean crop cultivated on 1.5 acres of land in 2014 due to the flooding and overflowing of the nearby canal,' he said. Namdev's crop was one among the several that were lost every time the canal flooded. It had to be given a certain path and direction so that such devastation would not occur again. After much effort, the administration had approved the project and decided to build a boundary wall to channel the waters. 'But by the time it was completed, the scheme changed. Now, the survey is useless and it might have to be done again,' explained Jai Prakash.

The family had repeatedly explained to the bank representatives the reasons for the non-repayment of their loan, but they were not convinced. As it became clear that he might lose the house, Namdev became increasingly anxious. In August 2013, the bank decided to take action and a possession notice was pasted on the entrance of the house. The eviction proceedings were next and the family lived in constant fear of being homeless. As the bank loan was in the name of Tarabai, the notices and letters were addressed to both of them, which further distressed Namdev.

'They spoke very badly to us,' Tarabai said, referring to the bank's agents who had come to seal the house. 'My husband used

FIGURE 32   Tarabai, Namdev Vyavhare's widow, January 2015
Source: Author

to be very sad and was lost in thought about the harassment he faced. That day in February 2014, he went to sit up on the terrace of the house in the late afternoon. When he did not return after some time, my son went to check on him.' Tarabai fell silent as she recollected those painful moments. Her son took over instead and said that he had found his father slumped on the terrace with a bottle of poison next to him. He rushed Namdev to a hospital where he was declared brought dead. The post-mortem had found he died of cardiac failure due to poisoning; he had consumed pesticides used in crops. The family pointed to the place where they had found Namdev; a spot on the rough, uneven surface of the terrace where he had killed himself.

Tarabai's eyes were melancholic as she remembered the weeks before Namdev's death. 'We were all so tense and anxious. When they put up the eviction notice on our front door, we were all worried about where we would go, how we would live,' she stopped. Tears welled up as she said, 'When we lived in the village, nothing like this ever happened. We have repaid loans

FIGURE 33   The terrace of Namdev Vyavhare's house where he committed suicide
Source: Author

before, every farmer does; but there was no pressure on us like this. He just could not take it.' Her grief for Namdev was mixed with the humiliation they faced. 'He was worried about what people would say,' she said, anguished.

There was a helplessness about her that must have added to her son's anger. 'I told the administration that it was because of the harassment of the bank that my father committed suicide. There was paperwork to prove it and also evidence of the bad crop yield,' Jai Prakash said. His younger brother, Naresh had been studying BA and left college midway when his father died. Life for Jai Prakash changed that day when he discovered his father on the half-finished terrace, which still awaited funds for building the parapet wall in 2016. The entire incident had left a sense of anger among the family members, not merely against the inhuman procedures that reduced everything to profit or loss, but also because of their experience of not being trusted. Their plight was evident to everyone; the state of the house spoke of shortage, and even their crop yield record could have established their dire straits. Despite every effort to tell their story, they were not heard or believed. It was as if they had no voice, as if the banks did not think of them any more than hands that should toil and repay the loans. The honesty of their hearts was useless until they stopped beating—for then, the state recognized that it had, indeed, been honest.

Tarabai, who had been 58 years old when Namdev died, understood Namdev's decision to end his life. She had been his constant partner, in good times and in bad. 'We had seen very tough times before but there was some dignity with which a crisis was dealt with. We struggled to repay the loans but no one threatened to complain to the police or throw us out on the street. I could not have imagined such things happening to us. He wanted to pay back the loan any way he could. He asked his friends for help and they were even ready to pay. But everyone needed some time to help, and there was no time,' she said, reliving the tragedy. 'It was the first time in his life that my husband gave up.' In her statement to the administration,[7] she had said that her husband had been worried by the crop failure and his inability to repay the loan. Even on the day of his death, he had just returned from inspecting the fields.

Jai Prakash ran a bookshop, but he also worked in the fields. 'I will not let go of that land,' he said with vehemence. 'We did not get much yield this year either, just 6 to 7 quintals of cotton. But I shall continue to strive.' He knew it took investment for agriculture, which the family could barely afford. 'Agriculture had never been enough, even during my father's time. Our family always had to work for daily wages to support ourselves,' he said. He was also through with striving for opportunities that had always been denied to the farmers. 'No one gives us jobs because we are not qualified enough; the only thing we are qualified for is agriculture,' he added. His brothers had all finished school but no one had finished college. They now worked in various shops in Prahaladpur and nearby areas, for salaries ranging from Rs 3,000 to Rs 6,000. A total of 10 members lived in that house, all belonging to the families of the two brothers, along with Tarabai. The monthly expenses for groceries of the household added up to about Rs 7,000–8,000, and then there were fees for the children's schooling, fuel bills, electricity bills, and other expenditure. In the end, there was no money left to save or invest in agriculture.

The role of the administration was significant in finding the case eligible for compensation. Although the local officers of the village had stated that there had been no pressure from lending agencies for loan recovery, their senior officer demanded to see all the pertinent documents himself.[8] Among the documents demanded was the crop yield of three years, along with details of the bank loan. It was possible, as Jai Prakash explained, that the matter of the recovery process by the bank had played an important role in the decision of the administration to declare the case eligible for compensation.

The truth was that Namdev had been credit–worthy in 2010 when he had borrowed a housing loan in the name of his wife. At that time, the bank must have assessed his financial status and found it to be sound. And yet, the actions of the bank showed that there was no attempt to understand the circumstances in which Namdev was unable to repay the loan. His sense of self-respect was evident from the way he and his family worked as farm labour on daily wages to support themselves; it was evident by the manner in which they toiled in their field with difficult crops. In his death, not just his family but the bank too had lost an honest man who would have repaid their loan if they had given him their time and their trust. But perhaps, money washed away the blemish of all guilt. Perhaps money could even return Namdev to his family. And to his house.

★★★

Jai Prakash was a changed man in 2016. He was no longer the rebellious youth of 2015 who had fought with the administration and the lending agencies for justice. He seemed to have lost his spirit somewhere in this fight against forces that were too large for a farmer to battle against. He had begun to clear his father's pending loan, but it proved to be a difficult task. He did not want to borrow from a bank ever again and explained that even the house loan was taken in 2010 as part of the bank scheme to promote housing with low interest rates. It had made him wonder why the loan had incurred so much interest, but the bank had been adamant.

The unhelpful attitude of the bank might have been the result of the suicide enquiry in which the recovery process was revealed. As the administration withdrew from the life of the farmer after paying the compensation of Rs 1 lakh to Tarabai, there was no one to monitor the bank's conduct towards Namdev's family. Jai Prakash explained, 'I pay for all the notices that were issued against my father, and the paperwork. I get to know how much I have to pay by looking at the figure on a computer screen. I have no option but to pay, even if it robs us of our normal life.' Of the Rs 2.4 lakh loan, Rs 2 lakh had been spent towards building the house. When there was an attempt made to seal the house before Namdev died, Rs 1 lakh was paid to buy some time. 'Even though I have repaid most of the loan, I still get messages of penalty being levied on whatever is left unpaid. I put every penny together to clear this loan and yet, it is not enough. Every minute of my day is spent in repaying the loan and yet, it is taking time.' The income of the family remained farm labour, agriculture, three cows, and Jai Prakash's bookshop. The family had sown onions, tur, and soybean, of which onion was wasted as the prices dropped due to high supply. The bookshop did not do good business and the sale of milk did not produce major profits.

The house had stopped evolving; there was no money to finish the structure. The uncured terrace created cracks in the ceiling, and the cemented walls were yet to be painted. Even though it appeared that life was standing still, Jai Prakash said that things were improving. He seemed to have inherited his father's

self-belief and faith in hard work. In his plans, he did not have
time for conflict. 'I wanted to fight, but who would then support
my family? I know we were wronged, but there is nothing I can
do about it. I must ensure that the bank has no hold over my
family and is never again in a position to hurt our dignity. I shall
ensure that at any cost.'

It was certain that Jai Prakash would succeed at his goal and
free his family of the bank loan. Tarabai would be proud of her
husband's achievements and the children would grow up in a
home built brick-by-brick by the sweat and blood of their family
members. The life of the Vyavhare family was a lesson for those
who equated capital with stature; not everything could be bought
for money, especially not dignity.

❧

Notes

1. Statement of record of the suicide of Namdev Vyavhare signed by
   the tehsildar, member of the panchayat samiti, sarpanch and the
   police in-charge of Chandur Bazar tehsil, where the village of
   Prahaladpur is situated.
2. Statement of record of the suicide of Namdev Vyavhare signed
   by the tehsildar, member of the panchayat samiti, sarpanch, and
   the police in-charge of Chandur Bazar tehsil, where the village of
   Prahaladpur is situated.
3. Notice from the bank in Chandur Bazar tehsil to Namdev Vyavhare
   in February 2013.
4. Notice from the bank in Chandur Bazar tehsil to Namdev Vyavhare
   on 1 March 2013.
5. Notice from the bank in Chandur Bazar tehsil to Namdev Vyavhare
   on 30 November 2013.
6. Statement of income of Namdev Vyavhare recorded by the talathi
   of Chandur Bazar, on 13 May 2014.
7. Statement of Tarabai Vyavhare recorded and presented to the district administration of Amravati, on 13 May 2014.
8. Letter written by the tehsildar of Chandur Bazar to the talathi.

CHAPTER TWELVE

Death at the Wishing Well

Anjana Katekar, Pedi Village, Bhatkuli Tehsil, Amravati District

A Widow Since 3 December 2011

What is a nation worth, if its citizens seek to escape their lives and commit suicide? The farmers of Vidarbha did not just commit suicide to be free of their circumstances, poverty, and helplessness. They also died silently amid the cacophony of election promises that glorified the farmer. What is a democracy worth when the vote merely exchanged politicians in power and never changed their politics?

The Vidarbha farmers, like their brethren elsewhere in the country, voted in free and fair elections that formed 16 governments at the centre since 1952 and 13 at the state level in Maharashtra since 1960. They were promised irrigation in five-year plans by experts; they were pledged water in lengthy budget speeches in hallowed elected houses but were yet to see even a drop delivered. And yet, the same governments and the state knew that rain-fed Vidarbha was involved in cotton cultivation with genetically modified seeds that required regular irrigation. Elected governments, on the lines of colonial exploiters, had overlooked the plight of the Indian farmers and even tried to minimize the crisis. Despite this, in every election the voter diligently carried his/her identity card to the polling booth and chose a candidate from the list who promised, if not a vastly improved future, at least a secure one. The voter created several influential politicians hailing from Vidarbha like Devendra Fadnavis (present chief minister of Maharashtra from the BJP), Nitin Gadkari (present minister for Road Transport and Highways, Shipping and Water Resources, River Development & Ganga Rejuvenation in the central government, from the BJP), Praful Patel (present Member of Parliament, and former minister of Civil Aviation from the Nationalist Congress Party), among many others. The list of the powerful was long, but longer was the list of farmers who had committed suicide every year in Vidarbha.

As Anjana, the widow of Shanker Katekar, said, 'No one really cares about poor farmers like us.' Her 46-year-old husband had committed suicide in 2011 because of debt; they had five daughters (of whom one remains unmarried), and an unmarried son. The official documents stated that the 'burden of debt', a phrase often used to explain the circumstances of a farmer's suicide, required enquiry. Why was it that farmers, some of the poorest people of this country, needed to repay loans with interest? One answer could be that if they had taken loans, then they must repay like everyone else. But surely, the deaths of the defaulters said something about this system. How many suicides would it take for the banks, the government, the experts, the economists, and others, to realize that farmers could not repay loans, not even at the so-called low interest rates? Every farmer suicide was a plea seeking to draw attention to the fact that rain-fed agriculture required a different system of crops, finance, markets, and other aspects—aspects that every farmer listed out each time he/she was asked.

The burden of loan also begged another question: why would a farmer commit suicide when millions of people defaulted on loans in this country? Farmers committed suicide, notwithstanding the various self-serving explanations of politicians and their supporting research, because they believed in fairness. They never questioned why they were subject to the same rules of banking as the affluent class or why were they harassed for repayment or why they were refused loans if they defaulted. Farmers believed that the state was fair. And, when they were unable to repay the loans, they preferred to end their lives rather than live with the burden. It was just as well that they would not discover how farmer suicides were subverted by the state afterwards; the death of an honest farmer had repercussions, even in this nation of hijacked headlines. The state minimized the damage it wreaked by questioning the character of the farmer, imputing some of the suicides in Vidarbha to alcoholism, gambling, depression, domestic quarrels, etc.[1] No visit to the state administration is complete without this version of farmer suicides being offered to researchers. In comparison, the state shares little information on harassment by

FIGURE 34 Anjana, Shanker Katekar's widow, January 2015
Source: Author

moneylenders, recovery notices by banks, household visits to ask
for money by cooperative societies, refusal by kisan kendras[2] to
lend farm material, threats by lending agencies, etc. If a farmer
who faced harassment for loan recovery committed suicide, who
would be held complicit in his death? That was primarily why the
burden of debt, besides being the truth, was also a simple guilt-
free description of a farmer's condition.

In the absence of political accountability through elections, the
administration remained complacent and inefficient. Instead of
modern irrigation techniques, the administration could get away
by sanctioning wells that either had little or no water. It rarely
helped the farmer to deepen or repair such wells. Shanker died,
according to the police report, a few feet away from one such well
in his field in December 2011. The well, a symbol of survival for
most farmers in Vidarbha, was the only hope for any yield on his
11.5-acre land. It was the harvest season and a low cotton yield
meant that he would not be able to repay the loan he had taken
that year. The police report of the suicide stated that Shanker had
died from poisoning; the bottle of pesticide he had consumed
was found at the spot. Spraying pesticide for the cotton crop was
critical as it protected the crop from debilitating pests that brought
down the yield. The crop in his field had reached the stage where
it was sprayed several times, and each spray cost Shanker money
he could not afford. These expenses were recorded at the kisan
kendra, to be recovered at the time of harvest. Along with irrigation, the high use of pesticide was another requirement for the
cotton crop that was not easy to fulfil. The cost of cultivation of
the advanced seeds of cotton contradicted the propaganda that it
was disease resistant and high yielding.[3]

Shanker was discovered in the field by his son Umesh. Apart
from the bottle of the pesticide, in which there was still some left,
there was also a steel plate that he used to consume the poison.
Shanker had taken the pesticide on the afternoon of 3 December
2011, and was declared dead on arrival at the government hospital

at Amravati. There was a reason that the well had been at the centre of Shanker's dreams for the future. It had materialized after many efforts, according to Anjana. The administration provided support to dig agricultural wells for poor farmers owning dry land and one such well was made in Shanker's land. It had been 10 years in 2015 since the well was made, and it was still dry. Anjana said, 'The administration has to ensure that a certain number of wells were dug in the village. This was a target they had to meet and they weren't bothered about the usefulness of the wells,' she said. 'The well was sanctioned when there was water at 10 feet, but that became scarce with each passing year. We kept asking the officials to sanction the deepening of the well, but that was not their concern. No one bothered to re-examine the location of the well or relocate it to a new place,' Anjana said, her lean face angry. 'It does not matter to anyone that we were losing our crops. How could we have repaid the loans if there was no water in our fields and no yield? We were ready to work on other's fields as wage labour and repay the loans. We just needed help.'

Ironically, even the compensation that the state had given Anjana had gone into repairing the well. The indifference of the administration was such that the relief provided for the death of the farmer was used by the family to do the state's work. Anjana explained, 'We used part of the Rs 30,000 that came to me as relief, to deepen the well.' The well that was dug to a depth of 10 feet by the administration was now 40 feet, and every inch had cost something of Shanker's life. On the other hand, it would have taken one signature of the administration on an approval letter to do the same.

Meanwhile, water is borrowed from a neighbouring field at an additional expense. Anjana's dark brown eyes were sarcastic as she said, 'We get power in the fields day and night, as if any of the poor farmers could afford it.' The bill for sparingly using power to draw water with a pump was Rs 2,200 for three months, which remained unpaid by the farmer if his crop failed. Unpaid bills, however, meant losing the electricity connection. The state provided nothing without a cost to the farmers, leaving them with no money to repay the loans. The electricity bill for the house where the Katekars lived was between Rs 400 and Rs 500 a month, while drinking water cost about Rs 1,100 per year. It did not take much imagination to ascertain where the electricity was spent, looking at the single light bulb in each room. The walls were bare brick and cement, and the portraits of the dead hung on the walls. The premises survived on things that had been used for years, and most of which were either made of plastic or other such material that did not degenerate. It was difficult to argue about environmental unsustainability where Anjana had to keep expenses to the minimum and could not use organic building materials that required regular repairs.

Shanker had an outstanding loan from a bank that sent notices for repayment. The latest notice, in December 2013,[4] was two years after Shanker's death, in which the bank stated that the loan of Rs 47,000 taken in May 2011, and amounted to Rs 56,427 and interest. It said that interest was being added to the principle amount and urged him to repay instead of incurring losses. It also stated that he had not honoured the agreement of the loan and the tenure was now over. While Shanker was beyond such threats now, Anjana was not.

'The bank people told us to repay,' Anjana said, referring to the letter. 'But there was nothing to repay them with.' Anyone could have discerned that just by looking at the way Anjana lived. Did the banks, perhaps, think that there were places to hide over Rs 64,000, the amount pending now, in that sparse, empty house? Anjana had preserved that letter, possibly to remind herself why her husband had killed himself. She had been sheltered from such matters throughout her life, as Shanker had never shared his burdens with her. 'The yield from our 11.5 acres for cotton had always been low because of lack of irrigation. Then he tried to plant cotton in one half of the land and soybean in another half in 2011, hoping that would help.' It did not; the yield was low even for soybean—4 quintals for 5 acres. They had to get one of their daughters, Swati, married in May that year, and Shanker had hoped that a good crop that season would repay the loan. Swati and her husband must have realized why Shanker had killed himself or where the expense for their marriage had come from. But such matters were not to be talked about in families; a daughter's marriage was always delicately balanced with the husband and his family holding it for ransom.

The gram panchayat had numbered the house that was barely standing, and in a corner of the plaque was the message to educate the girl child. This was unnecessary advice in the Katekar household; Swati was educated up to Class 12, but still worked in the fields. The gram panchayat did not mention in its message what a girl should do with her education. Like the expensive well that did not have water, the government supported expensive education for the poor without providing opportunities for employment. Perhaps, that was why Shanker's son Umesh had dropped out of school when he reached Class 7. Anjana said he wanted to pursue agriculture and tend the farm with his father. Now, Umesh took care of the field alone, and in 2015, had planted wheat in 5 acres that would serve for household consumption.

The rules of relief from the government left out farmers who had more than 5 acres of land in case of schemes such as the 2008 Loan Waiver, and it was an important criterion when the administration decided on the eligibility of a suicide case for compensation. Shanker's case was found eligible[5] as he had killed himself because the crop yield was low and his financial condition was bad. Before finalizing this, the administration checked on other possible reasons for the death, including any vices, addictions, domestic strife, etc. Although Anjana received bank notices two years after Shanker's death, at the time of the investigation the administration stated[6] that there had been no recovery attempts. It was clear that while gathering information, the administration placed higher dependence on banks than on the words of the farmer's family. The report,[7] which had been signed by all the important officials of the village and tehsil, informed their seniors that Shanker had not been sent any loan-recovery notices, and there had been no attempts to attach his property. It was now up to the experience of the senior officials of the administration to read beyond these signed documents, and to realize that the loan recovery process was painful and humiliating for the farmer. Once the farmer had committed suicide, the truth could not be revealed easily. Finally, after almost a year-long process, the compensation for the suicide had come to Anjana in the form of a cheque.[8] While Rs 30,000 was given to her in cash, the rest of the money (Rs 70,000 from the Rs 1 lakh received) was deposited in a bank to be released to her after six years.

Anjana's only complaint against her late husband was that he had never shared with her the troubles he faced about the pending loans. He had toiled with a difficult crop on an impossible land but kept all the distress to himself. She felt she could have shared the burden and supported him. But perhaps he could not share his plans with her. Perhaps he had planned to die next to the well, finally losing hope that there would be water in his fields. What if the well had to be deepened again? Who would have to pay for it with their lives? Certainly not the administration, which lived off a salary or even the government, which lived off the votes of the poor farmers.

★★★

In July 2017, the well was still dry. Earlier in August 2016, despite the good monsoons, the family stated that the well had remained dry and, once again, they got no support from the government to deepen it. A part of the roof of the house had collapsed in the heavy rains, and was yet to be repaired. Umesh had planted soybean, cotton, and pulses in the field, hoping for a good yield. Shanker's pending loan, though restructured, still remained, haunting Umesh. The bank had called him to discuss repayment.

Umesh said, 'I told the manager that there was no money as there was no crop last year. But he did not listen; he just said the loan must be repaid.' He had to borrow money for the new crop, and that loan of Rs 85,000 was pending with another lending agency. The aggregate loan amount now stood at Rs 1,49,000.

The manner in which he had discovered his father after the poisoning still bothered the 28-year-old. 'I was so frightened, I could not even accompany him to the hospital in Amravati. My mother went with him and I later got to know from the villagers that he had died,' he said. His three sisters were married before Shanker's suicide, one was married afterwards, and the family was looking for a suitable groom for the youngest one. One of the married sisters, 24-year-old Sharda who had studied up to Class 10, had a court wedding with Rajesh Khawde, a farmer. 'My brother-in-law knew there was no money and so the marriage was done simply, with minimum expense,' Umesh explained. The 22-year-old Swati, who had studied up to Class 12, was married in 2014. Neither girls had a job and worked as farm labour on daily wages, as did Umesh and Anjana. Education clearly did not improve the lives of farmers without suitable employment opportunities. A major source of support for the family was the subsidized food grain that the government provided through welfare. But the quantity was not enough and the family spent Rs 2,000 monthly to buy additional food grains from the open market. Anjana concluded that there had been no change in their situation. The troubles that claimed Shanker Katekar's life continued for his family, and like him, they too wished there was water in the well.

❧

Notes

1. Refer to the Introduction for the discussion on the 'other' possible reasons generally stated by the government for farmer suicides.

2. Kisan kendra or krishi kendra are agricultural input shops that provide farm requirements, sometimes on loan in lieu of produce.

3. Monsanto (www.monsantoglobal.com) is a US-based company that produces seeds for better crops, according to its website. Also see, Vandana Shiva, 'The Seeds of Suicide: How Monsanto Destroys Farming', *Global Research*, 9 March 2016. www.globalresearch.ca/the-seeds-of-suicide-how-monsanto-destroys-farming/5329947, accessed 5 July 2017. In 1993, Monsanto partnered with an Indian seed company MAHYCO to introduce Bt cotton seeds in India and in 1998, a 50–50 joint venture called MAHYCO-Monsanto Biotech (MMB) was formed. Bt cotton seeds were perceived as superior, with claims that they would not require pesticides for high yields, and were adopted mostly by small and marginal farmers. Anil K. Gupta and Vikas Chandak, 'Agriculture Biotechnology in India: Ethics, Business and Politics', *Int. J. Biotechnology*, Vol. 7, Nos. 1/2/3, 2005, pp. 212–27.

4. Notice from the bank in Bhatkuli tehsil, on 8 December 2013.

5. Letter from the SDO to the district collector of Amravati (Farmer Suicide Department), on 12 April 2012.

6. Statement of remark of Shankar Katekar from the tehsildar's office situated in Bhatkuli tehsil, in which the village of Pedi is situated.

7. Statement of record of suicide of Shankar Katekar signed by the talathi, sarpanch, senior police in-charge, tehsil agricultural officer, and tehsildar of Bhatkuli.

8. Cheque in the name of Anjana Katekar of Rs 30,000, on 23 November 2012, signed by the superintendent for collector of Amravati.

CHAPTER
THIRTEEN

The Immortality of Memory

Santosh Tingde, Kajli Village, Chandur Bazar Tehsil, Amravati District

Lost His Mother in 2006 and Father in 2014

When farmers commit suicide in Vidarbha, their children are taken care of by their mothers. But when the mother is already deceased, these farmers leave behind children without parents, like in the case of the Tingde family. Rekha Tingde had died in 2006 at the age of 37, from complications related to a cardiac condition, and their two children were brought up by her husband, Gyaneshwar. At that time, their son, Santosh had been 17 years old and daughter, Sheetal was 16. Then in November 2014, 45-year-old Gyaneshwar committed suicide because of the burden of unpaid loans taken to cultivate his 2-acre land. At the time of his death, he had an agricultural loan of Rs 50,000[1] pending since 2011–12, taken from a lending agency in the village of Kajli. He had consumed poison on the farm where he worked as a daily wage labourer, which was the only source of income left for him when the crops failed year after year.

Santosh was still submerged in the grief of losing his father when he was interviewed a few months later, in January 2015. He

FIGURE 35   The late Rekha Tingde, Santosh's mother
Source: Author

had grown up watching his father struggle to repay loans, and was determined to move away from agriculture forever. Gyaneshwar had ensured that his children were well educated, and had options beyond farming. Sheetal was studying for her graduation, held a diploma in Computer Sciences, had learnt typing and sewing, and wanted to pursue a bachelor's or master's degree in Education to become a teacher. Their mother, Rekha's family supported them through the years. They lived with their aunt in the nearby Warud tehsil, where presently Sheetal continued her education; Santosh moved between Kajli and Warud. He was a B.Com. graduate, and had done a certification course in Computer educa-tion[2] from a college in Amravati. In 2015, he was preparing for the Maharashtra Public Service Commission (MPSC) examina-tion. While Santosh used to work as a supervisor in a motorcycle showroom in Amravati to earn Rs 1,500, Sheetal taught tuitions to school children to earn Rs 1,000 per month.

FIGURE 36   Santosh Tingde, January 2015
Source: Author

'My sister and I don't have any other option but to find well-paying jobs,' Santosh said. 'We cannot depend on agriculture on the 2-acre field left to us. Those days are gone.' His grandfather had distributed the land among his three sons and Gyaneshwar's share had been the 2 acres. The size of the land meant that the financial situation of the household could not improve with the help of crops, and did not even match the loans taken for farming. Cotton was the main crop sown every season, and it failed regularly. In 2015, Santosh had just harvested 2 quintals of the crop that his father had sown in 2014. He said, 'There had been no water to irrigate the fields, and there were no rains. My father knew that the crop had failed even before the harvest. As a farmer, he could tell that the crop yield would be very low this year, and it was.' The state of the crop had been the reason for Gyneshwar's suicide; significantly, the farmer had waited until November, hoping that the rains would still come and help the crops recover.

These simple dreams turned out to be too impractical to material-ize, much like the support from the state for irrigation schemes to small farmers.[3]

The harvest had been so meagre that not even a cart was hired to transport it to the market. 'I sold the produce quickly, both quintals at Rs 3,500 each,' Santosh said, his eyes grim. The earn-ing was no match for the high cost of cultivation of the crop that began with the Bt cotton seeds, which cost Rs 800 per packet of 450 gm. The price was fixed by the seed companies that claimed they would make losses if it was sold at a rate lower than this. The government had contested the pricing in courts,[4] and managed to bring it down.[5] But even at Rs 800 per 450 gm of the seeds in 2015, it was still too steep for the poor among the farmers. In case of Santosh, for the 2 acres of farm, five packets of the Bt cot-ton seeds would have to be used at a cost of Rs 4,000. That was approximately equal to the price of 1 quintal of cotton, or half the total produce on Santosh's land.

Tur was planted in another part of the field, which yielded a low crop. Santosh explained, 'There is no well in the field and we are totally dependent on rain. We do not have electricity in the field as there is no need; we have no source of water. No crop can work in such conditions; this is not viable for agriculture.' Gyaneshwar had been deeply worried about this situation before his suicide and often spoke to Santosh about how impossible it was to repay the loan he had taken. 'He was always thinking of ways to repay the loan and worrying about where he would get the money,' he recalled. 'It felt bad that my father's account was closed in the lending agency. He could not repay the loan; everyone knew the state of the cultivation on our land. There was no money,' he added.

'I have concluded after watching my father's struggle with farming that it cannot be done. A farmer will get nothing out of it except for misery. Our future cannot depend on agriculture, it is impossible,' Santosh declared decisively. There was anger about the years gone by and the lives lost in trying to make agriculture work. 'Sometimes there is too much rain, sometimes there is no rain. We are victims of everything—the season, the market, the politics, and the prices. The odds are always against us.' Like his father, who had never waited for support from various schemes, Santosh also did not look to the government for help. 'How can a government, which is dealing with so much debt itself, help pay farmers' debts?' he asked. He highlighted the disparity in crop loans given to irrigated and non-irrigated lands and demanded to know how much of a loan burden could be eased by taking private loans. 'One reason for such indifference of the state towards agriculture could be that the industrialists need the farmer's land. They want to finish agriculture in this country, and they will succeed,' he said. Although as an educated man he had options other than agriculture, he also felt bad about leaving his occupation. 'We are an agrarian country and not everyone can leave agriculture. I feel bad for those who are trapped in the vicious circle of debt and lack of agricultural facilities,' he said.

He had often raised these issues in his village when his father cultivated the land. 'The officials always said that if we had a complaint, we should go meet the district collector. They said this for everything; for instance, if the loan was not enough, if the fertilizer was not available—anything. They knew we could not afford to go to the collector often, it cost Rs 80 to make one trip to the collectorate from my village.' He had to, however, meet the collector during the enquiry about the eligibility of his father's suicide for compensation. The administration had found the case eligible.[6] The enquiry[7] noted that there had been no recovery process initiated against Gyaneshwar for the pending loan, no notices issued, and no pressure brought to bear upon him for repayment. But there was no category in the enquiry sheet for the integrity of the farmer who did not want to have an outstanding loan against his name and no section that measured his honesty, which made him so anxious about repayment that he killed himself. Possibly realizing this, the administration found Gyaneshwar's family eligible for compensation for his suicide; part of the amount was given as cash to Santosh and rest was placed in a fixed deposit in the bank.

The compensation was more a reward for the farmer's sense of responsibility rather than an admission of the state's irresponsibility towards one of the weakest sections of the society. Santosh was aware of these interpretations, as he mentioned the process when the compensation was awarded. 'I had to go to the collectorate twice, and it cost me money. But I never mentioned this to the officials there,' he pointed out. He questioned the manner in which the administration conducted the enquiry of his father's suicide, as well as their perception that the families of the farmers were beneficiaries of patronage.

Santosh had plans for his future; he wanted to join the police force and had given the police recruitment examination, which he had failed to qualify only by a narrow margin. His next major target was the MPSC examination, but he was unable to study. He said, 'I miss my father so much. He was like a friend to me, and constantly encouraged me to apply for competitive examinations and study for them. I do not even feel like giving these exams in my present state of mind. But this is what my father wished for me, and I wish to turn his dream into reality.' Gyaneshwar had been educated only till Class 4.

Santosh carried within him a deep hurt from the events he had witnessed, which symbolized the struggle of his father, a man he loved and respected. He had to give up their cow, which has always held a special place in Indian villages, and which his father had been very fond of. As their financial situation deteriorated, it became evident to them that they could not afford to keep it; they had no money for its fodder. 'He had always said that if we could not keep the cow, then it should be donated to someone who could take care of it. He had insisted that it should not be sold,' Santosh said. The cow now was kept by a resident of the same village and reminded Santosh of not only his father's affection but also his helplessness. These reminders only added to his anger, and to his determination to never attempt agriculture. The same emotion was shared by his sister, who studied diligently and scored high marks in every examination. Santosh and Sheetal worked to support their own education; 'Despite that, my sister could not opt for Science in college as she did not have the money to pay the fees. Merit was not enough,' he added dryly. If there were expenses that still had to be met, Santosh took on work as a daily wage farm labourer at Rs 150 per day. This ensured that there was no further dependence on loans, although an earlier private loan of Rs 60,000 still remained, which the siblings were repaying.

Santosh represented the new thinking in Vidarbha, especially among farmers who struggled to continue with agriculture. The youth connected poverty and lack of opportunity with agriculture, and Santosh did not want to change it—he wanted to leave it for good. Additionally, he did not expect the government or politicians to change his life or agriculture. He was the new farmer of Vidarbha who strengthened himself with studies and patience for a future he could control. He was fortified by the sacrifice of his father and the memory of his mother; while grief weakened his heart, it also strengthened his resolve. As Santosh struggled to find the focus to prepare for the MPSC examinations, held state-wide for entry to various government jobs, it was unfair that his performance would be judged against candidates from better circumstances; such were the vagaries of the level playing field. The only advantage might be the anger he quietly nurtured within himself against the circumstances that had claimed his father's life. For now, he waited for outcomes with the wisdom of someone who knew justice would be done eventually.

★★★

In July 2017, Santosh had decided to take up employment with agricultural companies to fund his preparations for the MPSC examinations, including buying books and joining coaching classes. Earlier in August 2016, Santosh had appeared less burdened than before and there was even a smile on his usually serious face as he agreed to the interview. Sheetal had been married last year, and was now settled in Silvasa, Gujarat, where her husband worked as a supervisor in a company. She was happy, Santosh said with relief and satisfaction. He could deal with life alone; he knew he had a long struggle ahead of him and he was prepared for it. But he seemed to have wanted a less strenuous life for his sister and was glad she got it. He had himself found the match for his sister by placing an advertisement in his community's yearly matrimonial guide. 'The community has a book compiled for possible matrimonial matches, and has details of all the boys and girls ready for marriage, with their photographs and addresses. This book is printed once a year during the festival of Diwali and it takes Rs 250 to post an advertisement. I posted my sister's details in this book last year and we found a good match immediately,' he explained. The marriage was very simply done with the help of his aunt in Warud, who had cared for them after the death of their mother since 2006. 'I missed my parents so much during my sister's marriage. I wish they had been there, they would have been so happy,' he said, anguished.

As for him, he hoped to do his post-graduation in Amravati but could not afford the fees. The 2-acre land in Kajli was being cultivated by his paternal uncles, Suresh and Ramdas, who also kept the produce. 'Last year, the yield was 7 quintals, which barely covered the expenses. There is no irrigation on the field and added to that, the land is too small to support the family,' he explained. He had checked if there was any irrigation scheme available for the land but found they did not qualify due to their caste. 'The reservation of the schemes for certain castes means the farmers of other castes do not get the benefit of the government schemes even if they are poor and needy,' he said.

Santosh prepared to give the MPSC examination again in 2016, but could not afford to pay for tuitions. He used the public library provided in villages, but it was not very well equipped. 'The state of the public libraries is bad, even though they get a budget of almost Rs 2.5 lakh. I brought this matter to the notice of the department concerned and wrote to them a letter asking for books required for students preparing for competitive examinations.' According to Santosh, the tuitions for just Mathematics and English cost Rs 10,000 for six months, and those too were useful only if the candidate was good in other subjects like History. Santosh hoped to pay these fees with the help of employment. 'I am looking for a job that could pay for my preparation for the competitive examinations. In 2013, when I was pursuing graduation, I worked at a motorcycle showroom to partially support myself. I am not stuck on getting a *sarkari* [government] job,' he said. Santosh had not taken any new loan since 2015 and there had been no notices on the pending loan taken by his father.

For Santosh, the death of his father not only resolved the question of whether he should continue with agriculture as an occupation, but also showed the impossibility of depending on the state. 'I wanted to vote NOTA [None of the Above][8] in the last election. Instead, I voted for change because I was swayed by the political promises. However, it was of no use; nothing has changed. In retrospect, I was right in thinking of NOTA at first.' It was not the first time that promises he believed in were broken. 'Politicians had promised free seeds to the poor farmers. In my memory, nothing has ever been given free to the poor; there is always a cost directly or indirectly. Politicians promised employment in the new projects in the Vidarbha region. Again, I do not know of any instance where employment had been specially given to children of local farmers,' he said.

Santosh had also studied how government schemes failed. 'Irrigation is a major problem in this region and, as with agriculture everywhere, the yield is dependent on irrigation. It should be ensured that grants for irrigation must reach people who have never received such benefits. But these days, every elected member has a list of his own people to whom grants are given.' Asked about what he would have done to rectify the situation, he said that a survey should be undertaken of people who had received the irrigation grants and focus on those who had never benefitted from the schemes.

Similarly, in the case of farmer suicides, Santosh felt that the loan of the farmer must be waived. 'There is no point in continuing with a loan that had already cost the family a precious life. The family should not face such anxiety when there is no money to repay the loans. Also, the family of the farmer is considered a defaulter and no new loan is given by the bank. This practice must change. Procedures, at present, are not friendly to the poor farmer. Every farmer seeking a loan is required to get a no-due certificate from all the banks in the region at a personal expense. Then, every farmer must create a file that, along with all the paperwork, costs Rs 1,000. Do the banks expect farmers to get this money from the private moneylenders?' He also felt that the licensing of moneylenders should be strictly followed, as the unpaid private loans also led to suicides. He suggested that small farmers should be given an interest rebate, but not the large farmers. The cotton crop could be cultivated in the region but only with irrigation; the other options were crops such as soybean and tur. 'Whatever the crop, if it fails, the government must provide relief early so that it reaches the farmers during the season and not afterwards. Farmers would feel reassured if there was such timely relief,' he suggested. He also felt that the krishi kendra should be manned by people who were graduates in the subject of agriculture to be able to advise the farmers correctly.

Santosh's prime objective to join the administration was to bring about positive change. 'Every trick is used to deny benefit to those who qualify for it under the government schemes. We have seen so much corruption in such schemes meant for the poor and the farmers. If I get to a position of some influence, I would like to dedicate myself to solving these problems and to ensure that the deserving get their due,' he said. He did not

believe in public action or protests as a way of bringing about
change. 'Everyone is involved in corruption for four years out
of the five-year-government tenure, and then in the last year
before elections, others start protesting. There is a political
agenda behind every demand and every statement; the corruption is like an infestation in a crop. This must be changed from
within and not outside,' he said. Santosh had decided to pursue
his dream until he turned 30, after which he planned to begin
some business.

At a crossroad in his life, Santosh missed his parents the most.
He recalled his father's death with regret: 'He killed himself on a
day when I was away. I would have never let him think on those
lines if I had known how deeply he was affected.' He admitted that a farmer was under tremendous stress to provide for his
household through agriculture—a profession that was no longer
sustainable. He had to generate funds for education, health, mar-
riages, and also repay the loans. He said, 'Whatever the odds, I
believe that no one should commit suicide. I miss my father at
every step; we were very close.'

Santosh spoke about his mother, and her memory brought tears
to his eyes. 'I still remember that she wanted me to study well
and become someone important, someone who could do good for
others. In those days, the school in Kajli was only up till Class 4,
so I had to travel to the next village for my next class. She used
to work as a farm labour on daily wages and saved Rs 120 for me
for my monthly bus pass. Whatever the other expenses, she made
sure that there was no hindrance to my schooling,' he said. Rekha
Tingde had been educated until Class 10, but still found no suitable
employment in the village and worked as farm labour, a testament
to the lack of opportunities even for the educated in the rural areas.
And yet, it had not diminished her spirit. It was in her immortal
memory that Santosh continued on the path she had shown him.

1. Letter from the tehsildar of Chandur Bazar to the district collector of Amravati, on 6 December 2014.

2. Maharashtra State-Certificate in Information Technology (MS-CIT) is considered an essential course for any government job.

3. Under the prime minister's relief package, Rs 2,177 crore was allocated for irrigation, 9,105 check dams were to be constructed at a cost of Rs 192.66 crore, and 90,552 hectares of land were to be brought under the water-shed programme, costing Rs 55.83 crore. See Status Report of 'Rehabilitation Package for Farmers of Six Districts of Vidarbha for 3 years (2006–9)', Vasantrao Naik Sheti Swavlamban Mission, Amravati, pp. 3–4.

4. *Seed Industries Association of Maharashtra vs The State of Maharashtra*, W.P. No. 3255/2015, Bombay High Court.

5. The government's decision to reduce the price of a 450-gm seed packet by Rs 100 had disconcerted the seed industry. Before this, every state had a different price, and seed companies charged an extra fee for each packet of Bt seeds. See 'Maharashtra Bt cotton seed companies taken by surprise', *Financial Express, 2* June 2015, www.financialexpress.com/market/commodities/maharashtra-bt-cotton-seed-companies-taken-by-surprise/78957/, accessed 5 July 2017.

6. Letter from the tehsildar of Chandur Bazar to the district collector of Amravati.

7. Statement of record of the suicide of Gyaneshwar Tingde, signed by the tehsildar, Chandur Bazar, tehsil agricultural officer, police in-charge, sarpanch, and the member of the panchayat samiti.

8. None of the Above (NOTA) gives the Indian voters an option not to select any candidate contesting in an election. See www.eci.nic.in.

CHAPTER
FOURTEEN

A Farmer Standing Still

Bhagirathi Harale, Pala Village, Morshi Tehsil, Amravati District

A Widow Since 10 February 2013

A farmer in India lives in a different time warp, as if history has passed him by and the country has forgotten him. He has been left untouched by the economic reforms and urban revolutions that have captured the headlines of the world about India. The farmers stand still on the fast-fragmenting land of their ancestors to earn a living with crops that no longer make profit and through labour that is no longer respected. The farmers of Vidarbha, like the farmers elsewhere in India, must wait for the nation to eventually turn its focus towards them and their problems. But aspirational India does not want to look back at the villages from where it has emerged, and believes that the only salvation for the farmer is to leave the land that supports him. Many did, but those who stayed with their lands find that the cotton harvest does not allow for enough savings to invest in new land. As a result, every successive generation inherits farms that are smaller and progressively inconsequential.[1] The farmers who struggle to educate their children know that agriculture is the last resort for them, to be adopted only if the children are left with no other opportunity. In future, the land is to be sold or leased out, but not cultivated; it is now too small to sustain an entire family.

The increasing fragmentation of land also leads to the decline in the living standards of the younger farmers who have to survive under the same, limited roof in order to share household expenses. As the number of people dependent on the same piece of land increases without a simultaneous increase in crop yield, the lives of the younger farmers becomes worse than the poverty of the older generation. Given this scenario, unpaid debts are a major hurdle and their burden rests on the shoulders of the farmers who have no way to repay the loans. A farmer who defaults on loans lives daily through blame, fear, and embarrassment of the recovery process. The state is of little help, and the community, which is undergoing the same problems, cannot assist its fellow farmers. The only hope is from government schemes that have been designed to help small and marginal farmers.[2] But as the ranks of these farmers swell due to fragmentation, even the schemes do not reach people who need them the most. Agriculture on fragmented lands is only possible when the government supports the farmer at every level and when the farmer is not solely dependent on farm income. But if that is too much to expect, then history can wait and ignore the farmer a little longer. The lands will dissolve, like islands of sand, and the farmer will be gone; just like in the case of Daulat Harale.

Daulat Harale's widow, two sons, and their family were dependent on their 5-acre land. Their daughter, Vaishali, who had been educated up to Class 8, was married and lived away. Daulat had inherited about 2.5 acres of land from his father, who had acquired it sometime in 1960–70, when he had moved from the nearby tehsil of Warud to Amravati. Those were better times, and Daulat had planted 380 orange trees in it, a crop widely cultivated in Morshi. The cost of cultivation was low and the crops fetched a good market price in earlier days, making Daulat enough profit to buy another plot, about half a kilometre from the first. Together, the two made up his 5 acres. Then, the difficult times had begun and the bad seasons relentlessly returned, year after year. The cotton yield had remained below expectation between 2010 and 2013,[3] the year that Daulat committed suicide. He had been 55 years old; he had died on the evening of 10 February 2013, between 5 and 6 p.m., hanging himself from an orange tree with a 8-feet-long nylon rope. It seemed that he had planned his death carefully, choosing one of the trees he had planted 25 years ago. The branch, which had just borne fruit that season, supported his weight and the shades of the foliage had hidden his body until life was drained from it. The twilight of that evening must have filtered through his mind as Daulat died on his farm that stood witness to his final decision. He opted to escape from the fate of a farmer forced to stand still, and watch the slow death of his children's dreams.

The family said he had found it impossible to repay an outstanding loan of approximately Rs 1,39,673, which had been pending since 2011–12.[4] The loan was taken for the crop that year and also for installing drip irrigation. Daulat's wife, Bhagirathi was 50 years old, while her sons Umesh and Chhatrapati were 27 and 24 respectively. Bhagirathi carried a sense of disbelief about her husband's death. She was not surprised that he had the courage to commit suicide, but was stunned that he had given up the fight. 'He was anxious that he was unable to repay the loan,' she said; it had been outstanding only for a year. He could have waited for one more season to repay it. But he had given up waiting. 'Whatever topic we discussed, he would always end up raising the issue of the loan. It disturbed him that it would burden the family, and that his children would be troubled by it,' she said. Bhagirathi, like most widows of Vidarbha, had suffered the same circumstances that led to the death of her husband. These included not only low productivity of the crop, but also the loan recovery processes of lending agencies and the unresponsive state administration. As partial

FIGURE 37   Umesh (right) and his younger brother Chhatrapati with their mother Bhagirathi Harale, January 2015
Source: Author

atonement, Daulat's suicide was decided as eligible, and Bhagirathi was given the Rs 1 lakh compensation, of which Rs 30,000 was given in cash, in October 2013,[5] eight months after Daulat's death. The remaining was deposited in a bank.

Umesh clearly recalled the day of his father's death; Daulat's meticulous planning had dawned on him in retrospect. It had been a Sunday and there was no electricity in the field, which meant that the crops could not be watered from the 80-foot-deep well. Umesh had returned home to work on the house, which had been newly built in 2013. Even in 2015, the house was far from finished, as the work depended on the availability of funds. Umesh had decided to spend that Sunday on a few tasks to be done inside the house. 'At that time, there were no window frames and I told my father that I would get them fixed for the main room that day. He agreed, so I left him in the field alone and returned home around 5 p.m.' There seemed to be a deep sense of regret in Umesh for leaving his father's side. He said, 'People walking to the village from the direction of the field had found me working on the window and they said they had seen my father moving about the farm. That was usual, nothing was really amiss.' But soon afterwards, some other farmers discovered Daulat hanging by the tree and rushed to inform Umesh. The death had shocked the young farmer then and still hurt him to speak about it now. He said, 'I never thought he would take such a step. We were all concerned about the loan, and he was very worried. I thought I would somehow help him repay the debt. I believe that was what bothered him the most—that he had burdened me with a loan that was too large for us to ever repay.'

The 2012–13 season had been particularly tough for Daulat, as the cotton crop was devoured by disease. Umesh said, 'The cotton crop had taken three or four sprays of pesticide, and it cost us about Rs 3,000 per spray. The yield was still affected and we failed to recover our investment.' Additionally, the family had several illnesses, with some members needing to go to doctors in Warud, which cost money. Without any other source of income, expenses of this nature were paid with loan money, either borrowed from banks or moneylenders. The land was common for the two sons and they admitted that it was impossible to sustain their lives with the yield from the farm. Umesh said, 'The land is too little to support us, and we do not receive any welfare. We have no option but to work as farm labour for daily wages,' he said. The cotton crop was of no use either. 'Cotton in 3 acres yielded about 9 quintals. At Rs 4,000 per quintal, it just equals the cost of cultivation without any profit left,' he said. The yield further reduced as it had to be divided between the brothers, but Chhatrapati found a silver lining in the situation: 'When the land is divided, it may be easier to get loans and other schemes for small land holdings like pipelines, cattle, etc.'

The expense of the household, including all bills, fees, and other requirements, worked out to around Rs 6,000 per month. For the first time in generations, the family members were working as daily wagers to support themselves. This cemented the view of Umesh and Chhatrapati that there was no point in schooling or further education if the only employment they could get was as wage labour on farms. Umesh had studied up to Class 12, which he did not pass, while Chhatrapati had studied up to Class 10. On being asked why he had dropped out of school, Umesh said, 'I wanted to do a job but once I started agriculture, there was no time to think of anything else.' His wife, 26-year-old Vaishali, had studied up to the second year of graduation. He believed that she could have found a job but that had to wait as they had an 18-month daughter, Purvi, to take care of. These plans took effort and time, neither of which the family could afford in their constant struggle for survival.

In 2015, the orange orchard had produced very little fruit while the expenditure had been about Rs 50,000 for the upkeep of the 380 orange trees. The same year, the cotton yield was 10 quintals, which sold at Rs 4,000 per quintal. But the bills of a farmer's household did not wait for a good crop. The fuel and maintenance of his motorcycle cost Umesh Rs 200 per month, the cell phone cost Rs 100, the television charges were Rs 100, and cooking gas cost Rs 860, with a subsidy of Rs 350. The bill for electricity every month amounted to Rs 500, which was steep considering the usage by the family. The household had arrears of Rs 1.5 lakh on their electricity bill, which was difficult to repay. Umesh believed that it wasn't just his family that was over-billed on electricity but also the entire village. To address this, earlier in 2014, about 3,000 families had organized in protest and marched to the supply department of the government to complain. According to Umesh, this issue had been a cause for tension and even led to clashes with the officials. Citizen protests ensured that the electricity supply was not disconnected while the over-billing issue was being sorted out. Meanwhile, part of Umesh's 5-acre land that grew cotton was taken for setting up of a power transformer by the government, which was yet to be done.

As an experiment, the family had leased 4 more acres of land to cultivate cotton in 2014–15 at Rs. 20,000 per year and had earned about Rs 35,000–40,000 from this enterprise. The schemes of the government to help small farmers were directed by the panchayat samiti of the village. 'We had applied for poultry last year, and are awaiting a response. We got the cattle cart through one such scheme. But what we really wanted were pipelines for water in the field, and those we could not get,' said Umesh. He had considered selling the land that was clearly becoming unviable as a support to the family. 'I would be paid about Rs 10 lakh if I sell the land with the orange orchard. But what would I do then?' he asked. There was no clear answer to this question and that was why most farmers continued with agriculture; there was no other option.

'I always wanted to be a farmer, and I have seen that if I work hard, things will improve. I want to continue working on my field; I will not leave it and go away. I will improve the productivity and hope for a better future,' Umesh said. He was rooted to his land, his destiny, like his father had been. But as he struggled against the odds of agriculture, his fragile hope was tested by governments that did not fight for him, and by a society that did not care about his troubles. 'When my father died, everyone said we must have ceremonies and feed people. It would have cost us Rs 4,000, and that was money we did not have. We refused to borrow the money to do the ceremonies, and people were shocked. They tried to scare us, make us feel guilty, but how does it matter?' Umesh asked, smiling grimly. He said 'Since then, it has become a trend in this village. Poor people cannot pay for such things and more such people are refusing to borrow money to spend in this manner. After all, what is the meaning of these rituals for the dead? I do not believe in forgetting the dead. Anyway, it does not matter what people say because we do not matter to anyone. When we marched to the electricity supply department last year, they locked their offices and went away. That's because we do not matter to them. When political parties come to seek our vote, we tell them nothing. We know we do not matter to anyone.'

★★★

By 2017, Umesh's wife Vaishali had moved away to live with her parents to take care of their daughter Purvi.

Earlier in August 2016, the Harale house neared completion and appeared to be composing itself into a home. It had taken the family three years to put together the structure that still remained unpainted in parts and unfinished generally. But there were windows to the rooms and a name for the residence, Chhatrapati Niwas. The land and the house were in Umesh's name but he put his brother's name on the hard-earned house out of affection. Umesh's love for his brother was similar to the love Daulat had for his children; he had thus wanted to shield him from the outstanding loans that had made Daulat take his life. The memory of the event plunged the two brothers into melancholy and the new house suddenly felt empty. They recalled the day of his death and their decision to forego the rituals.

Umesh looked unusually fatigued and explained that his daughter was seriously unwell in a hospital in Warud. Quick tears filled his eyes as he explained that the doctors had given up on her. Purvi had developed a neurological disorder that came to light only in 2016; she had been fine in 2015. As a loving father, Umesh had looked into every little detail of his daughter's treatment and care. 'She still has baby food from a tin box and each box costs Rs 400; we use at least three boxes in a month. The doctors said that she should be given only buffalo milk for strength and that costs Rs 45 per litre. So instead, I bought a buffalo for Rs 10,000 to get her milk. I get about 2.5 litres a day, and the fodder is free as it comes from the farm. But I do not sell the milk as it is meant only for my daughter.' The family had all been together on 13 May of 2016, the date on which Purvi had turned two years old. Then, her condition worsened and she was sent away to Warud on August 18 in the care of his wife and mother. The buntings still hung on the walls of the room and reminded Umesh of his beloved daughter.

The outstanding loan, including that of his father that he had to pay was now Rs 6 lakh along with interest. Umesh had lost all hope of repaying the loan; he had harvested only 10 quintals of cotton in 2015, the crop on the 4-acre land taken on lease had been destroyed due to the red bug pest, locally known as lalya. There was also a new private loan in 2016 of Rs 1.5 lakh but there was no new bank loan. Most of the money now went towards Purvi's treatment, including Bhagirathi's savings from a cooperative society.

All members of the family worked as farm labour for daily wages. Umesh had implemented some of his plans for enhancing the family income. He had set up a small-scale flour mill in the neighbourhood and was planning to run a taxi to Morshi from the village. He hoped to get the benefit of the welfare schemes that the government offered to the poor but the only help they got was subsidized food grains through the Antyodaya Anna Yojana.[6] Even then, the quantity was not sufficient to meet the daily requirements of the family. He wished that his educated wife could get a job, especially as the village panchayat was headed by a woman. But Umesh was unhappy with how the panchayat system operated. 'All that the villagers are told when we enquire about government schemes is to wait. When we ask to meet the sarpanch we are asked to wait. Why must we wait so much?'

His father had never asked that question; he had just ended his life when he could no longer wait. Umesh, on the other hand, expected an answer to the question, from the panchayat, from the electricity department, from the state, from the politicians—and from the country.

1. 'All India Report on Number and Area of Operational Holdings', *Agricultural Census 2010–11*, Ministry of Agriculture, Government of India, 2014, available at www.agcensus.nic.in, accessed 2 July 2017.

2. Schemes like the Baliraja Chetna Abhiyan in Yavatmal and then those under the Vasantrao Naik Sheti Swavalamban Mission (VNSSM) in Amravati aimed to reduce farmer suicides by extending state support and resources.

3. Letter from the tehsildar of Morshi to the district collector of Amravati, on 13 March 2013.

4. Letter from the bank in Morshi to the tehsildar of Morshi, on 1 March 2013.

5. Receipt of Rs 30, 000 received by Bhagirathi Harale, on 18 October 2013.

6. Antyodaya Anna Yojana provided subsidised foodgrains for the BPL. See www.dfpd.nic.in

CHAPTER
FIFTEEN

The Rules of Dreaming

Sunita Utkhede, Utkhed Village, Morshi Tehsil, Amravati District

A Widow Since 20 March 2012

There are unwritten rules for the poor farmers of Vidarbha—rules about how they should live, how they should die, and how they should learn to reconcile with poverty and hopelessness. Breaking these rules usually proved to be fatal, especially the rule about dreaming for a better future. Strangely, despite the risk of failure, this was the one rule broken most often, in the hope that they could change the other rules. Such defiance, however, was never possible, and each death of an honest and hardworking farmer proved it. Dreams costs lives in Vidarbha.

The brick-lined house in Utkhed village of Amravati appeared far too fragile for the story that had unfolded within its walls. The structure was bare, as if all the hopes of a better life had been washed from its surface, leaving behind the stark outlines of a plan that had been too good to be true. Four brothers used to live in that house with their families; only two were left now. The 11 acres of family land had been divided among the four brothers, with each cultivating roughly 2 acres. It had not been enough to sustain the family, but they lived together and shared their burdens. That was how they thought of building a dream together, how they dared to think they could educate their children and, maybe even provide them comforts of a better life. Chandrashekar, the third son of Keshavrao Utkhede, had committed suicide by consuming poison on 20 March 2012. He was only 45 years old at the time of his death. His widow, Sunita had been 41, and they had two teen-age sons—Rushab and Prajwal. The land was in Chandrashekar's name, like it was in the name of the other brothers. At the time of his death, Chandrashekar had an outstanding loan, taken from a lending agency in 2011, of Rs 17,534.

According to the district administration,[1] the land had con-sistently yielded below average since 2009–10. It was clear from the pattern of cultivation that about half of the land was not even cultivable. Chandrashekar used to mix the crops; he had planted cotton in half his field, and soybean and tur in the rest. In 2011–12, he had planted cotton and tur in just half of the land. There was no ambiguity about the fact that agriculture had failed in this case, as indicated in the report from the tehsildar to the district collector through the SDO.[2] The lack of productivity had made it impossible for Chandrashekar to repay the farm loan that he had taken in 2011. That was all that the official documents stated and, as always, they did not mention the private loans or the pressures faced by the farmer families from the moneylenders. The reality was different, and only the farmer's family was witness to the circumstances that had led to the suicides. Sunita spoke about what had killed her husband.

First, there were the loans taken from different lending agencies, ranging from local self-help groups to cooperatives societies—places where the farmers were themselves members. Sunita said, 'We had a pending loan of Rs 3 lakh and the recovery agents came to demand repayment. These were embarrassing moments that created anxiety for my husband. He was also under pressure

FIGURE 38   Sunita, Chandrashekar Utkhede's widow, August 2016
Source: Author

because we needed the money to continue farming.' It was a vicious circle of debt into which the farmer was hurled without choice. Loan waivers given by the state were designed to assist the farmers in escaping this circle by either cancelling or reschedul- ing the loans. Neither happened in the case of Chandrashekar, even though he should have qualified for the 2008 Loan Waiver, announced by the Central government.[3] Sunita's eyes filled with tears as she remembered those difficult times. 'No one was ready to give us a new loan unless we cleared the old one. My husband was a member of a lending agency from where the loan had been taken. But the office-bearers refused to lend further to him, unless he cleared the old debt. There was nothing to repay the loan with; there had been very low yields from the crops.'

The second reason was the low productivity of the land, a fact known to the administration through its representatives in the villages, and should have been known to the lending agencies as well.[4] The farmer still had to argue the truth of his losses and in most cases, he was not believed. However, from the perspective of lending agencies, they could survive only if the outstanding debts were recovered. That was the reason why the recovery process of loans from poor farmers was harsh and brutal in its relentlessness. It was no wonder that the family of the farmers often mentioned the recovery enquiries as a cause of distress for the farmers who committed suicide.

The third reason was the productivity of the fields, which was the result of several factors, and the farmers had to deal with the other problems as much as they had to deal with the quality of the soil. Sunita explained, 'There were fruit trees of orange in the field that required the drip system of irrigation. A loan was taken a few years ago and the pipes were laid to get water to the trees. But since then, the pipes have been chewed up by mice, and now we have no money to reinstall them or get a new irrigation system. So, there is once again no irrigation in the field. These and other such problems have to be addressed in farming. But along with that, there is the constant feeling that none of our efforts will really help as the yield will still be low.' It was not surprising that Chandrashekar started losing faith when the crops failed in 2012, and there was no money for even sowing the next crop. The only hope for a poor farmer in such conditions was the lending agencies, but they conveniently distanced themselves from him. She recalled, 'He was always tense in those days before his death. He used to be lost in plans of how to fund the next crop and repay the debt.' She questioned the injustice of it. 'We lost the irrigation system in the field, the productivity was low and the banks were not lending us money. And yet everyone expected us to repay our loans. How did they even think we could?'

The case was found to be eligible for compensation by the administration, and Sunita was paid Rs 30,000[5] in December 2012, nine months after Chandrashekar's death. The remaining compensation was issued in January 2013, which was kept in the bank as a fixed deposit and gathered an interest of 8.5 per cent at

Rs 492 per month.[6] The amount would remain in the bank until 2019, when it would be paid to Sunita. This staggered payment of compensation ensured that the widow could plan the expenditure and had control over the funds. From Sunita's point of view, this seemed to be a good arrangement as it provided her financial security and independence from the uncertain fate of agriculture. But she knew it was not a lasting answer to her problems or substantial support for her children's future. It was in pursuit of such solutions that Chandrashekar had worked hard, and failed.

In her statement to the district administration,[7] Sunita had said that Chandrashekar consumed the poison on the afternoon of 20 March 2012 and had committed suicide. He was worried about the low productivity of his farm and the outstanding loans, she had told the representative of the administration who had taken her statement. There were details behind this statement that the state had no time to get into, but nevertheless, were etched in her mind about that day. 'We had planted a little wheat for the family and he had gone to water the crop,' she said. 'I brought him lunch in the afternoon and found him lying in the field. There was a container of poison next to him. I was worried when he failed to respond, so I put him in a cart and brought him to the village.' She paused, as if the panic of that moment still filled her mind. 'My brother-in-law, Dilip, was working in his own field and I called him for help. We decided to get my husband to the hospital, but he died on the way.'

Chandrashekar's decision to end his life made it clear why her husband had been forlorn for some time. 'For four or five days before his death, he had been preoccupied with some thought. I wanted to know what it was but he never told me,' she said. 'He had even stopped eating, and I could tell he was very anxious.' Tears sprang to her eyes again as she recalled that she had been away in the village when he had committed suicide on the farm. She felt she could have prevented him if she had known his intentions. Chandrashekar must have known that, the reason why he took the step at that time and that particular place. The post-mortem report[8] had found no injuries on his body and no other visible signs of trauma. The conclusion was that he had died of a cardiac arrest caused by poisoning. According to the police, the poison was a pesticide[9] primarily used in cotton farming.

Dilip Utkhede, Chandrashekar's elder brother, had taken him to the hospital and identified the body. Dilip and Arun were the two brothers left of the four; Rajendra too had committed suicide a few years ago because of debt following a bad yield from scarcity of rainfall. Dilip recalled the time when all the four brothers worked together and managed to share the expenses of the house. Now, only Dilip and Arun worked on the farm. Dilip had seen his younger brothers grow up, and had shared the dream of a happy and contented life together. The impossibility of this dream became vivid when the cotton crops started failing farmers across Vidarbha. He said, 'The cost of sowing cotton in 2 acres was Rs 40,000 and it yielded 4 quintals, which earned between Rs 3,500 and Rs 3,800 per quintal.' Other crop options were equally dismal, as the cultivation report showed.[10] 'We got about 1 quintal of tur from 2 acres, which sold at Rs 5,000. How does a farmer's family support itself on such returns?'

Dilip does not focus on agriculture anymore; the loss of his two brothers was a steep price to pay for that one elusive good crop. He now looked for support from welfare and other government schemes for Sunita, like anganwadi,[11] or the widow pension of Rs 600 per month, and sops that the state provided to dependents. This was difficult to admit for a person used to earning a livelihood through his or her own agency and hard work. The loss of crops was, in a way, the loss of the spirit of a farmer. 'Monthly, the children's school fee is about Rs 1,000–1,200, the tuition is Rs 500. The electricity bill annually is Rs 6,000 and then there are bills for groceries, water, house tax, etc. These cannot be cut down, and cannot be paid through agriculture,' he explained.

The only source of income for the family now was farm labour. Dilip earned Rs 200 a day for working two shifts, while other members of the family earned Rs 100. Dilip held a master's degree in Mathematics, but had opted to do agriculture as it used to be an equally good opportunity. In those times, it was enough to know the art of tilling the soil, but that was redundant in today's India. For the Utkhede family, the question was no longer about the dream of a better future, it was about survival. 'I could sell the land,' Dilip said without any sentimentality. 'I will get Rs 3–4 lakh per acre. I could bring the entire struggle to an end.' But he belonged to that land, that village of 4,000 people and that house of bare brick and broken dreams. Even he carried a debt of Rs 20,000 from the local krishi kendra[12] for sowing cotton and tur, and could not raise a new loan without repaying the old ones.

Chandrashekar's two sons had finished schooling, although 19-year-old Rushab had quit his studies after Class 12 to do farming. He contributed to the family income by working as a daily wage farm labourer from 7 a.m. to noon every day. He believed that education was a waste of time and wanted to support his family through other means. This lack of hope from education appeared valid, considering the unemployment figures among rural educated youth.[13] Sunita's younger son, 18-year-old Prajwal was good at studies and had wanted to join either the railways or the police force in 2015. The children knew what it cost the family to educate them, and they were also aware of the reasons behind their father's suicide. It was difficult to imagine how the youth looked at life, or where it turned to for hope and belief. But Sunita seemed to know that the tragedy of losing their father was a preparation in itself for her sons. She was proud of their resolution and their strength. She noted, 'They are tall like my husband. They are determined to take care of their family.'

The future was full of struggle for Sunita and she wished she was not alone as she battled the odds. 'I miss my husband all the time,' she said, as she struggled to deal with the fervour of the

Sankranti festival in 2015. For Sunita, her husband's 2-acre land was also the graveyard of his dreams. These were buried there forever, somewhere near where Chandrashekar had fallen and where the poison had spilled onto the soil, killing it as well. Such were the deadly rules of dreaming in Vidarbha.

★★★

In July 2017, the family waited to explore if the state government's loan waiver applied to them. No one informed them and the only way to find out was through a visit to the bank, which the family was budgeting for.

Earlier in August 2016, the brick house where despair used to lurk in the corners now had hope. Sunita's younger son Prajwal was training to be an engineer at an Industrial Training Institute, and was preparing to find a job in either the railways or any of the private sector companies that dealt with heavy machinery. Sunita looked weak but smiled as she heard him speak. Prajwal said, 'I will not wait unendingly for a *sarkari* [government] job. I will work in any company that has a job for me, from ordnance to the power sector.' There was the impatience of youth about him for solutions as he listened to Dilip speak about the problems of the onion crop, which had been planted so extensively in 2016 that its prices fell in the market from oversupply. Disturbed by the lack of attention on the farmers' plight, Prajwal said, 'There are so many programmes on television, and there is a channel dedicated to agriculture. But these cover only Uttar Pradesh or Bihar, as if there are no farmers in the rest of the country. I have never seen a telecast that told us anything about onions, when most of Vidarbha has cultivated it this year.' He did not blame anyone for the circumstances; in his positive world view, there was no place for such things. He said that farmers should be supported in subsidies, where crucial and expensive inputs were involved, like irrigation.

Dilip heard his nephew in silence, as if letting him hope. Then he said, 'We need an additional business to run our households, as agriculture is no longer enough. At the moment, the banks do not lend to farmers who do not already run a business. That is unfair and unjust to farmers like me who want to start something new to augment our income.' He wanted to begin a dairy farm and had applied for support from the state in 2014 but was told there was no government scheme for people of his caste. He had taken a new private loan of Rs 60,000, and had sown cotton, tur, soybean, and onion in 2016. There was a plan behind this crop diversification. Dilip explained, 'We need to cultivate smaller crops like fruits, vegetables, etc., instead of depending on one large crop that could fail for any reason. In case cotton is cultivated, then it should be priced at a minimum of Rs 6,000, only then will the farmers survive. Otherwise, there will not be a next generation of farmers to work on these fields.'

Meanwhile, the house stayed still, as if it waited for the rules to change. No new repairs took place and in the summer light, it was clear that the bricks had been gathered from broken-down structures, some blue, and some brown. Only the two brothers and their families, and Sunita and her sons lived in that house. Vanita, Rajendra's widow, had not borne a child, and returned to her parents' house when he died. Dilip seemed to know that the young would once again leave the house, but unlike before, they would return. He waited, like his house, for the rules to change about dreaming.

ॐ

Notes

1. Letter from the tehsildar of Morshi, through the Morshi SDO, to the district collector of Amravati, on 17 April 2012. It is signed by the tehsildar (Morshi), the agricultural officer of the taluka, the sarpanch of the gram panchayat, and the police in-charge.

2. Letter from the tehsildar of Morshi, through the Morshi SDO, to the district collector of Amravati, on 17 April 2012.

3. In 2008, the Government of India announced the loan waiver for farmers. According to the report by the Public Accounts Committee, 2013–14, the scheme sought to assist farmers who had outstanding loans taken between 1 April 1997 and 31 March 2007. The beneficiaries were divided into three categories: farmers with land up to 2.5 acres qualified as 'marginal farmers', those with land up to 5 acres qualified as 'small farmers', and those with more than 5-acres qualified as 'other farmers'. The scheme was estimated to cover 3.69 crore small or marginal farmers and 0.60 crore other farmers. Hundred per cent of the loan taken by a marginal or a small farmer was waived off, while for other farmers, 25 per cent was waived off if they gave an undertaking to pay the remaining 75 per cent by June 2008. 'Ninety-Fifth Report of Public Account Committee on 'Implementation of Agricultural Debt Waiver and Debt Relief Scheme, 2008', Ministry of Finance, Government of India, 2013–14, pp. 1–5.

   However, the Comptroller and Auditor General of India's (CAG) report of 2013 observed that the scheme did not achieve its intended goals due to corruption and malpractices like errors of inclusion and exclusion of beneficiaries, poor documentation, tampering of records, non-issuing of benefits, etc., in many cases. See www.cag. gov.in, and www.rbi.org.in

4. Letter from the tehsildar of Morshi, through Morshi SDO to the district collector of Amravati.

5. Receipt of Rs 30, 000 received by Sunita Utkhede on 7 December 2012.

6. Term Deposit Receipt of Rs 70, 000 received by Sunita Utkhede, on 17 January 2013.

7. Statement of Sunita Utkhede recorded and presented to the district administration of Amravati by the talathi of Morshi, in which the village of Utkhed is situated.

8. Memorandum of a post-mortem examination of Chandrashekar Utkhede held at Dispensary Hospital, on 20 March 2012.

9. Crime Details form of Chandrashekar Utkhede, on 20 March 2012.

10. Letter from the tehsildar, Morshi, through the SDO, to the district collector of Amravati, on 17 April 2012.

11. The Integrated Child Development Services (ICDS) describes an anganwadi worker as a community-based worker chosen from the local community to work for the ICDS programme. She is expected to mobilize support for care of young children, girls and women. See www.icds-wcd.nic.in

12. Kisan kendra or krishi kendra are agricultural input shops that provide farm requirements, sometimes on loan in lieu of produce.

13. 'Report on District Level Estimates for the State of Maharashtra (2013–14)', Labour Bureau, Ministry of Labour and Employment, Government of India, Chandigarh, 2014, p. 24. Available at: www.labour.gov.in, accessed 27 May 2017.

    According to the report, the unemployment rate is 2.4 per cent for the rural male and 1.7 per cent for the rural female; this does not account for landless labourers or daily wagers.

CHAPTER
SIXTEEN

Of Death and Second Chances

2015: Archana Dhawde, Kharpi Village, Chandur Bazar Tehsil, Amravati District

A Widow Since 19 January 2013

2016: Archana Deshmukh, Adula Bazar Village, Daryapur Tehsil, Amravati District

Married Since 27 May 2015

Time had forgotten this address in Kharpi village. So, when asked about Gajanan Dhawde, his parents appeared surprised that anyone wanted to know the story of their son who had killed himself two years ago. The small house seemed waylaid on the road that led to better places, at a turn that passengers rarely took while travelling through Chandur Bazar, a district known for its picturesque orange orchards. The road connected the district to the neighbouring tehsil of Daryapur where Archana, their former daughter-in-law lived at her parents' home in 2015. Although nearby, it was a journey too painful to retrace, as it travelled back into their past. And yet, it was a road that could not be avoided, by either the Dhawdes or Archana.

Rajkanya, Gajanan's 55-year-old mother, recalled the time when they decided on Archana as a bride for Gajanan. 'We were very happy to have found a suitable match for our son from a respectable and hardworking family. She had no father, only her mother, and our son-in-law knew the family very closely.' Rajkanya had two married daughters, and Archana's match was suggested by one of the sons-in-law. The marriage had taken place in April 2012 and the new couple began to build their own little world in the Dhawde house. It had been a good time for the family, and they all looked forward to a future that brimmed with possibility and promise. Just eight months into this idyll, however, certain incidents prompted Gajanan to kill himself by consuming poison.

On 19 January 2013, 28-year-old Gajanan was rushed to the sub-district hospital in Kharpi at 5.05 p.m. only to be declared dead.[1] A case of suicide from poisoning was registered on 21 January 2013 at 9.05 p.m. On the day of his death, Gajanan had visited the Bhairav temple in the neighbourhood, a manifestation of Lord Shiva, the Hindu god of destruction of evil. Ironically, the name Gajanan is the name of Shiva's son or Ganesha, the elephant god. As always, Gajanan returned home in the afternoon and went to his room to rest. It was a fragile brick-lined room that was designed to provide privacy without any degree of comfort. That was, however, true for most farmers' homes as they were built incrementally and with generations of the family enduring the inconvenience. After his death, Gajanan's home remained unfinished, as if now it had no particular reason to rush it. According to his 60-year-old father, Bhimrao, the house had been in the making for 15 years.

On that fateful day, the door of his room had been closed and after some time, Archana entered to check on her husband, only to discover that he had committed suicide. She had been just 22 years old. He had worn a white shirt and black trousers at the time of his death,[2] the same clothes in which his body was sent

FIGURE 39   Rajkanya and Bhimrao, Gajanan Dhawde's parents,
January 2015
Source: Author

for a post-mortem. He had also worn a white shirt in the framed
photograph that hung at home to which the family paid tribute:
a garland of fresh flowers and a red *tilak* adorned it. His parents
had kept his memory alive, along with the sorrow of the struggles
they had witnessed of his life and his death. They knew his deep
sense of duty had made him feel responsible for his failures. 'The
mistake was my son's,' Rajkanya stated quietly. 'He did not have
to throw away his life; he did not have to lead his life in the manner he had.' It was *usual* for a farmer to carry the stress of unpaid
loans and the humiliation of being a defaulter; it was *normal* for a
farmer to fail. But that had not been acceptable to Gajanan and
his mother knew that well. 'He believed that no money could be
made through agriculture. Four years ago, he stopped counting
on the farm,' she said. This had not seemed surprising; she had
expected her son to lose his faith in agriculture. 'The 5-acre land
yielded just about 2 to 4 quintals of cotton. And that had never
been enough.'

The family had struggled with the land for the last 30 years. There had been two loans pending at the time of Gajanan's death.[3] One loan, in Bhimrao's name, of Rs 56,498 had been due in September 2011.[4] Rajkanya also had a pending loan of Rs 30, 940 in her name at the time of her son's death.[5] After ascertaining the circumstances, the administration had decided that Gajanan had been forced to commit suicide due to the burden of the unpaid loan and low productivity of his farm. He had tended to his parents' land, and taken over the responsibility to repay the loans for agriculture. 'There is a well on the land for irrigation, but the terrain is so rocky and uneven that it is very difficult to cultivate it. We seem to be always in debt and struggling to repay it with the meagre yield from the farm. Even now we have a pending loan that cannot be repaid because of low productivity this season,' Bhimrao said. They usually sowed cotton and pulses. Gajanan had been aware of the trouble with farming, but he had not accepted the struggle as an unchangeable fate of the family, as his father had.

'I have another son who works on the farm and toils hard, and yet, does not get enough returns. Gajanan wanted the situation to improve for the entire family,' Bhimrao said sadly. 'And in the rush to change things for the better, he got into the habit of gambling.' Poverty and the certainty of despair made Gajanan try to change his prospects. Sometimes, he won, and with the winnings, he set up businesses that he thought would support the family when agriculture failed. His father explained, 'He set up a *bhatti* [brick-making kiln]. Like any business, it was going to take capital and time to settle down and start yielding profits.' But Gajanan did not want to wait. He had seen the result of his father's waiting; waiting for a better crop, waiting for the rain, waiting for fate to change. He wanted to put an end to all the waiting by counting on something different—luck. But for him luck proved to be even more treacherous than fate.

'When he won the gamble everything was good. But when he lost, he lost everything,' Bhimrao said. 'It was something we could not afford; our household was not geared to lose money. Gambling can have very serious consequences when people start betting money they do not have.' Everything of value that he had acquired was liquidated to allow Gajanan to gamble, including his brick kiln. 'We even sold the utensils of the kitchen,' Rajkanya said, as she recalled the urgency of these debts. 'In the end, my son felt he had destroyed the household.' It had been a serious setback for Gajanan but the family regrouped and supported him. The farmer's household was used to failure, but had never anticipated the suicide. 'I never thought my son would kill himself. He just shut himself in the room and ended his life,' Rajkanya recollected with anguish.

There was an aspect of Gajanan's nature which was strong and uncompromising; he hated outstanding debts. He disliked being constantly reminded of the money he owed, and when he lost repeatedly in gambling, they snowballed, with the amounts multiplying. 'There was a gamblers' den where he was promised great returns. We could see that he had fallen into wrong company and we warned him about the consequences. But he was adamant that our lives must improve and that it could not be done through agriculture. There were loans to be repaid, but now, there was no money.' She paused for a moment and continued affectionately, 'He had been my best child. He was always the most understanding and sensitive to all aspects of a problem or a situation. He created trouble for us only in the last three years of his life when he tried to fund his businesses through gambling,' she said. Bhimrao added, 'He used to say that because of his actions, he had made beggars of his entire family. Death was like a punishment he imposed up on himself.'

Ten days after Gajanan's death, Archana left her in-laws' home after completing the last rituals. She could have stayed and continued living as his widow, but even his parents wanted her to begin a new life and put the past behind her. Bhimrao said, 'It was not her fault, it was our son's fault. He should not have destroyed his life chasing impossible dreams. She had no role to play, she was innocent.' They had sent her back to her parents' home in the hope that she would marry again. They had even returned the gifts the marriage had brought for the household; about Rs 2 lakh was spent on the occasion. Rajkanya and Bhimrao did not explain these facts to elaborate on their own sense of justice but as a tribute to their son's memory and his widow's future. This quiet gesture would stand in stark contrast to the traditionalists who would oppose the remarriage of a widow. This simple fairness was common to the nature of an ordinary Indian and it made the Dhawdes send away Archana with a sense of regret, and their blessings. As the case was found to be eligible, Archana had received the compensation from the state, out of which Rs 30,000 was deposited in her bank account.

The condition of the family remained the same; they held a ration card, and obtained 15 kg of wheat and rice for Rs 60 a month. In 2015, less than two years after Gajanan's suicide, each member had to work to support the family; some did it through agriculture on the farm, others as daily-wage labourers. The yearly income of the family through agriculture as discovered by the administration was Rs 25,000[6]—five members had survived on this amount every year. In 2015, there had been no improvement in either their income or the productivity of their land. For Rajkanya and Bhimrao, the only expectation of happiness was from Archana. Smiles lit up their faces as they spoke about the possibility that she could be married again. Archana had kept in touch and visited them on festivals or special days. It was a bond of affection and love that was strengthened by shared tragedy. In a way, Archana reminded his parents of their son, and their dreams for him lived on in her life and achievements.

★★★

Archana was married in 2015 and had a child, Aradhya, in 2016. They lived in Sakri village in Daryapur tehsil in 2017.

Earlier in 2016, 28-year-old Rameshwar, Gajanan's younger brother, had been at home in Kharpi. He worked on their 10-acre land and also as a labourer for daily wages. He recalled the circumstances before his brother's suicide. 'Gajanan was a good man, but he had taken a loan in the name of our parents because of which he was under a lot of pressure. The recovery process had begun, and when he could not repay the loan, they seized the tractor he had bought.' The instalments per month of Rs 72, 223[7] were almost impossible to pay, he said. 'I suggested to my brother that we should sell the land to repay the tractor loan. But he refused, and said that the land could not be lost in this manner.' The family still struggled with the pending loan and was even summoned by the lending agency that demanded the repayment. Rameshwar did not expect the future to be any different from the difficult past, and said that there would never be enough profit to increase the size of the land even by one acre. He expected to get married, but only after there had been one good crop to count on.

Archana had remarried in May 2015, and although the Dhawdes were all invited, no one had attended the event for her sake. 'It might have been awkward for her. She knew we all wish her to be happy. We told her family that we wanted Archana to be remarried and hoped our relationship continued,' Rameshwar said. Rajkanya appeared more fragile in 2016 than before. 'Perhaps, I miss my son more because I stay at home and get the time to remember him. And now, even Archana is married.'

The affection the Dhawdes still had for Archana was evident among her own family that gathered for the interview in 2016 at her mother's home in Daryapur tehsil's Adula Bazar village. The small residence had a difficult access through a narrow lane along an open drain. The low doorway led to a front yard and the dark house was lit by a single bulb. Archana was married on 27 May 2015 to 26-year-old Sunil Deshmukh, a farmer who owned 4 acres and cultivated pulses. He was educated up to Class 10.

Referring to her own education—she had studied up to Class 12—Archana said, 'I wanted to study further and become someone of consequence in my life. But what could I do, I had to get married.' She wore a subdued green printed sari and new jewellery. Sunil remained silent, listening to her with attention and respect. When asked about his marriage, he said, 'I believe this should be the norm, not an exception. I hope more people follow this tradition and remarry.' He had refused to accept any gifts at the wedding, a step that had gathered him great admiration in the community. There had only been the *mangalsutra*[8] for Archana, a wedding ring for him, and a few new clothes. There had been 700 guests on the occasion. 'I live with my brothers and their families. We all cultivate the land together and we are happy,' he said, referring to Archana's new home, in the nearby village of Sakri, 10 km away.

At her home in Adula Bazar, were also Archana's younger brother, Gyaneshwar, younger sister Sadhna, and their mother

FIGURE 40   Archana with her husband Sunil Deshmukh, August 2016.
Source: Author

Subhadra Bhawne. Sadhna was completing her graduation and awaited an eye-correction operation before continuing her studies. Gyaneshwar was educated up to Class 12. About Gajanan, Gyaneshwar said, 'He was a very good man, always respectful and quiet. He wanted to do business as he felt there was no profit in agriculture, and invested in the tractor and the brick kiln. Unfortunately, neither worked out.'

It was 45-year-old Subhadra who had brought Archana home after Gajanan's last rites. A mutual relative, aware that Archana had returned home, spoke about the match with Sunil. Subhadra said, 'Sunil's family had met Archana before. It worked out perfectly, as Sunil and Archana are well matched.' The couple had been blessed with a daughter, Aradhya. About a year old in 2017, she was growing up to be healthy baby. Archana said she was happy, and that was easy to believe going by the way Sunil wanted to fulfill her wish for a sewing machine.

Subhadra herself was educated up to Class 10 and had never been a beneficiary of any government welfare scheme. Her husband, Bhaskar, had died of an illness about 15 years ago. The household survived due to Subhadra's agency, which had also made Archana's remarriage possible. There was a calm force and decision about her that was reassuring to her family. She explained, 'After my husband died, I went through very difficult times. I worked as a farm labourer and, when there was no work on the farms, I carried bricks on my head at construction sites so that I could feed my children.' These experiences had taught her hard lessons: 'Everything is transitory. We may face bad times, but even they shall pass.'

Perhaps this was a higher level of humanity that lived in the lightless rooms of poverty in rural India—men like Sunil who did not accept dowry for marriage and women like Subhadra who did not accept defeat. Or, perhaps, this was the real India.

Notes

1. Police statement of the death report signed by the police in-charge.
2. Memorandum of a post-mortem examination of Gajanan Dhawde, on 20 January 2013.
3. Letter from the tehsildar, Chandur Bazar, through the SDO, to the district collector of Amravati.
4. Letter from the tehsildar, Chandur Bazar, through the SDO, to the district collector of Amravati.
5. Letter from the tehsildar, Chandur Bazar, through the SDO, to the district collector of Amravati.
6. Statement of income of Gajanan Dhawde recorded by the talathi on 11 March 2013.
7. Demand notice of loan agreement signed by Bhimrao Dhawde, on 11 December 2010.
8. The sacred thread is a symbol of Hindu marriage usually worn by women with gold embellishments.

CHAPTER
SEVENTEEN

The Dependent World
of a Widow

Vaishali Sambde, Ganoja Devi Village, Bhatkuli Tehsil,
Amravati District

A Widow Since 17 August 2007

Each death leaves a space that can never be filled. This was never
truer than in the case of Vaishali Sambde, widow of Om Prakash,
who killed himself in August 2007 just three years after their marriage at his home in Ganoja Devi village. Vaishali was 30 years old
at the time, and the mother of two-year-old daughter, Gayatri. In
an instant, her life had changed. A widow's position in Indian society has always been tenuous; without a male member of the family
to support her, patriarchal society seems at a loss about how to
account for her. Her participation in social and religious practices
in the community is restricted, but even within the family her existence is the responsibility of other male members who have their
own families to care for. Her husband's death immediately plum-
meted the widow into this position of dependence, and she was
subject to the generosity of others and on her own 'good' conduct.

A widow could lighten the burden on her family by supporting herself and her children financially. But as poor parents sought to invest in the education of boys rather than girls, many widows were not qualified for employment and were forced to work as farm labourers. Welfare schemes like anganwadi[1] were designed to support the income of women. In most cases, however, the widow, owing to her lack of education, did not qualify for the job. Even when she was qualified, she needed the help of a male member of the family to do the paperwork for such schemes, get approvals and recommendations, and visit the government offices.

The only scheme that helped the widow directly was the compensation that the state offered in case of a farmer suicide due to debt and crop failure. To get the Rs 1 lakh compensation, the widow had to provide evidence about how her husband had been unable to repay loans and, therefore, committed suicide. This process took place in the wake of the death and while the widow grieved for her husband. In Vaishali's case, she herself had to go to the administrative offices of the area to get her compensation; the state machinery had called her to process the paperwork. The compensation was given to her in the form of a cheque, of which Rs 30,000[2] was released immediately and Rs 70,000[3] was given after six years of Om Prakash's death. This division of the compensation seemed a tacit recognition of the difficult circumstances in which a widow lived where the money could be wrested away from her control. The money was sanctioned in December 2007, four months after the suicide, with the tehsildar of Bhatkuli witnessing the payment of Rs 30,000 to Vaishali. The second part of the payment of Rs 70,000 was put in a fixed deposit[4] for her to access after a period of six years. This was conveyed by the tehsildar to the postmaster of Amravati in a letter[5] that also explained how Rs 30,000 had been given to the family for their use. The passbook showed that the account was jointly held with the tehsildar so that the amount could not be released without his knowledge or approval.

Vaishali had been married for three years when Om Prakash died, leaving her amid people she was just about getting to know well. He was 30 years old when he killed himself by consuming poison at his home and was rushed to a hospital in Amravati where he had subsequently died. The records stated that he had supported six members of the family, had taken a loan of Rs 37,300 from a lending agency that had been pending for at least two years, cultivated cotton on an 8-acre land, and killed himself when the crop failed to make profit. In her statement, Vaishali said that he had struggled to repay old loans[6] and had even sold some of her jewellery to fund agriculture. As the size of the family was large, and it was his responsibility to support it, he was under constant pressure to sustain the household. Since loans were crucial for survival, and defaulters were not given new loans by banks, private moneylenders charged exorbitant interest rates. When the cotton and soybean crops failed consistently for two years, Om Prakash's hopes failed as well. He had shared his anguish with his wife that he had no money left; aware of their precarious situation, Vaishali already worked as farm labour on daily wages to support the family. In the days before his suicide, Om Prakash had been listless and silent, she said in her statement. She felt that he might have taken the extreme step because he believed suicide to be the only way out of his situation.

In 2015, she had sat alone in her room, which was a little away from the rest of the household. Only one portrait hung on the walls, the picture of her late husband. The single shelf in the room held objects of religious importance representing various pilgrimages in the country. This set-up was consistent with the traditional notion that a woman should focus on religion once her husband was dead. She was eager to speak about the conditions that had led to his suicide. Vaishali said, 'There was no water on my husband's farm, because it was not irrigated. There was not even a well and he struggled to keep the crops from dying. It took hard work to get a proper yield, which had always been very low.' While the fields yearned for water, when the rains did come, they washed away the crops in 2007, along with Om Prakash's plans to earn enough profit to support his family and repay the loans. In retrospect, however, the crisis that killed Om Prakash seemed to be much lesser than the one Vaishali faced after his death. 'I am now always dependent on someone or the other. People help me financially sometimes, but no one has that kind of money in these parts to help me all the time. But I understand the compulsions of other people,' she said.

It was possible that the community had expressed its inability to help her, just as her parents might have. They lived in the same tehsil but she said they were poor. The widow, in any case, was the responsibility of her husband's family; that was how the burden of the daughter was shed by her parents. It was unlikely that it would be taken up again, especially if there were other unmarried girls in the family. Vaishali, however, was at peace with such a world and did not grudge anyone the choice of ignoring her. She did not speak extensively about her experiences, but her long and frequent silences did. She knew she needed an identity beyond being a widow, and that could only come through an income. 'I earn my own living. I have bought a second-hand sewing machine for Rs 2,000 and I do what I can to earn from it. But I do not get enough work, so the income is not regular,' she said. It was difficult to imagine that she was member of a family that owned a ration shop for the last 31 years, once allotted to her father-in-law. A ration shop, which was not an easy licence to get, provided subsidized food and fuel to the poor. The Sambde family itself had a card that said they were a BPL[7] family. 'I have to live by what I earn, I have no option,' she continued. 'I have a child and I must contribute to the family in any way I can.' Her daughter, Gayatri, was 10 years old in 2015 and studied in Class 5 at a private, English-medium school in Bhatkuli.

FIGURE 41   Vaishali Sambde with her daughter Gayatri (centre),
January 2015
Source: Author

At the time of Om Prakash's death, his younger brother Ashok
had been 25 years old. In his statement to the administration, he
said that the low crop yields in 2005 and 2006, and lack of money
to either repay old loans or fund the new crop, might have led
Om Prakash to commit suicide. He reiterated this view when he
spoke to us in 2015. 'We have had the land for 30 years or more.
The only help with irrigation we ever had was when, once under
a government scheme, we got Rs 10,000 for sinking a well after
waiting for two years. But that amount was only partially useful
as the cost of the well was much more.' The scheme for the well
was given to the poor and dry-land farmers who had no source
of irrigation.[8] The crop cultivated on the land had always been
cotton, soybean, and tur. He said, 'The earlier local variety of
cotton did not require as much irrigation as the new seeds do.
We stopped cultivating cotton for almost 10 to 12 years when the
new seeds were introduced. Then when we began again, we got
only four quintals of cotton from four acres.'

So why cultivate cotton at all? He said the options were worse; the soybean yield had been even lesser than cotton at 1.75 quintals for 4 acres. 'We keep sowing cotton hoping that next year, maybe, the crop will be better. But we have not yet got that one year of good crop that would take care of us for some time.' They got relief for low productivity of Rs 4,500 per hectare[9] and their land was 8 acres or roughly equivalent to a little over 3 hectares. That was not much of a relief, but Ashok was happy that he did not have to run around for the paperwork. 'The patwari [village official] knew the yield of the land and so the relief amount came directly into our bank accounts,' he said. It was difficult to pay for the expenses of the family solely from the earnings of the ration shop. 'All we earn from the ration shop in profits gets paid in bills,' Ashok said, and added that electricity cost Rs 500 per month while the water bill was Rs 2,000 annually. It was still a large family, with four children, three of whom went to school. 'The school fee for all the children together is about Rs 1 lakh annually, and the cost of commuting to the school in Bhatkuli is Rs 15,000,' he said.

Agriculture continued to be the only hope for Ashok to support the family, even if it had led to the death of his brother. As with all farmers, he lived on hope. He hoped that if there were irrigation facilities provided through a borewell, the problems of low productivity would be solved. Added to that, he wished there would be some provision for building a boundary wall around the fields so that the crops were not ravaged by wild animals. Presently, a guard had been employed at a salary of Rs 5,000 together by all the farmers of the neighbouring fields to protect the crops from the menace of monkeys and other animals. Ashok knew that these requirements would never be fulfilled by the government and he could not afford to get a borewell on his own or build a boundary wall. Even the state could not afford the proliferation of borewells and the associated problems of contamination, along with low water yields. But no official or politician had the time to address Ashok's requirements and educate him on the right choices.

Vaishali knew the cost of the neglect on the part of the state and she knew the price Ashok paid by waiting. She had stood through the interview with her eyes lowered most of the time, as if lost in some other place, in some other grief. But now she glanced up and the sadness spilled into the room. She asked if there was no one who could help farmers like them, people who were ready to work hard but whose lands were uncultivable. She had been a silent observer of the failure of the administration to help the farmers, and asked who would provide redress if the state did not even notice their problems. She wondered about the local elected representative's negligence of the village. 'There are a total of 250 houses in this village with an approximate population of 5,000 people,' she said, with her impressive knowledge about the village. 'And yet, I have never seen the elected representative to the state Legislative Assembly return to check on those among his voters, who struggled to even survive.'

The vote should have been a tangible choice to improve her future. She disagreed, and said, 'I vote for one candidate, and when that person does not deliver, I vote for the other. What else can I do? Things do not change for us. They [the candidates in elections] make lofty promises about things that really do not make an impact to our lives. They never promise us things we need, and things we should have already had.' She referred to farmers like her husband who toiled hard on dry lands with crops that did not yield without proper irrigation. She remarked help-lessly, 'I hope someone will improve our lives someday so that farmers do not kill themselves.'

Throughout the interview, the young Gayatri heard every word intently. She might not remember her father, but over the last nine years she had repeatedly heard that his death had been for nothing. She must know by now that his suicide had not changed anything for her or her mother; in fact, it had only made things more difficult. Also, it must be evident to her through the con-tinuing struggles of her mother that the state was absent from their life, as if their troubles were of their own making. It was unlikely that Gayatri would become a farmer; girls did not inherit their father's land. In this case, that would be a blessing. On her part, Vaishali seemed to ensure that Gayatri would never be dependent on anyone, as she herself had been. Education was her blessing to Gayatri, and Vaishali lived every moment to fulfil that.

★★★

Vaishali's humble plans, however, were not easy to achieve. In July 2017, Gayatri could not afford tuitions due to which, according to Vaishali, her daughter's grades suffered in school.

Earlier in August 2016, it had been raining heavily in Ganoja Devi, as if the monsoons were making up for the last two very dry seasons. Vaishali had lost weight and Gayatri, had grown taller—and quieter.

Vaishali felt the situation had remained the same as 2015, and she did not expect any improvement. But she recalled how her world had changed since the death of her husband. 'In those days, I did not know about the income or loans, and my husband never told me. Now I do. I work on the sewing machine now and work as farm labour for daily wages. There is not enough work, except during the festival season,' she said. She had never trained for sewing and learnt on the job. A vacancy for an anganwadi scheme had opened in the village but the job had gone to a woman who was a graduate. She felt it should have been allotted according to need and not qualifications. But she still did not fight her battles; her brother-in-law Ashok did on her behalf. 'I go to the panchayat samiti [committee], the patwari office, and other places but Ashok speaks and I listen,' she said. Eleven-year-old Gayatri was in Class 6 and was learning to speak English. Vaishali said that her daughter got a scholarship of Rs 5,000 for one year and received Rs 400 per month as part of the Bal Sangopan Yojana (scheme),[10] which was yet to be paid for 2015.

The ration shop continued to support the family, along with the land on which soybean and tur were cultivated, and there was a new unpaid loan of Rs 50,000. The family had once again abandoned cotton due to lack of yield. A proposal for a common boundary wall around the fields never materialized as the neighbouring farmers could not share the financial burden.

Vaishali's mother-in-law, Suman Sambde, explained that the land had been in her name since the death of her husband, Triyambak, 15 years ago. She recalled how her husband had bought the land after toiling hard for 20 years and from the profits of selling vegetables. 'But now when my son is gone, I do not see the point of the land or agriculture. If these conditions continue, there will be no farmers, and no agriculture. We will have to just buy food, like they do in the cities,' she said. It will not matter, perhaps, if everyone has enough money to buy everything. But what about those who have no money? Even the rains did not care for the poor. Perhaps, that was why it rained with remorse in Ganoja Devi that afternoon.

☙

Notes

1. The Integrated Child Development Services (ICDS) describes an anganwadi worker as a community based worker chosen from the local community to work for the programme. She is expected to mobilize support for the care of young children, girls, and women. See www.icds-wcd.nic.in
2. Receipt of Rs 30, 000 received by Vaishali Sambde.
3. Receipt of Rs 70, 000 received by Vaishali Sambde.
4. Account under the Post Office Savings Scheme, which is signed by the postmaster.
5. Letter written by the tehsildar of Bhatkuli tehsil to the postmaster of Amravati, on 26 December 2013.
6. Statement of Vaishali Sambde recorded and presented by the talathi to the district administration of Amravati, in which the village of Ganoja Devi is situated, on 27 August 2007.

7. The Below Poverty Line (BPL) yardstick has been used by the Indian government as a tool to decide the economic status of a poor person. Those earning less than Rs 32 a day in a rural area or less than Rs 47 a day in an urban area fall under the BPL line. 'Report of The Expert Group to Review The Methodology For Measurement of Poverty', Planning Commission, Government of India, 2014, available at www.planningcommission.nic.in and 'New Poverty Line: Rs 32 in villages, Rs 47 in cities', *Times of India*, 7 July 2014, available at www.timesofindia.indiatimes.com/india/New-poverty-line-Rs-32-in-villages-Rs-47-in-cities/articleshow/37920441. cms?from=mdr, last accessed 12 December 2017.

Broadly, the debates over the BPL and APL (Above Poverty Line) are that it is difficult to qualify for BPL benefits, as 74.52 per cent of the rural population lives on a household income of less than Rs 5,000 per month (see 'Social Economic and Caste Census 2011', Government of India, available at: www.secc.gov.in, last accessed 12 December 2017); that the international standards set to measure poverty are unfair to developing countries (see Sanjay Reddy and Thomas Pogge, *How Not to Count the Poor, 2005,* available at www. papers.ssrn.com, accessed 6 July 2017); and, that large-scale corruption, government irregularities, and bureaucratic malpractices were affecting the issuing of BPL cards. Therefore, the BPL list failed to capture ground realities of the poor, as also observed in the 18 cases in this book.

8. In January 2014, the Government of Maharashtra approved Rs 20,000 crore to the Dryland Farming Mission under the Bharat Nirman campaign to integrate central and state schemes to improve the condition of dry-land farmers. See PTI, 'Maha to Undertake Rs 20,000 Cr Programme for Dryland Farming', *Business Standard,* 9 July 2014. Available at www.business-standard.com/article/pti-stories/maha-to-undertake-rs-20-000-cr-programme-for-dryland-farming-114010901200_1.html, accessed 6 July 2017.

9. The Government of India announced relief package of Rs 3,750 crore for the families of farmers who had committed suicide in Vidarbha. It included waiving of interest on overdue loans and rescheduling of interest for three to five years. Additionally, the state government announced a relief package of Rs 1,075 crore for affected families. This was followed by the announcement of the 2008 Loan Waiver. Narendra Jadhav, 'Farmers' Suicide and

Debt Waiver: An Action Plan for Agricultural Development of Maharashtra', Farmers' Suicide Prevention Packages Evaluation Committee, Government of Maharashtra, 2008, pp. 1–16.

10. According to the Government of Maharashtra's Women and Child Development Department's website, the Bal Sangopan Yojana (scheme) provides assistance to children whose parents are not able to take care of them owing to difficult circumstances. See www. womenchild.maharashtra.gov.in

CHAPTER
EIGHTEEN

Her Place under the Sun

Lata Patil, Borala Village, Chandur Bazar Tehsil, Amravati District

A Widow Since 2 March 2003

When the status of the woman is mainly dependent on her marriage, the death of the husband leaves her in a grey area that has no contours. Not only does society impose ambiguity on the widow and curtail her rights, but it expects her to welcome such conduct. The status of the woman, always dependent on circumstances, is untenable when she becomes a widow. Within her in-laws' household, where most widows live, she is an anomaly who does not fit into any social, religious, or cultural structure. Her lack of identity is also permanent and seen as the work of destiny that cannot be altered. More importantly, she cannot improve her destiny because anything she achieves will always be unequal to what she has lost. Therefore, she requires the benevolence and kindness of her in-laws who provide her not only with shelter and security, but also a place in society. This is not easy; she faces discrimination as much in her home as she does outside. But for a woman with barely any education and almost no awareness, this facilitates a safe, albeit, dependent life. Women accept this because the difficulty they face in their husband's household is less than the challenge of surviving alone in the world.

Lata Patil was not one such widow. At my first meeting with her in 2015, though, she appeared to be exactly the kind of woman who would tolerate the injustices of her life for the sake of her children and their future. But by 2016, it became clear that she was made of sterner stuff.

The paved lanes of Borala village served another purpose on that day in January 2015; a festival feast was laid out under the resting shades of trees, and laughter and conversation filled that shimmering winter afternoon. Lata's house was deep inside the village, a brown spot of crumbling mud walls that fought a losing battle with nature. The boundary was thick brown vegetation that had now dried to a twig and a gate opened into the narrow front yard that held a well. It had been 12 years that she had lived in that house with her brother-in-law and his family. She had not cultivated cotton on her 2-acre farm for 10 of those 12 years. She explained that was because there were no irrigation facilities on the farm, and she did not want to waste money on a crop that required water. Instead, she planted soybean and pulses, which yielded 6 to 7 quintals. It was never enough, she said, but at least she did not make losses.

The land was transferred to her name after the death of her husband, Sahebrao Patil. He had killed himself by consuming poison on his farm; Lata had been home with the children at that time. She had discovered later that he had an unpaid loan of Rs 44,000, which had since then become her responsibility. In 2011, finally, she had managed to repay half of it. Besides farming, the only other source of income for Lata had been from work as a farm labourer on daily wages. In 2015, her daughter, Poonam was in Class 11 in school; her son Pratik was in Class 8. Their education was her main expense and she struggled to meet it. She spoke confidently despite the difficult circumstances, 'I would like to do all I can, and for as long as I have strength in my arms. I can work hard to ensure the dreams of my children are fulfilled.' Her daughter wanted to be a graduate and Lata encouraged her to study well, while her son had begun getting a grant of Rs 5,000 per year under the Bal Sangopan Yojana (scheme).[1] The bus passes of both children cost Rs 400, roughly equivalent to the amount Lata earned by working for two to four days as daily labour on the farms.

Sahebrao had died in 2003 because of a decisive crop failure that had left all his expenses unpaid and made funding the next crop impossible. She remembered him with affection as she said, 'He used to think out everything carefully before implementing any decision. He was deeply concerned for his family and, when things got worse financially, he could not bear to see us suffer.' His suicide was found eligible for compensation by the administration. Of the Rs 1 lakh that Lata was awarded, she had invested Rs 30,000 on the farm and kept Rs 70,000 in the bank. Her children remembered little of their father; Poonam had been five years old and Pratik had been only two-and-a-half years old at the time of his death.

In a way, Lata's mind was the last repository of her husband's memories. There had been times in the past several years when she had lost hope and wanted to merge with those memories. Her eyes turned moist as she said, 'It was difficult to survive with two young children and there were times when I too wanted to end my life. Then I forced myself to live one day at a time, for the sake of my children.' From absolute despair, she learned to hope again. However, she said, 'I found that times changed and things improved. Nothing happens by itself, and hope is not enough. I had to learn to think about the future of my children and plan for them. I discovered that I need not be dependent on the family for survival. I could fight my own battles.' She had negotiated the hurdles of life through the assistance of the community more than her family, and learnt to deal with the helplessness of her situation.

The old hut and the decrepit premises were where the families of the two brothers spent their life in close proximity and shared the bills for power, water, and groceries. The space shrunk when there was conflict, and when relationships were strained with unhappy compromises. Lata appeared weighed down by the troubles of living in the household, and reconciled to the desperation for an escape. As a habit, she derived relief from looking beyond immediate problems, but no solution appeared possible even in the future. At least, not in 2015.

★★★

In 2017, Pratik was in Class 11 and worked in the fields, while Poonam had continued with graduation in Home Science.

Earlier in August 2016, the little brown hut had appeared to still face impossible odds and an indifferent fate. Its pessimistic walls seemed resilient enough to dampen the spirit of the residents, and it seemed that Lata could have been lost within this structure. However, Lata was not to be found within these premises in 2016; she lived in a house across a small lane. It was a house of her own, constructed with the loan given to her under a government scheme for widows.[2] While she had applied several years ago, Lata had lost all hope and was surprised when unexpectedly one day, she was sanctioned the loan. It had changed her life.

There was a sense of justice about the location of the house that stood across the lane from the old hut where she had spent over a decade struggling to find an identity. The house was built on a small unoccupied plot of land in 2015. It had no boundary wall and had served as storage for fodder for the cattle from the neighbouring houses. When the loan was sanctioned, she bought this land and started construction on it. It had not been easy but Lata was no stranger to difficult times. She explained, 'I got Rs 95,000 under the government scheme as a loan, and then I sold my portion of the old hut to my in-laws for Rs 40,000. Using that money, I bought the 800 square feet of land for Rs 1.5 lakh

FIGURE 42 Lata Patil at her new house, August 2016
Source: Author

and, with an additional private loan, constructed my house.' Her
house contained three rooms and a smart stable for a new cow
she had named Kapila. There were two entrances to the house,
and Lata wondered if she should shut the gate that opened out
towards her old hut, and her old life.

The transition had not been smooth; widows in Vidarbha were invisible, inaudible shadows. There was friction as Lata demanded a place of her own under the sun. Her thinking was too incisive not to address the source of the problem. 'There is an issue about dealing with widows in our society; everyone is used to seeing them as dependents who live a subordinate life and die in vagueness. I could sense that my family was uneasy with the positive transformation in my life. They accepted me when I was in the grey world of the widow who had no voice or rights, but they did not know how to support me when I sought a better destiny. I have understood that now,' she remarked. Ironically, she explained that Sahebrao's family had wished many times since 2003 that they did not have to carry the burden of Lata and her children. The arrangement had been that she should share the cost of living equally with others, even though she was the only person to take care of her children. And yet, when she became independent of the family, they resented her freedom. She reflected on those times, 'I never expected the men in the family to think for me; how would they know what it was like to be a single, unsupported woman? But even the women in the family did not take my side and that always hurt me. And when I sought to leave them and move away, I was criticized even more.'

She remained the sole earner for her family, and the results of her efforts to cultivate her 2-acre land were not very happy in August 2016. Owing to the heavy rains, soybean had to be sown twice at a cost of Rs 20,000 each time and even in 2015, she lost the crop to disease. She hoped that the continued good monsoons might help the second crop to recover enough to balance the losses that she had already incurred. She continued to work as farm labour on daily wages, but had been unable to clear the rest of her husband's loan that continued to grow with interest. She said, 'The bank tells me every time they see me that I should repay or I will not get a new loan. I ask them how I am supposed to repay them. Everyone knows my financial condition, then how do they expect me to repay?' She was content to manage without a formal loan and borrowed from private moneylenders.

Poonam was then in her first year of graduation in Home Science; she had also learnt sewing and hospitality at an Industrial Training Institute in Chandur Bazar, also the tehsil's headquarters, about 20 km from the village. It was clear that Lata wanted an education for her daughter that could financially support her in life. She explained, 'Every moment of my life is spent in planning on how to pay for my daughter's education. I want her to find a career for herself and get a job. I do not want her to be dependent, the way I had been. I want her to do something with her life and not be at the mercy of others. There is nothing else I can give her except for education.' But education cost money; both Poonam and Pratik, who was in Class 10 in 2016, studied in Chandur Bazar. The total expense for the children was about Rs 40,000, which Lata paid mainly through private loans and farm labour. She expected both children to move out of the village and find paying jobs. About her future, she said, 'I will go and live with my children wherever they are to help them with their lives. I have proved a point to the community and my family by building this house and now I can leave this place and strive for a better life.' Agriculture did not figure in her future scheme at all. 'I have never even taught my children how to work in the fields—I have never even taken them there. Without irrigation facilities, what would I have taught them anyway? That they should cultivate the soil, sow the seeds, and wait for the rains?' That was a crucial question and she seemed to have found the only answer. 'My children cannot do agriculture and will not work as farm labour; they do not know how to. The only thing they know is education and what they learn in school, and that is how I want it to be.'

As she carefully planned the future, Lata constantly drew her strength from the past. She said, 'I keep thinking that if only my husband had told me about how anxious he had been about the loan, I would have helped him somehow. But in those days, no one really knew I could think of solutions. It was, perhaps, my mistake that I never tried to explore how he paid for food and other expenses, or how he ran the household. I was like any other woman who is taught only to manage the children and stay at home. I wish I had been much stronger then, like I am now, and perhaps, I could have helped my husband live.'

As she moved from one goal in her life to the next, the need for a companion was more practical than emotional. She wished there was someone to follow up on the complaints or applications but in reality, she was independent and supported by her own intelligence. Also, she no longer thought of death herself, as she had done in 2015. 'I often wonder what my husband was thinking when he killed himself. Did he think about how we would eat, where we would live, and how we would survive without him? He escaped and did a favour to himself. But where did that leave us?' There was no anger as she articulated these thoughts. Then she smiled and explained, 'I too have pesticide for the farm. It is so easy to die, but I want to win in a situation, and not escape.' Her house was the evidence of her conviction and she requested that she be photographed next to it. It was a good photograph, and Lata was very pleased to see it. That bright afternoon at her house, there seemed to be no place for shadows in Vidarbha.

❧

Notes

1. According to the Government of Maharashtra's Women and Child Development Department's website, the Bal Sangopan Yojana (scheme) provides assistance to children whose parents are not able to take care of them owing to difficult circumstances. See www.womenchild.maharashtra.gov.in
2. The Government of Maharasthra's Gharkul Yojana (scheme) provides financial assistance for homes to widows, members of Scheduled Castes and Scheduled Tribes, next of kin to defence personnel killed in action, minorities, and BPL category households.

The district rural development agencies and panchayats identified the beneficiaries, and the house was allotted in the name of the woman of the family. See: DNA, 'Maharashtra Govt to Build 1.86 Lakh Houses for Backward Class', 26 July 2011, available at www.dnaindia.com/mumbai/report-maharashtra-govt-to-build-186-lakh-houses-for-backward-class-1569571, last accessed 18 December 2017. Also see: www.pmayg.nic.in

Conclusion

'There is no choice but to succeed.'
A widow of Vidarbha

Part I

The stories of the widows of Vidarbha were studied in this book through the narratives of the families of the farmers who committed suicide. The narratives were gathered between 2014 and 2017, from Yavatmal and Amravati districts of Maharashtra. Farmer suicides committed between 2001 until 2014 were considered in the study, and the widows were in the age group of 26 to 63 years (see Appendix 1 and 2). For every family, expenses, loans, yield, gains, and losses were recorded along with qualitative descriptions about the state of their lives, successes, failures, and expectations. The research yielded findings about the lives of the widows and their children after the farmers committed suicide in Vidarbha, and about the impact of state intervention.

The 18 suicides explored in this study took place between 2002 and 2014, with four cases in 2013, three cases in 2014, three cases in 2012, two in 2011, three cases in 2007 and one each in 2005, 2003, and 2002. A representative number from earlier years was taken to learn how the widows had fared over a decade since the death of their husbands, while higher numbers were chosen from later years to address more contemporary problems.[1] Among the differences observed in the narratives between the earlier and later years of the farm crisis were a marked increase in the minimum support price of cotton, from approximately Rs 1,675 per quintal in 2002[2] to Rs 3,750 per quintal in 2014;[3] increase in its cost of cultivation from Rs 21,083.24 per hectare (roughly equivalent to 2.47 acres) in 2002–3[4] to over Rs 73,232.07 per hectare in 2013–14;[5] decrease in rainfall, the falling yields of cotton and soybean, and the increase in crop diversification. The three widows from the earlier years, Jayashri Sawankar of Sirasgaon, Lata Patil of Borala, and Mira Dike of Dhabdi, were found to be strong and confident, with a clear vision of what they wanted for their children and how to achieve it. In all the cases, they sought education for their children as a way to provide them security against difficult times. Every widow from the earlier years had struggled for state support and had partially achieved it. While Lata had built a home for herself with the assistance of a government scheme,[6] Jayashri held on to her part-time attendant (PTA) work at the medical dispensary and Mira saved the money awarded by the state as compensation for the death of her husband to marry off her daughter.

The widows from the later years seemed to be at the beginning of their struggle and faced rejection by the state or their local village representatives of their applications for welfare. While Vandana Rathod of Ajanti and Anjana Katekar of Pedi had not yet applied for any welfare scheme until the writing of this book, Manjubai Rathod of Son Wadhona, had just begun to enquire about the paperwork. A similar reluctance to explore the schemes, along with lack of awareness about them, was found among two of the three women who had been widows since 2007. As an experiment, all the widows and their families were given details about how to contact the departments concerned with welfare, either for families of farmers who had killed themselves in Yavatmal and Amravati, or for farmers facing distress. During this research, only one family each in the two districts had approached the relevant officers in the administration to enquire about the paperwork. The trend also revealed an indifference towards the state's schemes and its promise of assistance, along with an assumption of the prevalence of corruption in the selection process. Poor families did not want to waste limited time and resources in chasing such schemes without any hope of success. Widows from recent years shared a higher degree of pessimism than those from earlier years, which was indicative of their conclusions based on experience of the state apathy towards those who needed welfare.

Of the 18 cases, only four widows were educated up to Class 12 and four more were educated up to Class 10, while the rest had dropped out during school. Most of them had been married when they reached or passed out of Class 10. The older women, like Gayabai Zhambre of Sonkhas and Bhagirathi Harale of Pala had not received any schooling at all. Education—or the lack thereof—had a considerable impact on a widow's circumstances, but did not receive enough attention during her childhood. In cases like Vaishali Sambde of Ganoja Devi, Jyoti Bhumbar of Ashtgaon, and Sunita Utkhede of Utkhed, they did not qualify for government schemes like anganwadi due to lack of adequate educational qualifications. This limited their opportunities and decision-making capacity about the future of their children. There were cases like Sunita Dhale, who said that she could have written her own statement to the administration but was denied due to the procedure. Lack of education created dependence among the widows as they were deprived of qualified positions and had to depend on the guidance of the more educated among the family and society.

The most common occupation among the widows was, therefore, farm labour, besides cultivation of their own field. In almost all cases, widows worked as farm labour on daily wages earning between Rs 100 and Rs 150 for six hours, and usually did two shifts, in the morning and afternoon. In all cases, working as farm labour constituted an important source of income for the family; in this, even the children and elderly were involved. Children who were studying or were very young were exempted from working on the farm, which was seen as a training that could be useful when required. It was only in case of Lata Patil that she particularly kept the children away from agriculture and believed they would not need to work as farm labour. Where the children were old enough to work on the fields, they worked on weekends when their schools were shut. Labour on daily wages was the only dependable source of income for the widows, even when they had school education. Based on their own experience, the widows ensured that the children were trained as farm labour so that they could work for daily wages, if required. It showed a deep distrust of the education system and employment opportunities that left the rural poor with no other option but to work as labour.

Land fragmentation was found to be a crucial factor weighed against the survival of the widow and her children on agriculture. Of the 18 cases, four widows held less than 3 acres of land, nine held less than 6 acres of land, two had less than 10 acres of land, and three had 10 acres and more. Children of two among the four widows who had less than 3 acres—Pushpabai Raut of Ghatanji and Rekha Tingde of Kharpi—no longer depended on their land for support, and sought to either lease better land or leave agriculture for good. The three widows who owned between 10 and 15 acres shared the profits with the entire household, therefore, diminishing individual advantage to themselves and increasing household risk in case of crop failure. None of the farmers had enhanced their farm holdings since the 1970s–90s, and had not been able to buy new acres to add to their farms. Farmers of the earlier generation, like Suryabhan Nandagawli of Adgaon, still argued that agriculture contained a certainty that no other occupation did, while those of the new generation, like Rajesh Bhumbar of Ashtgaon had already moved on to other businesses. In comparison to other occupations, agriculture appeared to be highly risky and was increasingly being conducted either out of helplessness or sentiment, rather than choice.

Notably, the farmers who had committed suicide had, on an average, defaulted on bank loans of approximately Rs 67,000 (inclusive/exclusive of interest*), and of the total 18 cases, only one loan was over Rs 2 lakh, which was taken under a housing scheme and not repaid due to crop failure. In all cases, the farmers had been extremely anxious about the unpaid loan and did not want to face the humiliation of the recovery process. However, in all cases, the farmers were refused new loans as they were default-ers and that closed their only avenue for repaying old loans—a new crop. The rules of the formal lending agencies were strictly followed in case of poor farmers, who eventually killed them-selves. The rules were followed even after the farmers' suicides and the loans were restructured for repayment by their families. As the Yavatmal administration explained during this reserach, there was no provision or scheme for waiving loans of farmers who had killed themselves because of inability to repay them. The rules of lending and repayment, notoriously violated by the wealthy and influential defaulters in India, squeezed every rupee out of the hands of the poor throughout their life and even after their death. Such disparities might have been hidden before from the citizens in earlier times, but this was a changed countryside that was fully informed through the social media. Such disparities were known to every last poor farmer and widow of Vidarbha.

The impact of the perception of these 16 women in 18 cases, especially after the death of their husbands, must have been expressed in their vote in several elections. There were 13 wid-ows between the ages of 30 and 50 years, who had been eligible to vote since 2004 and 1984, respectively. Those who could vote since 1984 would have, till the 2014 elections, participated in the Indian democratic system nine times to elect the Lok

---

* Please refer to Appendices 1 and 2.

Sabha in Parliament and seven times to elect the Maharashtra Legislative Assembly. Those who could vote since 2004 might have participated in three elections each for the Lok Sabha and the Maharashtra Legislative Assembly. Except for the turbulent 1990s of short-lived coalition governments, every vote had cost the widows five years of their life and had failed every time to bring about change for the better. The women, as Vaishali Sambde articulated, knew that their vote did not matter, and that their life could not improve through elections. The contempt expressed by farmers' families uniformly for forgotten election promises relegated the political class, as also the role of democracy, to the margins of the lives of the poor.

The legacy of disillusionment being passed on to the next generation was what the farmers and their widows desperately fought against. Altogether, 52 children were studied from 18 families, and their aspirations tracked for the period of research. Except for one post-graduate, the highest level of education among the children was graduation; the youngest was in Class 4. Many of the children were too young to remember their fathers' lives, but they had grown up listening to the causes for their death; the failing agriculture, the indifferent state, and the helpless community. The older children experienced the loss of their fathers' guidance and affection, witnessed the struggles of their mothers, and grappled with the despair they inherited. Where the children continued with agriculture, it was because they had dropped out of school, like in the case of Umesh Katekar in Pedi or Umesh Harale of Pala, to work with their fathers in the field.

There was a different destiny for boys and a different one reserved for girls, and neither was easy to achieve nor to live through. The girls were married in their late teens or early 20s, and usually when they turned 18. As a result, there were only two cases in which the daughters were enrolled in graduation. The fate of the daughters was also sealed because the government schemes that supported children's education did so only until

18 years of age. The widows sought further education for their daughters but were unable to afford it, especially in view of the expenses they would incur for their marriage. Typically, girls who passed out of school aspired to specialize in subjects that would get them a job, like Sushma Zhambre of Sonkhas who wanted to be a nurse or Payal Dhale of Chincholi who wanted to study Law. But like Sneha Dike of Dhabdi, the girls at this age knew their aspirations were futile and that they would be married in a short period of time. It was also unlikely for the daughters to continue any education after their marriage, as was seen in the case of Sneha who got married and had a child within the period of this research. As she herself had predicted, Sushma, too, got married despite her best efforts to train as a nurse. Growing up, however, the daughters believed they would get the opportunities denied to others, including their mothers. The younger among the children wanted to be airline pilots or policewomen, while the older children wanted to find a job as soon as possible, mainly through technical training courses.

Significantly, only daughters of those women who had been widows for a longer duration, studied for graduation. As mentioned before, the widows themselves were educated mostly until school, with no graduates among the 18 cases, and except in two cases, the same pattern was followed for the daughters. It was likely that the widows would opt to marry away their daughters rather than help them study further, despite their own unhappy experience due to lack of proper educational qualifications. This was mainly due to the uncertainty of the unmarried daughter's position in the community and to ensure she had the identity and security of her husband's name. Although it appeared that the widows put their daughters in the same position as themselves, it was not so in reality. Most of the young girls who had to stop their education or knew they studied only because a match for marriage was not yet available, carried a deep discontent in their hearts that did not bode well for the future of Vidarbha.

The destiny of the boys was equally based in assumptions, whether the children shared those views or not. The mothers played a limited role in deciding the future of their sons while their fathers were alive, and the difference could be seen between the earlier and the recent cases of farmer suicide. In the case of recent suicides, or those from 2011 till 2013, the farmer himself had the opportunity to guide his sons. Sons who had studied beyond school either opted away from agriculture or found an additional source of income like a business or employment. This was evident in the case of the families in Prahaladpur and Ghatanji, where the sons had moved away from agriculture much before the suicides had taken place. It was clear that their fathers had encouraged the sons to find occupation other than agriculture, which they had considered increasingly futile. After the farmers' suicide, the humiliation of unreturned loans only strengthened the conviction of the sons to leave agriculture for good. However, where the sons were not good with education, the fathers had encouraged them to work on the farms, like in the cases recorded in Pala, Pedi, and Utkhed. After their fathers' suicides, even these sons looked for different avenues of incomes that could reduce their dependence on agriculture, like a backyard flour mill, or local transportation. Notably, although there was anger among the older sons about the indifference of the state towards the troubles their fathers had faced before they died, it did not translate into an ideological position.

The role of the widows was more apparent in the case of younger sons, who considered their fathers' suicides to be either an act of helplessness or response to injustice. There was commitment to excel at education, unmediated by any role in agriculture, like in the case of 14-year-old Gaurav Bhumbar of Ashtgaon or 17-year-old Rohit Rathod of Ajanti (age as of 2017). Like in the case of daughters, the aspirations of the younger sons were far more diverse and ambitious than the sober plans of the elder ones. But even then, the sons brought up by the widows were committed to excel, like Aniket Dike of Dhabdi, Prashant Rathod of Son Wadhona, or Prajwal Utkhede of Utkhed. The mother was the voice of sons too young to decide, like in case of Adgaon and Borgaon, and pushed them to do better in their studies with the hope that they would find an alternative to agriculture. Like in the case of daughters brought up by widows, even the sons carried a sense of responsibility early and believed that failure was not an option in the struggle for survival.

In this struggle, however, the state played a marginal and unsteady role, especially as a source of support. Notwithstanding this, the state promoted its achievements as being uniform and regular, belying the reality on the ground. The most recent efforts of the state are discussed here. In 2015, the state supported a mission[7] in Amravati that proposed new crop loans to farmers in all 14 districts of the region with a fund of Rs 40,000 crore.[8] The mission also sought to relax the rules of loans to farmers to bring down suicide rates in the district. Similarly, Yavatmal had launched a campaign[9] in 2015 to address the requirements of families affected by farmer suicides and advertised that they provided assistance with the education of children, loans up to Rs 20,000 crore without interest, and assistance for higher education to all poor farmer families. According to documents provided by the Yavatmal administration, this three-year campaign had a fund of Rs 32 crore per annum through which every village was given Rs 1 lakh to be spent on the most distressed and needy in the village. The campaign already claimed to have had an impact in bringing down the suicide numbers by 45 per cent, a claim that was yet to be methodologically examined. It appeared rather unlikely that the state's claim would stand such a test as the deep-rooted problems of Vidarbha were more likely to be brushed under the carpet than solved in one year (inception in 2015). However, as it was one of the most damning empirical evidence of distress and of the state's neglect, the number of farmer suicides might be vulnerable to state reinterpretation and, perhaps, 'adjustment'.

The government schemes aimed at farmers and their families gave rise to, at first, hope and later, disappointment. Loan waivers, however, were popular with politicians for what they implied and not very popular with farmers for what they covered up. Loans typically were not cancelled under such schemes and were only restructured for the farmers to pay at a later date. The 2008 Loan Waiver proposed to address all outstanding loans given between 1 April 1997 and 31 March 2007. The audit reports found that the scheme had failed to achieve its goal due to errors in identification of beneficiaries, poor documentation and records, among other causes. In the 18 cases studied, none was given a loan waiver, although as the narratives showed, a majority of cases should have qualified for it. A similar disconnect between the state and the farmer led to the widows being deprived of not only benefits of the welfare schemes, but even information about the process. In many cases, the widows blamed the corruption at the level of panchayat samitis that led to such schemes being cornered by a select few in the village. Of the 18 cases, nine were identified as BPL and five got support for the education of their children. Most widows did not pursue the schemes as it meant incurring the expense of travelling to another village or town. At the same time, none of the widows reported that any representative of the state had voluntarily provided the paperwork or information about the schemes to them. The widows counted less on welfare to support their lives and more on the work as farm labour for daily wages. The narratives exposed the truth of welfare among rural poor being waylaid by the state at every level, from information to disbursal. Importantly, the few cases where the widows did derive the benefit of welfare, it was mainly through their persistence and not through state initiative.

Finally, the state played a direct and important role in identifying the death of farmers as suicides due to rural distress, which made them eligible for state compensation of Rs 1 lakh. In all cases, the compensation had been meaningful for the widows and their families, even though the amount was low and remained unrevised since 2006[10] when it was first instituted. The state unofficially provided various arguments against even continuing this compensation; that the money encouraged suicides, or that regular deaths were misrepresented as suicides by farmers. The desperation of the farmers and their helplessness was a routine matter that the state dealt with and adjudicated. It also explained why the process of ascertaining farmer suicides' was patronizing, insensitive, and even selfish. It was difficult to comprehend—while reading through the 43 questions of the administrative enquiry—the mental and emotional state of the widow when she must have answered them just a few days after the death of her husband. The widow was also aware that her answers were not merely for information but to establish the distress that had caused the farmer suicide. As was seen in the narratives, her word was often doubted by the administration, and led to extensive cross-checking with official facts. While every level of the administration was aware of the proceedings and the statements of the widows and her family, many widows said they were not given the entire copy of the file. The state on its part, displayed unusual vigilance against the possibility of misrepresentation of normal suicides as farmer suicides, and the main reason appeared to be the poverty of the families, which made them welcome the relief.

It was in the interest of such a state to maintain the invisibility of the poor who demanded a share in the accumulated profits of a nation. As half the poor are women, this formed one of the six invisibilities of the widows discussed in the next section.

The stories of the 18 cases of Vidarbha and their battles through life that were documented from 2014 to 2016 revealed a world that had to remain unacknowledged so that it stayed invisible. The widows were reconciled to the invisibility that they inherited because they were women, and such invisibility was executed through tradition, status, procedure, opportunity, value, and vote, all of which claimed but failed to represent their interests and their rights. The inherited invisibility provided women of poor, rural families an accepted, even though disenfranchised, path for survival in life. The only challenge came from the educated young girls aware of other, less exploitative paths, and sought the freedom to become visible. As this subversion threatened the status quo, there was a serious price to be paid by those who demanded it; for instance, the withdrawal of support and security by the community. Subversive women were not seen as reformist or progressive, but merely as aberrations brought about by extraneous factors like education, awareness, attitude, or age, which seemed to promote dreams of visibility that were appropriate only for men. Such young women were expected to return to the fold of the normalized invisibilities, and let the community represent their interests instead. Invariably, the community established superiority of the opinion of the visible over the invisible, which was necessary for power and control over their rights and aspirations. Therefore, even when thus represented, the invisible were never allowed an independent existence with boundaries of their own sovereignty, as that would produce a difference. A widow embodied the 'difference' that had to be made invisible so that it did not have to be addressed. The narratives showed how the six invisibilities forced the woman to remain in the shadows of Vidarbha with a promise of representation, which failed at various levels.

The first invisibility was brought about by tradition, which failed to represent the interests of the widow through her family and community. Marriage was seen as a crucial transition for young girls into the invisibility of being represented by their husband, who was born as the visible part of the community. Without an identity separate from marriage, the women themselves merged with the background, to be identified only in accepted roles, such as a wife or mother. Women could challenge traditions only by becoming visible, which was, once again, subversive conduct and incurred risks. Visibility came at a price that the women usually could not afford to pay. Widowhood did not return the control over her life to the widow, but merely provided a joint ownership to the family and community, who now represented her instead. Without an alternative identity, the inherited invisibility of tradition was a status quo that the widow preferred to keep. Such conformity was hailed as 'correct' conduct and was rewarded with security and respect, which revealed the second invisibility of the widow—status.

The conformist invisible widow was identified as leading a pure and pious life that was unmediated by desires that should have died with her husband. Widows were often hailed as sacrificing and selfless, and constantly concerned about the welfare of their children and families. The farmer who committed suicide never faced such an evaluation, even if he was also a husband and a father. The status of the widow, which also claimed to represent her interests, did not help her to navigate life any better than her husband had. She was thrown into the same crisis he had faced before his suicide, and with no prior information and much less experience. This led, therefore, only to the exchange of dependence of the widow from the husband to another male member of the family rather than her own independence; it was also not sought by the widow weighed down, as she was, under the debt of welfare received from the family and the community. The state should have not only assisted widows to be free of such debt, but also facilitated their independence. That constituted the third invisibility of the widow when the state failed to represent her rights and interests—procedure.

The state that provided welfare to the widows by recognizing them only through their husband's identity played an unfortunate role in making her incapable of traversing the visible world without a man to represent her. Many women in the narratives in this book mentioned their reluctance to visit banks to get loans or even to the local panchayat offices to check on welfare schemes, mainly because they were not expected to do such work. The state endorsed the invisibility of the widow when it did not facilitate procedures that allowed the widow her own identity. Even when the state enquired into the suicides, it provided only partial visibility to the widow as she established the circumstances of her husband's death, and withdrew it once the enquiry was over. For the state, it was easier to deal with the visible patriarchal system of standardized procedure and predictable outcome rather than cater to different procedure for widows, which resulted in a 'difference' in outcome. Like the family or the community, even the state sought to deal with those who indirectly represented the invisible rather than engage with the invisible directly. It achieved this by procedure designed with the expectation of dealing only with men, and women who were represented by men. The welfare schemes for widows, the marginalized, and other underprivileged sections of the society aimed at empowerment without defining it for them. The widows were denied the chance to represent themselves, which revealed the fourth invisibility of the widows—opportunity.

As a young girl, a widow was given basic education that provided her an introduction to the visible world to which there seemed to be access through opportunity. Although employment for those with limited education was uncertain, education provided girls an alternative destiny to their inherited invisibility. However, the education of the girl and her access to opportunity was considered unnecessary for leading her life as a dependent housewife or a mother. Most girls in the narratives had expressed their desire to study further and to find jobs. Though their mothers did not contradict them at that time, through the period of research, girls who had completed their schooling found it tough to remain unmarried and continue their education. Widows with limited financial means found it more secure to fund a conventional life for their daughters than a subversive one, except in cases where the widow herself had found visibility. As the widows were not educated enough to qualify for either welfare schemes or employment opportunities, they most often worked as farm labour. With agriculture failing to make profits, farm labour eventually became the only source of income for a widow to run her household and support her children, even if it imposed the fifth invisibility on her—value.

When compared to the efforts of the man, the woman's contribution to the household was unaccounted for, as was her role in moulding the future of her children. This did not change in the case of widows, even when they made all the efforts that a man did to support the family along with all the work they did as women. The allocation of value to a woman's labour might provide her a visibility that was incompatible with her invisible universe. She had to be represented indirectly through the life of her children or the opinion of her family but not directly through her work, even if she worked on the same farmlands as the men. The widow seldom had rights over property or the farm, and would face difficulty finding bank loans. And yet, it was the widow's daily wages that paid household expenses and the children's school fees. The earnings of the invisible were also categorized as invisible, and the widow did not derive any financial freedom because of her labour. While the farmer was hailed for his efforts to earn a livelihood on the farm, a widow did the same in the shadows without acknowledgement. This revealed the sixth and last invisibility of the widow that had come with the failure of the democratic promise of equality of all citizens—the vote. As mentioned earlier, the widows of Vidarbha described in this book had the opportunity to vote at least three times in the elections for forming state and central governments. This was a representation that the widow should have been able to count on; it did not come to her because she was a widow or a woman—it came to her as a citizen. The vote equalized the visible with the invisible in a moment of decision-making about power, which was the inherent promise of democracy. However, the electoral process with the first-past-the-post system allowed candidates to win on minority percentage votes that did not provide a level playing field for widows. They were not represented in the visible world of assertive politics of organized vote banks and engineered equations, in which the invisible did not count. The unchanged life of the widow proved that, like her, even her vote was invisible.

★ ★ ★

In the end, the widows and their children were asked a set of questions to ascertain prevalence of trends through common experiences. A majority blamed the government for their circumstances, followed by agriculture and debt, and stated that they anticipated difficulties in fulfilling their dreams of further education, housing, employment, and better agricultural profits. Ten out of the 16 widows were unhappy with the future they provided for their children and 12 widows stated that agriculture was not an option for the next generation and preferred employment or business. Most widows mentioned they did not want to be born again as women in India, while their daughters said they did. Perhaps the lives led in the twilight awaited the dawn of a different day in Vidarbha.

1. Refer to the Introduction.
2. Department of Agriculture and Cooperation and Farmers Welfare, Ministry of Agriculture and Farmer Welfare, Government of India. Available at www.eands.dacnet.nic.in, accessed 4 July 2017.
3. Department of Agriculture and Cooperation and Farmers Welfare, Ministry of Agriculture and Farmer Welfare, Government of India. Available at http://eands.dacnet.nic.in/, accessed 4 July 2017.
4. 'Selected State-wise Estimates of Cost of Cultivation/Production of Cotton in India (2002–03)', Ministry of Agriculture, Government of India. See www.indiastat.com/default.aspx
5. 'Selected State/Crop-wise Estimates of Cost of Cultivation/ Production in India (2008–2009 to 2013–14)', Ministries Statistics and Programme Implementation / Agriculture & Farmers Welfare, Government of India. See www.indiastat.com/default.aspx
6. The Government of Maharashtra's Gharkul Yojana (scheme) provides financial assistance for constructing homes for widows, members of Scheduled Castes and Scheduled Tribes, next of kin to defence personnel killed in action, minorities, and BPL category households. The district rural development agencies and panchayats identified the beneficiaries, and the house was allotted in the name of the woman of the family. See: 'Maharashtra Govt to Build 1.86 Lakh Houses for Backward Class', *DNA*, 26 July 2011, available at www.dnaindia.com/mumbai/report-maharashtra-govt-to-build-186-lakh-houses-for-backward-class-1569571, last accessed 18 December 2017. Also see www.pmayg.nic.in
7. The Vasantrao Naik Sheti Swavalamban Mission (VNSSM) was set up by the Government of Maharashtra to help reduce farm distress by facilitating credit availability and disbursal. Headquartered in Amravati, the Mission proposed to assist crop loans in 14 districts of Vidarbha.
8. 'Maharashtra Panel Moots New Crop Loans to Arrest Farmers Suicides,' *Mid-day*, 24 August 2015, available at http://www.mid-day.com/articles/maharashtra-panel-moots-new-crop-loans-to-arrest-farmers-suicides/16480169, accessed 11 July 2017.
9. Baliraja Chetna Abhiyan, according to the documents provided by the district administration of Yavatmal in 2016, was a scheme approved by the Government of Maharashtra in 2015. It was

proposed to run for three years on a fund of Rs 32 crore annually. Every village would be given Rs 1 lakh to spend on libraries;
distressed farmers; public festivals; and on loans of up to Rs 20,000
without interest for two or three months for sowing and for medical
treatment.

10. Government Resolution on 23 January 2006, based on Farmers'
Suicide Information, Amravati Division, Maharashtra.

APPENDIX 1

Yavatmal

Name of Widow	Age[1] (in years)	Education (in school)	Children	Below Poverty Line (BPL)	Above Poverty Line (APL)
Vandana Rathod	35	Class 5	4	×	×
Manjubai Rathod	38	Class 5	2	√	×
Mira Dike	44	Class 7	2	×	√
Pushpabai Raut	63	Class 4	2	×	√
Savita Ade	40	Class 6	2	√	×
Anita Nandagawli	33	Class 7	2	×	√
Sunita Dhale	41	Class 12	3	√	×
Gayabai Zhambre*	58	No schooling	8	×	×
Jayashri Sawankar	40	Class 12	2	×	×
9	–	–	27	3	3

[1] Ages have been revised up to July 2017.
[2] Antyodaya Anna Yojana provided subsidised foodgrains for BPL families.
[3] (0–2.47 acres) Marginal: Ma
(2.47–4.94 acres) Small: S
(4.94–9.88 acres) Semi-Medium: SM

Bal Sangopan Yojana	Antyodya Anna Yojana[2]	Size of Land Holding[3]	Loan Amount at the Time of Husband's Suicide[4]	Other Sources of Income
×	√	10.61 acres (M)	Rs 41,706 (P)	Daily labour
×	×	5 acres (SM)	Rs 91,462 (P+I)	Daily labour
√	×	4 acres (S)	Rs 67,000 (P)	Anganwadi worker + Daily labour
×	×	2 acres (Ma)	Rs 43,625 (P+I)	–
×	×	5.63 acres (SM)	Rs 55,044 (P+I)	Daily labour
√	×	9 acres (SM)	Rs 60,000 (P)	Daily labour
×	×	4.5 acres (S)	Rs 44,371 (P+I)	Anganwadi worker
×	×	4.94 acres (S)	Rs 56,042 (P+I)	–
√	√	3 acres (S)	Rs 50,000 (P)	Part-time Attendant (PTA) at dispensary
3	2	–	–	–

(9.88–24.71 acres) Medium: M. (However, among the sample, the maximum land in this category was 10.61).

[4] Principal Amount: Principal (P) + Interest Amount (I)

★ Deceased in 2014.

APPENDIX 2

Amravati

Name of the Widow	Age[5] (in years)	Education (in school)	Children	Below Poverty Line (BPL)	Above Poverty Line (APL)
Jyoti Bhumbar	41	Class 10	3	×	√
Tarabai Vyavhare	61	Class 3	6	×	×
Anjana Katekar	46	Class 3	6	×	√
Rekha Tingde★	37	Class 10	2	√	×
Bhagirathi Harale	54	No schooling	3	×	×
Sunita Utkhede	46	Class 10	2	×	√
Archana Dhawde	26	Class 12	×	×	×
Vaishali Sambde	40	Class 12	1	√	×
Lata Patil	41	Class 10	2	×	×
9	–	–	25	2	3

[5] Ages have been revised up to July 2017.

[6] Antyodaya Anna Yojana provided subsidised foodgrains for BPL families.

[7] (0–2.47 acres) Marginal: Ma

(2.47–4.94 acres) Small: S

(4.94–9.88 acres) Semi-Medium: SM

Bal Sangopan Yojana	Antyodya Anna Yojana[6]	Size of Land Holding[7]	Loan Amount at the Time of Husband's Suicide[8]	Other Source of Income
×	×	3.5 acres (S)	Rs 36,863 (P + I)	Daily labour
×	×	4 acres (S)	Rs 2,41,931 (P)	–
×	×	11.5 acres (M)	Rs 47,000 (P)	Daily labour
×	×	2 acres (Ma)	Rs 50,000 (P)	–
×	√	5 acres (SM)	Rs 1,39,673 (P + I)	Daily labour
×	×	2 acres (Ma)	Rs 17,534 (P)	Daily labour
×	×	10 acres (M)	Rs 87,438 (P + I)	–
√	×	8 acres (SM)	Rs 37,300 (P)	Daily labour
√	√	2 acres (Ma)	Rs 44,000 (P)	Daily labour
2	2	–	–	–

(9.88–24.71 acres) Medium: M. (However, among the sample, the maximum land in this category was 11.5).

[8] Principal Amount: Principal (P) + Interest Amount (I)

★ Deceased in 2006.

Index

About the Author

Kota Neelima is a political author and has been a journalist for over 22 years. She holds a Master's Degree in International Relations from Jawaharlal Nehru University and was Senior Research Fellow, South Asia Studies at The Paul H. Nitze School of Advanced International Studies (SAIS), Johns Hopkins University, Washington DC. She is former political editor for *The Sunday Guardian* and writes on farmer suicides, rural women, and electoral reforms in India. Her bestselling books include *Shoes of the Dead*, *Death of a Moneylender*, and *The Honest Season*.

Neelima is also an artist. Her works are impressionist-abstract, oil on canvas and attempt to deconstruct contemporary reality through spirituality. Over the last decade and more, her paintings have been presented at several solo exhibitions in Delhi, and featured in art shows in India and abroad. Her work is also part of the permanent collection at the Museum of Sacred Art, Belgium.

Neelima lives in New Delhi. For more information, visit www.kotaneelima.com.